East Sussex Library and
Information Services

LEWIS
STORE

East Sussex
County Council

This item is satisfying requests

before going to its home library

Please return/renew this item by the last
date shown.
Books may also be renewed by phone or
internet.
www.eastsussex.gov.uk/libraries

COMMON GROUND

AROUND BRITAIN IN 30 WRITERS

Edited by John Simmons,
Rob Williams and Tim Rich

CYAN

Marshall Cavendish
Editions

First published in 2006 by:

Marshall Cavendish Limited
119 Wardour Street
London W1F 0UW
United Kingdom
T: +44 (0)20 7565 6000
F: +44 (0)20 7734 6221
E: sales@marshallcavendish.co.uk
www.marshallcavendish.co.uk

and

Cyan Communications Limited
119 Wardour Street
London W1F 0UW
United Kingdom
T: +44 (0)20 7565 6120
E: sales@cyanbooks.com
www.cyanbooks.com

A CIP record for this book is available from the British Library

ISBN-13 1-978-904879-93-0
ISBN-10 1-904879-93-4

Designed by Grade Design Consultants, London
www.gradedesign.com

Printed and bound in Great Britain by TJ International Ltd, Padstow, Cornwall

Contents

Preface

I cannot pinpoint the exact moment when the idea for this book came. That's almost certainly because ideas rarely come in that cartoon lightbulb way. Ideas emerge from an accumulated mass of information that our brains take in, store away and retrieve when randomly prompted. Part of that mass for me was the knowledge that, on three summer visits by car to the southern parts of France, I had failed to make a detour to a place I still yearn to visit. For each time I had passed within 30 km of the forest where Alain-Fournier had lived and which he had supposedly used as the setting for his novel *Le Grand Meaulnes*.

If you have read *Le Grand Meaulnes* you will recognise how perfectly apt it is that I should never reach that place. But the idea started to form. I liked the extreme case of searching for (and perhaps never finding) the lost domain that had inspired one of my favourite books. It seemed to me that this searching for something that is probably unattainable could itself be a metaphor for writing.

I also recognised that I had always been attracted to the places where writers had lived and written. It hardly mattered whether I knew the author's work. For example, on one of those French holidays, I found myself visiting the house in Provence where Petrarch had lived for a time. I remain blissfully ignorant of Petrarch's poetry but I loved being in a place that had played a role in defining the form of a sonnet. Then I thought of the places where I had visited and felt closer to authors whose work I did know. Haworth, of course, as evocative on a misty autumn day as *Wuthering Heights* itself. Wandering with the clouds through the Lake District and entering Dove Cottage with the lingering presence of William and Dorothy Wordsworth. Visiting Dylan Thomas's cramped wooden hut in Laugharne, Dickens's glowering house in Rochester, even sitting in fuggy Edinburgh pubs where Ian Rankin might have huddled in miserable comfort with Rebus and a pint in hand.

The potential of the theme became more and more encouraging. My fellow editors Rob Williams and Tim Rich sharpened the idea further, in particular to spread the literary range wider but narrow the geographical focus to the British Isles. We then invited the membership of 26 – an organisation created to inspire a greater love of words – to submit proposals to write a chapter on writers and places that have inspired and informed their own work, to explore the common ground that they share. We were nearly overwhelmed by the flood of proposals. Our next challenge was to whittle down the proposals and commission the 30 chapters that make up this book.

I am enormously grateful to those 30 contributors who demonstrate here the power of the theme. The simple, unsurprising truth is that writers admire and learn from other writers. The not-for-profit association called 26 brings together everyone from literary writers to journalists, copywriters and others who work with language. As you will discover, these are people in love with words that poets, novelists, storytellers, screenwriters, playwrights and lyricists have created, it seems, especially for them. There is a very personal relationship between the writers and their chosen subjects. Words, written and read, have enormous power to shape lives. We all feel that power, but we question it and celebrate it too rarely. Here was a chance to do that. What influence have those words and works had on our own writing, on our own lives, characters and choices? And what was the influence of the places that nurtured those works – on ourselves and our subjects? Can we find similar spirit in these landscapes, streets, houses and passing places that we might share for only the briefest or even deepest of encounters with these writers?

You will find variety here, a variety that reflects the range of literary inspiration available to anyone who aspires to be a better writer. There is variety in the places. As well as the solidly expected scenes – Hardy's Dorset, for example – there are the shifting and unexpected interchanges with Will Self's motorways, Richard Long's landscapes and HW Tilman's seas.

There is variety in the writers who are the subjects. Van Morrison in Belfast shares a stage in this book with Harold Pinter in Hackney and Shakespeare in Stratford. Milton's shadowy confined cottage in a Buckinghamshire village can link by storytelling to the wide-eyed spaces of Stevenson's Highlands. As well as the justly famous such as Charles Dickens and Virginia Woolf there are the unjustly neglected such as Hugh Miller, Mary Butts and FW Lister. And there is variety in the writers who contribute: an award-winning novelist such as Ali Smith, a cult writer such as Niall Griffiths, John Mitchinson who co-created the word-obsessed TV quiz *QI*, William Easton who is Rektor of Sweden's leading school of marketing.

Above all, this book is a chance for each of us to discover or rediscover writers while learning something unexpected about ourselves. And the way we do that is by going on a journey, real or imagined, to the place where the work of a writer emerged into life and changed the way individuals think about the world.

John Simmons
August 2006

MURDOCH
F.W. LISTER
PAUL ABBOTT
KEITH WATERHOUSE
ALAN GARNER
DAVID LODGE
DYLAN THOMAS
WILLIAM SHAKESPEARE
WILL SELF
JOHN MILTON
HAROLD PINTER
GILES SMITH
EDWARD THOMAS
JULIAN HAM
PATRICK HAMILTON
BARNES
REV W AWDRY
T.S. ELIOT
JASPER FFORDE
HILAIRE BELLOC
MAN LONG
MARY BUTTS
VIRGINIA WOOLF
CHARLES DICKENS
THOMAS HARDY
RICHARD

How Camest Thou in Such a Pickle?

Shakespeare's Stratford

by Jim Davies

From: j.benedick@tempest-tv.co.uk
To: l.shakespeare@muchadoo.com
Subject: Lost the plot

Hi Liam,

Thanks for your latest scene-by-scene outline. There's the germ of something here, but to be frank, it's not really floating my boat. We're building a reputation for hard-hitting, high-stakes drama at Tempest, so this is probably a bit too light for us.

Also, the discovery of the handkerchief doesn't work. No one uses them any more, particularly the monogrammed ones. I'm not even sure you can still buy them …

Best,

Johnnie

From: l.shakespeare@muchadoo.com
To: j.benedick@tempest-tv.co.uk
Subject: RE: Lost the plot

Hi Johnnie,

Of course you can. I saw some in a gentlemen's outfitters window the other day. And there was an ad in the Sunday paper for personalised handkerchiefs last week – £9.95 for 12 inc p&p – 100 per cent Egyptian cotton, with 20mm initial embroidered in classic blue thread.

What do you suggest instead, a soiled tissue?

Regards,

Liam

From: j.benedick@tempest-tv.co.uk
To: l.shakespeare@muchadoo.com
Subject: RE: Lost the plot

Liam,

At least that would add some gritty realism. That's the problem. You've pulled it back too far. It's all a bit twee now. Unfortunately, we don't live in the kind of world where a black guy can work his way up to be a top general in the Italian army. And if he thinks his wife is sleeping around, he's not going to be so reasonable and forgiving about it. "It's just a phase ..." The man's supposed to be a killing machine! Where's the jealousy, the aggro, the domestic violence?

I don't understand why it has to be set in Venice either.

Johnnie

From: l.shakespeare@muchadoo.com
To: j.benedick@tempest-tv.co.uk
Subject: RE: Lost the plot

Johnnie,

Before, you said I needed to tone it down, that the indiscriminate bloody rampage was too violent for prime-time TV. So I thought I'd turn it into a romantic comedy instead. But with an edge.

Liam

PS What about Colin Powell? It must be even trickier in the US.

From: j.benedick@tempest-tv.co.uk
To: l.shakespeare@muchadoo.com
Subject: RE: Lost the plot

Liam,

Look, a spot of advice. Why don't you set it in a hospital? O'Teller could be a successful black surgeon, who's just married Desdemona, the fragile-yet-beautiful daughter of the registrar. That way you've got it all under one roof – life and death, blood and tears, power and corruption, class conflict, pathos, comedy, nurses' uniforms …

And another thing. You really need to fork out for a scriptwriting programme, it makes you look like you know what you're doing. Try Action!Pro or Director's Chair. They're only a couple of hundred quid.

J

From: l.shakespeare@muchadoo.com
To: j.benedick@tempest-tv.co.uk
Subject: RE: Lost the plot

In my day, all you needed was a sharpened goose feather and a pot of homemade ink.

L

* * *

A plague upon all their production houses! What the devil do they know about drama anyway? I could serve them up a dish fit for the gods and they'd tell me it was overcooked. Toad-spotted promise-breakers. But hark, what's this?

From: SaladDays.com
To: l.shakespeare@muchadoo.com
Subject: message from an old friend

Dear Liam,

You have a new message. But you'll need to upgrade your membership before you can read it.

Click here to upgrade now

Kind regards,

The SaladDays team

Just to remind you, your login email is l.shakespeare@muchadoo.com and your password is H****t.

SaladDays – because time cannot wither true friendship.

Now let's see … Zounds! A week on Saturday in Stratford? Well, well, well … every dog will have its day.

Stratford-upon-Avon is a small gold mine in Warwickshire, the so-called Heart of England. If England actually was a person, it's slightly down and to the right of where the heart would be, but if anywhere has a licence to be poetic, it's Stratford.

Screaming Lord Sutch kick-started his raving lunatic political career here. Jack Profumo, whose well-tailored trousers couldn't resist the Earth's gravitational pull, was once its MP. JB Priestley, no mean scribbler himself, spent his last days in the ancient town before shuffling off this mortal coil. It boasts a butterfly farm and a bandstand, a museum full of old cars and another full of old teddy bears, a race course fit for the sport of kings, and a barge upon which you can buy baguettes.

But there's simply no getting away from it. One person has left his distinguished inky imprint on virtually every street in Stratford. And that's me.

I'm not laying it on with a trowel. Some are born great, some achieve greatness, and some have greatness thrust upon them ... I'd say mine was part thrust and part achievement. But these days, I've become accustomed to the grubby reality of London, so the more I roam the mock-mock-Tudor avenues and alleyways of this town I once called home, the more my teeth are set on edge. Artifice and authenticity play fast and loose in a spot where even Pizza Express is half-timbered, and the townsfolk's idea of olde-worlde charm is to be profligate with their use of the letter "e." No wonder I left. If only the rest had been silence.

I say "roam the streets," but this isn't actually possible any more. The sheer volume of pedestrians means you're snatched along like a small boat in a ceaseless storm, whirred by eager tourists from all corners of the globe, buffeted by rucksacks, street maps and camera cases, drowned in a babel of exotic, far-flung accents and less-than-exotic local ones.

What's more, wherever I look, I'm reminded of mine own none-too-pretty visage, emblazoned on the most ludicrous of gewgaws. By now I'm immune to the mugs, tea towels, and the miscellaneous stationery that kids can't get enough of on school trips. I've even come to have a grudging admiration for people who can bring themselves to wear those cringe-worthy "Will Power" T-shirts.

But some of the little shockers make your hair stand on end. Fridge magnets. Ceramic thimbles. Little tin crests to attach to walking sticks. Night caps. I even came across a lusty five-and-a-quarter-inch William Shakespeare vinyl action figure with removable book and quill pen. The *pièce de résistance,* though, is undoubtedly the £1.99 glitter "snow storm" in which a crude and understandably pissed-off-looking bard-bust is trapped forever and a day to ponder the slings and arrows of outrageous fortune. I can empathise – shipwrecked with no apparent means of escape in an uncouth, uncultured age where precious talent is given such short shrift.

Nevertheless, here I am ... cutting a surprisingly inconspic-uous dash through the tat and the tour parties. And do you know why? Because I bear no more than a passing resem-blance to that ill-favoured caricature, which is based on an engraving of an engraving of a painting by a decidedly untalented Dutchman. Comparisons are odorous. OK, I'm thinning a bit on top, there's a poet's gold hoop dangling in my left lobe, and I sport the tidy jazz beard favoured by the burghers of Clerkenwell, EC1. But the smug, dome-headed, bug-eyed creature trying to pass himself off as the great "Swan of Stratford," looks no more like me than a plucked goose.

I'm making my way to Precious Times in the old town, a photographic studio-cum-costumiers which purveys over 300 types of outlandish fancy dress. You can't miss it, there's a six-foot mannequin posing as a bipedal white rabbit guarding the front door. On the way, I stiffen my sinews as I pass the dodgy reminders of my glorious past – the Pen & Parchment pub, Thespian's Indian restaurant, Bard's Walk shopping arcade, The Food of Love café, the Shakespearience, and Mexican Hamlet. Forty-odd plays (yes, there are more), some of the most haunting poetry the world has ever clapped eyes on, and it's come to this.

My choice of disguise for the night is a foregone conclusion. When in Stratford ...

* * *

The evening air is thick with bravado and basso profundo. With their mangy, hop-coloured locks, full-blooded beards and pinch-tight leathers, these are the fearsome knights of the road, sitting bestride their growling, gleaming chargers. Passers-by on Waterside glance over anxiously, but these tattooed speed-chasers are supremely uninterested, lost in an arcane kingdom of their own, where chrome and horse-power are the only currency.

I scuttle past them self-consciously in my bard's outfit, glancing over at the glinting Avon, bejewelled with midsummer sunlight. The sky is champagne pink, the atmosphere charged with a strange, invisible perfume that hits the senses. In the car park just outside the Royal Shakespeare Theatre, a domed, gently billowing marquee rises upwards, its flower-soft fabric at odds with the brutal red brick of the theatre building. I'm greeted at the entrance by a pair of Elvises (or should that be Elvi?) – their respective girths suggesting different reference points in the King's career. The young pretender hands me a fizzing glass, and they usher me in to a strange, enchanted indoor garden that beggars all description.

The centre-piece is a massive, gnarled oak tree, hung, like a blossoming spider's web with flowing canopies of luscious woodbine, sweet musk roses and eglantine. Skirting the tent's edges is a long, elevated ha-ha of grass and moss, prick'd with oxslips, primroses and violets, on which an unlikely cast of characters loll and laugh and look back in languor.

The place is already heaving, a dreamlike collision of personae from every conceivable era and genre. On the far side of the marquee, Caliban has set his sights on a passable Marilyn. Groucho Marx vainly tries to out-aphorise Oscar Wilde under a leafy sylvan bower. Cleopatra, provocatively stroking her asp, tilts her head back and snorts heartily at an illogical quip from a scaled-down version of Mr Spock.

How will I know her? There were precious few clues in her suggestive message on the SaladDays website. A place, a time, a promise. To complicate matters, there seem to be two of everyone. The alpha-male duo who both hired gorilla suits are desperately trying to avoid eye contact. At least there's some textual basis for the Tweedle Dee/Dum double-act. And there holding court, and truly lapping up the attention, is my alter ego. Clearly, he's modelled himself on the five-and-a-quarter-inch vinyl action figure, complete with removable book and quill pen. Pah! What does he know? And yet, there they all are, the ignorant fools, hanging on his honey'd words, and dancing his attendance.

I weave my way tetchily to the refreshments table, festooned with ornate finger-food and leafy decoration that are hard to tell apart. The sweetmeats appear tempting enough, but the jellies look vile. In pride of place, like a precious stone set in a silver tablecloth, there's a huge ice sculpture of a swan peering majestically over the proceedings. Three witches are hunched over the punch bowl, uttering delicious incantations. Though they've done their utmost to make themselves look foul and filthy, their girlish vanity has kept them in check, so for all the amateur prosthetics and stick-on warts, beauty still hangs upon their cheeks.

"All hail you secret, black and midnight hags," I venture, hoping I haven't gone too far. "Where can I find the Dark Lady I dream of amongst this pleasing throng?"

"She is here, yet she is not," says the first, in an unsteady voice that seems to belong to an able seaman one moment and a prima-ballerina the next.

"Double, double, toil and trouble, she'll come and go like a bursting bubble," warns the second, slightly more convincingly.

"She's over there talking to Bjorn Borg," says the third.

My gaze follows her crooked finger. And my heart stops dead ... Did I ever truly love till now? Forswear it, sight! For I ne'er saw true beauty till this night. I pick my tongue off the floor, and stride over as casually as I can given the tightening of my trousers.

"What took you so long?" she asks in a voice that's soft, gentle, low, and could melt the stoniest of hearts. "I have plans for the night ahead."

Her powder blue dress is a wanton explosion of silk and taffeta that tapers into an impossibly small waist. The décolletage reveals a perfect olive skin, and a barely contained cleavage ready to burst out like a pair of greyhounds in the slips. Oh that I might live one hour in that sweet bosom! I try desperately to look behind the white player's mask she's holding to her face, but she's careful to keep up the façade. Her ample black ringlets provide further camouflage, but I convince myself that her lips are quite as plump and inviting as the painted counterfeits that gash her crude disguise.

* * *

How my raven-haired beauty persuaded me to don the blind-fold, I still don't know. But that night, her beck might have commanded me from the bidding of the gods. Her tender hand pulses intoxicating electricity through my entire body as she gently leads me through the sultry streets of Stratford. Hours pass, or is it mere seconds? My sense of time has vanished into thin air. We're floating, weightless in our own private bubble, warm and wonderful, immune to the weary world outside.

I catch short snatches of conversation, the tinny reverb of distant laughter, hear the quiet lapping of the river, the sweet breeze dancing insistently with the leaves overhead. But these sounds are hollow distractions. My heart is tied to her rudder by the strings, carried on her mellifluous voice, at once coquettish and soothing, mysterious and like home.

We arrive at a doorway. Then breathlessly climb some steep stairs. There's total silence, but somehow, it's charged with a trembling anticipation. She sits me down on what I can feel is the edge of a downy-soft bed and removes my blindfold. Not that it makes any difference. The room is as black as pitch. Then she loosens my hired ruffle and tunic, and with the most eloquent of giggles, bids me hop in. My heart is pounding like McDuff knocking desperately at the castle gates, as I hear her gently pad across to the other side. Was that a whisper? I can't be sure. What's taking her so long?

As we finally lock into a fiery embrace, it strikes me that something's amiss. Her hair smells quite different, like apples and cinnamon. And I surmise that her dress, though exquisite, must have been particularly bulky – she's quite a few pounds of flesh lighter, and her greyhounds fall well short of the proportions I'd envisaged. What's more, the sweet nothings she whispers waft over in a shy, girlish voice, more of a trilling piccolo than the melodious flute I remember. But by now, my ardour is well stoked, so I decide not lose the name of action in the pale cast of thought. Things won are done, joy's soul lies in the doing. Or as the more contemporary slogan tells us, "just do it."

* * *

Suddenly, the heavy velvet curtain pulls back, the sun-bright stage lights come up, and the packed Royal Shakespeare theatre audience bursts into rapturous applause. The guy who always whoops and whistles is there too, bringing his familiar descant to the throbbing hum of clapping hands.

I'm still cocooned in the night's rapturous delirium, spaced out and propped up in the bed I'd been lured to earlier. Next to me lies a strange yet familiar figure. A pale, smiling, fragile-yet-beautiful blonde. Her discarded nurse's uniform is a crumpled heap on the boards. We find ourselves in a theatre designer's vision of an NHS hospital ward, surrounded by outsize medical paraphernalia, the over-grown, exaggerated children of an inspired props department.

Almost instinctively, as if I've been rehearsing it for the past 400 years, I know the next line.

"Pass the tissues, Desdemona."

I smile ruefully and think of what might have been. But clearly, it wasn't written in the script.

PAUL ABBOTT

MISTER

KEITH WATERHOUSE

ALAN GARNER

DAVID LODGE

DYLAN THOMAS

WILLIAM SHAKESPEARE

WILL SELF

EDWARD THOMAS

JULIAN

JOHN W

PATRICK HAMILTON

BARNES

REYN

RICHARD LONG

HW TILMAN

THOMAS HARDY

JASPER FFORDE

MARY BUTTS

ANDRY HILAIRE B

VIRGINIA WOOLF CH

Still Not Much Going On

Edward Thomas and Adlestrop

by Richard Medrington

Yes, I remember Adlestrop –
The name, because one afternoon
Of heat the express-train drew up there
Unwontedly. It was late June.

The steam hissed. Someone cleared his throat.
No one left and no one came
On the bare platform. What I saw
Was Adlestrop – only the name

And willows, willow-herb, and grass,
And meadowsweet, and haycocks dry,
No whit less still and lonely fair
Than the high cloudlets in the sky.

And for that minute a blackbird sang
Close by, and round him, mistier,
Farther and farther, all the birds
Of Oxfordshire and Gloucestershire.

(from Edward Thomas, *Collected Poems,* Faber & Faber, 2004, p. 27)

Of course when I get to Adlestrop, it's not as I remembered it – sorry, not as I *imagined* it. The mental image was so vivid – the feel of the velour seats, the smell of pipe smoke in the carriage, the red neck of the chap who cleared his throat, the shimmering stillness of the platform – paint peeling on benches, creosote bubbling from the hot sleepers. It had that wrong-end-of-the-telescope clarity that certain memories acquire with age, only more so because I was looking through the extra lens of someone else's mind.

No train has stopped at Adlestrop station for forty years. Sleek, bullet-nosed machines thunder past on their way to Worcestershire or Oxfordshire, their schedules tight, their windows sealed against the unnecessary friction of birdsong. On the platform no one comes and no one goes. Well, actually that's not quite true. I am about to come and go: a return ticket from Edinburgh to Adlestrop – a brief 24 hours in Gloucestershire. The owners of the guest house were excited to hear that I'm to write something about Edward Thomas and have arranged for me to meet some of the local characters – in particular Dorothy, who has lived in the village all her life and whose father worked for the railway in 1914, and John, an Edward Thomas expert.

But the truth is I know relatively little about Edward Thomas. Apart from *Adlestrop* – which happens to be my favourite poem and which I have often recited on the performance poetry circuit, I know a smattering of his poems and prose and some details of his life. I will probably be a disappointment to them. On the other hand, I have the books and a six-hour train journey ahead of me. To work!

The village itself is quite beautiful, and seems not to have changed that much since 1914. Its seventy inhabitants mostly live in pretty golden stone cottages. I walk up the hill behind Adlestrop on a crisp winter morning and, in spite of the map on loan from my kindly hosts at "Lower Farm," manage to get lost. I never was much good with maps. There is a momentary panic, reminiscent of school days and the horrors of compulsory orienteering. Then I relax, slow down and decide to follow my nose.

There is a glen near my home where I walk often – usually very slowly. I have been there hundreds of times, but it is always a new experience. When I go there with so-called serious walkers they say: "You'll never get fit that way." But I don't walk to get fit; I walk in the hope of finding … something. I want to tell them to slow down, to match the pace of the place, and the pace of that place is *slow*. It asks you to take the time to stand and stare, or as Thoreau called it, to *saunter*. He suggests that the word derives from pilgrims who wandered about the countryside in the middle ages, seeking for charity and claiming they were going to the Holy Land or *Saint Terre*. They were seen as being rather lazy, pausing to look at this and that, taking detours as and when the spirit led them:

> "I have met with but one or two persons in the course of my life who understood the art of Walking, that is, of taking walks – who had a genius, so to speak, for SAUNTERING."
>
> (from "Walking," *The Atlantic Monthly,* 1862)

Thomas himself was a great walker – he knew large areas of Wales and the south of England intimately. His good friend Eleanor Farjeon, who later wrote the famous hymn *Morning Has Broken* (with its reference to a certain blackbird), said of him:

> "To walk with Edward Thomas in any countryside was to see, hear, smell and know it with fresh senses. You would not walk that road again as you did before. You would know it in a new way."
>
> (from *Edward Thomas: The Last Four Years,* Oxford University Press, 1958)

Evidently he didn't like the railway, and always chose to live as far from it as possible, but on a hot June afternoon in 1914 he found himself on the express train from Paddington to Worcester when it made an unscheduled stop at a small country station. *And nothing happened.* History tries to convince us that life is made up of a series of events, but actually it is made up of centuries when nothing much happens and a few years, or even days, of feverish activity. So here nothing happens except for the things that go on while nothing is happening: bodies function normally, breathing proceeds uninterrupted. The train exhales, then someone coughs. Apart from that there is a moment of absolute stillness.

When was it that we came to equate success with speed and mobility? Whenever you see a "successful" person on telly they're always going somewhere – in the back of a fast car or on a yacht or a private plane. Like dogs straining at the leash we are always trying to get to the place where we're not. Rarely do we pause and breathe in and experience the joy – or the gloom – of being fully present. Some people find such moments vaguely disturbing. They fidget, unfold the newspaper, clear their throat, anything to break the stillness, to fill the void. But it strikes me that it is when nothing is *happening* that we have a chance to get in touch with what *is*. I find that the best ideas come in times of stillness, the most creative stuff happens when I'm not trying to be creative.

I wander back through the village, past the bus shelter, which now houses the original railway sign – the only surviving first-hand witness to Thomas's transcendental moment. As I look at it I imagine him rolling this evocative new word around in his mind. Apparently he was a lover of curious sounding place names. Where does a name like Adlestrop come from? How does it evolve? Often in the frequent repetition of a word one loses touch temporarily with meaning – the word melts and becomes merely a collection of sounds. In *Old Man* (Andrew Motion's favourite poem, incidentally), Thomas says:

"Even to one that knows it well, the names
Half decorate, half perplex the thing it is:
At least, what that is clings not to names
In spite of time. And yet I like the names."
(from *Collected Poems*, Faber & Faber, 2004, p. 9)

I wait for some kind of powerful feeling to overwhelm me – but it doesn't, so I take a few photos of the sign to show to my wife. Perhaps Thomas didn't feel anything overwhelming during the unwonted pause at the station. It may have been one of those revelations that take root and grow gradually in the memory. At the time it seems a thing of no importance, but later, when you casually recount the story, the room grows quiet as people listen, and you realise that you have entertained angels unawares. It reminds me of something Patrick Kavanagh said about the subjects poetry ought to deal with:

> "What seems of public importance is never of any importance. Stupid poets and artists think that by taking subjects of public importance it will help their work to survive. There is nothing as dead and damned as an important thing. The things that really matter are casual, insignificant little things, things that you would be ashamed to talk of publicly. You are ashamed and then after years someone blabs and you find that you are in the secret majority ..."
>
> (from *Self Portrait*, The Dolmen Press, 1963)

It seems that Thomas didn't write *Adlestrop* until at least six months after the event (if it can be called an event). I find that memories often lurk for years in dark corners of my mind. They watch like ghosts from dingy doorways, and then it turns out that they just wanted me to write about them. As we begin to communicate, they open a door to a warren of interesting thoughts and revelations. These reminiscences are rarely of deeds or actions, more of things I felt or observed. The times when I *was* – not when I *did*. The times when I *saw* – even though at the time I may not have realised that I saw anything.

Thomas thought he was seeing only a name, but the train window opened onto another dimension, where the blackbird was speaking "like the first bird." Did he trill a three-note song? And did Thomas hear in it a transliteration of what he could see: *Ad-le-strop* ... *Wil-low-herb* ... *Mead-ow-sweet* ...

Glouce-ster-shire? The poem is full of such dactyls – as if the bird were calling out like an efficient station master, listing all things, as his ancestors had done since long before the Anglo-Saxon Johnny-come-latelies got in on the act. Before he knows it, the poet's consciousness is soaring out over the English countryside and beyond. He finds himself rising above the realm of what can be understood into the realm not of the meaningless but of that which is beyond meaning – what the ancients might have called *the peace of God which passes all understanding.* I came across this description of a bicycle ride in one of Thomas's prose works:

> "At that time I was a great deal nearer to being a disembodied spirit than I can often be … I fed through the senses directly … through the eyes chiefly, and was happier than is explicable or seems reasonable. This pleasure of my disembodied spirit was an inhuman and diffused one, such as may be attained by whatever dregs of this our life survive after death."
>
> (from *In Pursuit of Spring*, Thomas Nelson & Sons, 1914, p. 210)

A year after Adlestrop, Edward Thomas joined the Royal Garrison Artillery and trained, appropriately enough, to be an observer. Reading through the diary he kept in the trenches in 1917, I'm interested by his preoccupation with birds and planes – it's as if he were scanning a wider and wider horizon. In a letter to his son Merfyn he describes how, on 15 March, he climbed up the inside of a tall chimney to get a better view of enemy positions. He had to come down before he reached the top, due partly to the shells bursting around him and also to the fact that he knew one rung of the ladder was unstable, but not which one. A few weeks later, on the first morning of the battle of Arras, he was killed by an enemy shell. It was Easter Day, 1917. One of his senior officers wrote to his wife Helen describing the funeral: "As we stood by his grave the sun came up and the guns seemed to stop firing for a short time. This typified for me what stood out most in your husband's character …"

But I must tell you what I found when I reached the station. There was a tall wire fence and the following notice:

FOR YOUR INFORMATION

This is the site of the former Adlestrop Railway Station, the inspiration for Edward Thomas's famous poem *Adlestrop*.

British Railways closed the station in 1966 and all the buildings, platforms and infrastructure were demolished and removed.

The land is now privately owned and you are asked NOT to trespass onto this land NOR disturb the occupants of Station Cottage with enquiries.

Thank you.

I got as close as I could and viewed a scene of desolation:

Adlestrop 2006

They have forgotten Adlestrop
Again. All hopeful I began
To wander by the railway line
One afternoon. It was late Jan.

A wire fence, a terse, official note
Ensured that no one came
To the old platform. What I saw
Was *entropy!* That and the shame

Of motor-coaches sprouting grass
And rubbish scattered carelessly,
A layering of negligence
Upon a poet's memory,

A ruined double-decker bus
And dismally, round it, rustier,
Sadder and sadder, rotting hulks
From Bedfordshire and Lancashire.

Where are the blasted railway enthusiasts when you need them? If only the land had been sold to someone who wanted to restore it, instead of someone who didn't give a damn. How hard would it be to erect a shelter and replace the old sign, to make a place where people could sit for a while, as restless commuters whistling past look and think – "Ah yes, *Adlestrop*"? And of course there should be a copy of the poem in each carriage of every train that uses the line – *Poems on the Overground.*

On the other hand, shouldn't the saunterer be able to find Adlestrop wherever he or she is? Actually it's probably more to do with Adlestrop finding the saunterer. You can go out wandering on your own (it is generally a solitary thing, a lonely-as-a-cloud experience), you can slow down, you can keep your eyes and ears peeled, you can even do nothing, but in the end you can't make it happen. It comes to you. It is a gift. It is the present. It is here and it is now.

Sauntering back through the village I meet a man with a pot of paint sprucing up the village hall. This is Terry, who tells me he has escaped the rat race and come to Adlestrop seeking a quieter life. I tell him what I'm thinking of writing about – those moments when you see through a layer and touch something, you're not sure what. He seems to know what I mean: "I remember coming down the hill through the village one evening on my bike and seeing a stag in the wood. I stopped and stared at him – and for a moment he stared back. It was like something passed between us. It was just a moment and then he was gone. I don't know what it was."

I spend a fascinating hour chatting to Dorothy Price about her memories of the railway and later I sit with John Gillett, the Adlestrop church organist and Edward Thomas expert, who has strong Quaker leanings. When I explain my theory of inactivity he comments that it's a very Quaker-like idea, this waiting in silence for the spirit to move. Mostly we rush around trying to do stuff – to boost our standing or make a living – then the train stops (sometimes with a bump) due to circumstances beyond our control, and while we clear our throats, look at our watches and curse the inefficiency of the service, we notice a fellow traveller staring out of the window with what can only be described as a faraway look in his eyes.

Notes

Collected Poems by Edward Thomas is published by Faber & Faber. The latest 2004 edition contains Thomas's prose War Diary of 1917.

"A Legendary Lazy Little Black-Magical Bedlam by the Sea"

Dylan Thomas's Laugharne

by Niall Griffiths

Laugharne is a small town on the coast of South Wales, not far from Carmarthen. The poet Dylan Thomas lived there, off and on, throughout his life. His last house is now a museum dedicated to his life and work on the muddy shore of the estuary. The town has made much of its connections with the poet; Brown's Hotel, one of his favourite pubs, has an image of him on its signage and photographs of him cover the walls inside. There is a five-star hotel called Dylan's. The actor Neil Morrisey has invested much money in the town, including, allegedly, buying Brown's. The setting for Thomas's most famous work, *Under Milk Wood* – a town called Llareggub (read it backwards) – is undoubtedly modelled on Laugharne, as well as Newquay in Cardiganshire, where Thomas also lived, for a much briefer period. His rotund and crapulent features dominate the town now as much as the huge castle does (and where novelist Richard Hughes once lived. But that's another story).

FIRST VOICE *(very softly)*
Let's begin:
It is mild, wild winter, February in the small seaside town, sunless, herring-smacks abob under a bruised-blue, contused-maroon sky, cobblestreets silent and only the lover's wood snuffling and shuffling and rustling bow-legged down to the –

SECOND VOICE *(loud)*
Shite! It is 2006! He's been dead half a century! And the only reason the place is so quiet and not full of gawking Yanks (whose homeland he died in) and be-tweeded scholars agog for the mystique of presence as if a fifty year's dead ghost could ever offer such a thing is cos it's so fucking freezing. I've been here before, and I've seen them peering dewy-eyed into the shed where he wrote and hoping to absorb something of the shore all mussel-pooled and heron-priested and the black cap of jackdaws that dons Sir John's just hill and the hawk on fire hanging still and never do you hear them cry look! There! Those are the steps he fell down pissed and cut his head open or *that's* the tree he vomited on or *that's* the bush he pissed his pants under on one of the many nights he spent here parabloodylitic. I've seen them, ghoulish, worrying the bones of the talcum dead. I've heard them, foolish, blustering and fustian in their attitudes and words. They *want* him, they do. They've *always* wanted him. They need him desiccated in their studies and they hope that somehow It will rub off on them, the ecstasy that has left him as it always does rotted down to mulchy marrow in the sloping graveyard on the hill. All proxy and vicarious it is. You're talking shite.

FIRST VOICE *(softly still)*
No, listen; only you can hear their dreams. Only you can hear the –

SECOND VOICE *(loud)*
Banging techno from the chav-wagons.

PASSING CAR
Dumph dumph dumph dumph DUMPH DUMPH dumph dumph

SECOND VOICE
And, in the Cross House pub divided now into Polly Garter's Lounge and Captain Cat's Bar and where every standing or sitting space is occupied by a close cramped crowd watching Italy play England in the Six Nations on the big screen, the silent local grumbling in his skull:

LOCAL 1
Them faces I dunno but them faces I've seen cos all the same they are; another bunch of Yanks or Sais queer for the ghost of the fucking poet.

LOCAL 2
C'mon Italy c'mon the Eyeties.

PINT OF LAGER
Ssssssss.

THROAT
Glug glug. Aaaaahh.

SECOND VOICE
And taken by a booze-buzz you are *out* of that pub and *up* the hill and down a wet-stone alleyway past the white clock tower that has a Mediterranean tale to tell and doesn't ring in the mornings any more. In search of food you are but not yet and the Stable Door restaurant (which, you recall, does good

tapas) bears an advertisement for the Dodo Modern Poets, £18.50 including two courses and *fuck me* you think, *eighteen flippin' quid*, and you bend to stroke a friendly cat and hear a high humming like mad wasps caught in a bottle and you look up and you see two propeller planes looping-the-loop over Sir John's Hill and it is like a small visitation from another age and you wish you had a topper to toss in the air. *Who was Sir John?* you think and for a while you watch the aerobatics.

FIRST VOICE *(softly)*
Yes, oh yes, you watch the weakening sun slice silver from their wings.

SECOND VOICE
And you go down the of course Dylan's Walk past the commemorative bench-stroke-shelter that bears lines from *Under Milk Wood* and you stop at the Writing Shed which, on a plaque outside, has lines from "Poem on his Birthday," the last of which is "as I sail out to die." You think two words: *Melodramatic arse*, and you peer in through the window and see the desk and the empty bottles and the crumpled papers and the images of Blake and Lawrence on the walls and the shells and the stones from the beach and the oil lamps and the fireplace with paper balls and dry sticks in it and the whole thing looks half a century old and just as you're wondering how much at auction those crumpled and discarded worksheets would fetch the alarm is activated either from some remote point or from a timer-switch and it bleeps and pips in your ear as if it has read your thoughts so you go further down the walk to the Boathouse itself (past a sign that cries "SAVE DYLAN'S WALK!") which is closed now but you've been there before and you remember thinking what a wonderful place it would be in which to live and write and –

FIRST VOICE
die

SECOND VOICE
at the age of 39 younger than you are now no I don't think so.
I mean being alive is so fucking –

SEAGULLS
Laa-ger! Laa-ger!

FIRST VOICE
On down slow to the hushed and wave-washed, scalloped
shore where –

SECOND VOICE
there's another bleedin' monument thing, this one a pair of
wooden benches adorned with wooden fish and birds and a
central totem between them with the letters "DYLAN'S
WORDS" wriggling vertically down it like a worm. "ON MY
SEA-SHAKEN," it says, and "BREAKNECK OF ROCKS," and
the castle looms above it like castles always do. Looming is
why they were built. And crows man or rather *bird* the battlements and you feel like you can see their eyes but you can't,
of course. They're too far away.

FIRST VOICE *(softly)*
Oh yes but you can hear them, can't you? Heed their bird-
thoughts my lost one bounced from a good home. Only listen
to how they fly:

CROWS
Drink! Drink! Drink! Drink!

FIRST VOICE
Bugger.

SECOND VOICE
And see the marsh from where the Llansteffan ferry once
sailed but not any more. And see the buoy in the waves which
for one hopeful moment you think may be a seal or a dolphin
and yes there *are* some boats, yes, not bobbing because they're

stuck in mud waiting for the tide to free them. And wonder if those waves lap over any drowned and dreaming sailors and if those drowned ones could talk what words would they utter or what *do* they murmur in their briny dreams? Maybe just one:

THE DROWNED (*in a slow, low voice, like a 45 rpm record played at 33⅓*)
reeeeeeeeeeggreeeeeeeeeeettt

FIRST VOICE
But oh the songs they sing! Oh the sadnesses and raptures of their salty celebrations and psalms! Listen, and you'll –

SECOND VOICE
hear the splat of the shit that leaves the crow like a soft white bomb and lands on the wooden bust of the poet that stands in the little garden beyond the castle carpark. Dark wood now run with white shite over the accurate bulbous nose and across the full and blubber lips. "LAUGHARNE YOUTH CLUB" says a sign and sitting on that sign is a young lad in trackie and Burberry pecking with his thumb at his mobile phone.

YOUNG LAD
S BORIN ERE U WANA MEET L8R GOT SUM GANJ

SECOND VOICE
And you leave the carpark and cross the road and go back into the Cross House pub.

BARMAN
All go so quick they do once the rugby's over. Which the fucking Sais won. But they'll be back after they've done the rounds, up to Brown's and The Mariner's and then back down the hill to here unless they go off to St Clear's for the change or off to a club in Carmarthen or Tenby like the young ones do. Don't know what they see in the oh good evening, what can I get you?

CUSTOMER
Drunk.

BARMAN
Yes, and what would help you achieve that aim?

CUSTOMER
Vodka Red Bull.

BARMAN
Vodka Red Bull it is, then. Just passing through, is it? Not local then?

CUSTOMER
No.

BARMAN
Suit yerbloodyself then. Another one wanting the fucking poet. Three pounds.

STOMACH
Gurgle, hoip!

SECOND VOICE
And three vodka Red Bulls for the energy because no food has been eaten and with that energy you –

FIRST VOICE
need to eat. Why don't you eat while drinking?

SECOND VOICE
Because of the appetite suppressant qualities of the alcohol. Because of the delirium. Because of the euphoria.

FIRST VOICE
He was like that, you know. *He'd* never eat while he drank. I watched him starve himself.

SECOND VOICE
Oh yeah? Well how come he was such a porker?

FIRST VOICE
That was probably one of the things that killed him so young,
the weakened body –

SECOND VOICE
bouncing jaunty up the hill to –

FIRST VOICE
Brown's Hotel where he'd meet his father of a morning to
share a beer with him as they pored over *The Times* crossword.
See the photographs of him on every wall. See the Augustus
John portrait of him on the swinging inn sign above the door.

GUIDEBOOK VOICE
One of the most famous taverns in the world now thanks to
its connections with the dissolute Welsh poet who died in
1953 in New York at the age of 39. His table still sits in the
alcove of the bay window surrounded by memorabilia, yet the
barstaff and regulars will leave you in no doubt that this is first
and foremost a pub, not a shrine.

FIRST VOICE
Yes but this tavern on a tourist trail, heritaged here, this listing
building listed now –

SECOND VOICE
and inside; more bloody rugby.

TOURISTS *(a discordant choir of clamouring voices)*
Where's Neil Morrisey? Where's Neil Morrisey? Man behaving
badly with the cheeky grin?

SECOND VOICE
And up at the bar the snaggle-toothed old feller orders. Would
call him a salty sea-dog type if that meant anything at all.

SALTY SEA-DOG TYPE
Whisky and a pint, Rhi.

RHIANNON THE BARMAID
What kind of whisky, Bill?

BILL THE SALTY SEA-DOG
Makes no difference.

RHI THE BARMAID
Double, is it?

BILL THE SALTY SEA-DOG
Better make it a small one. Started on the stuff earlier, see.

RHI THE BARMAID
Oh aye? When?

BILL THE SALTY SEA-DOG
Nineteen sixty-seven.

FIRST VOICE
And yes oh yes now you are drunk the living you can see in this man and the living to come in her. Born another time perhaps she might be saying to him and he to her: "Oh let me crash and come to grief, oh let me shipwreck in your thighs."

SECOND VOICE
Take pint and peanuts to the bright bay window seat and drink that pint and several more as dark velvet rises over the rooftops and the sounds of the outside night-time blare and blur.

PASSING CAR *(same as before)*
Dumph dumph dumph dumph DUMPH DUMPH dumph dumph

SECOND VOICE

And you like *him* love that slow-lapping alcohol rush. And the blurred heiroglyphics on the TV screen that when you squint to read them tell you the best story you've heard today: WIG 0 LIV 1 and MID 3 CHE 0. Something else to drink to.

FIRST VOICE

Yes, ahgh ye fuckaaaahh! And drink they do all over the town, beer and spirits in the pubs and wine and green tea in the houses where once it would've been –

SEAGULLS

Laa-ger! Laa-ger!

FIRST VOICE

in The Mariner's, yes, where –

SECOND VOICE

to me because I can see a terrible sadness prevails. This is the pub where after *he* died his wife would seek to drown her griefs (which learnt to swim) in beer and men (which burnt to *him*, for her, for her). Queue up they would to lance her loneliness. There is a tale concerning one of *their* children seeing her mother's legs straddling the arse of a visiting navvy across a garden wall next door to the pub and his workmates forming a jostling queue up the street. Imagine the spread legs of your mother and that pimply arse and the –

FIRST VOICE

nuts, salted, in a bowl on the bar. You remember reading or being told something about nineteen different traces of urine found in a bowl of shared nuts cos of the, cos of the men who don't wash their hands after peeing and then eat the nuts. Dirty friggers. Those men over there with the suspicious eyes and urinous hands. The dirty little friggers.

SECOND VOICE

And only you can hear their thoughts:

LOCAL 3
More of them queer for the fucking poet.

LOCAL 4
He's fifty years' dead, boy. Leave him be. Let him rest –

FIRST VOICE
under the sod like the boundless others and their alone-ness never even stifled by earth or worms. Hear them:

DEAD HUSBAND
Never leave me.

DEAD WIFE
I can't, now. We're in the same grave. You've got me forever, now.

SECOND VOICE
Oh to be free of the everyday obscenities, this smear of someone else's excrement on the toilet bowl. Wiping your arse you hear someone enter the toilets and approach the urinal and then the trickle of their piddle and then a thunderous breaking of wind:

ARSE
BRAMPFT!

FIRST VOICE
And you go back out to the bar through a foul miasma unsteady on your legs now and you drink more and drink more and leave Brown's for another pub and when the clock in the tower if it still worked would ring twelve times you –

SECOND VOICE
can hear their thoughts, now, yes. All the voices in this small town and all the songs they sing but in such a drunkenness as this it all sounds like one wailing, just one wailing. And there is an ecstasy that must burn itself out and there is a joy that

will pillage as much as it awards and there is a long dark trailing shadow that will always leech off a certain kind of happiness. That's easy to understand now.

FIRST VOICE
And accept?

SECOND VOICE
And accept, yes. Cos now I'm drunker than the crows on the battlements like short black soldiers but I don't understand how, I mean it was *you* that was drinking how can I –

FIRST VOICE
fall into sleep and only I can hear the song in the earth:

VOICE IN THE EARTH
But I'll always think as I tumble into bed
Of the silly little ones who are dead, dead, dead.

FIRST VOICE
Hear it? No? You will. Just listen.

DYLAN THOMAS
ALAN GARNER
EDWARD THOMAS
REV W AWDRY
JASPER FFORDE
MARY BUTTS
THOMAS HARDY
RICHARD LONG
H W TILMAN

Footnotes

Living a Richard Long life

by Peter Kirby

Keep going. Everything is cyclical, all things loop, even those without a tail. Believe in motion and the starts, middles and ends will, by force of nature, play musical chairs. "Time" does little more than coerce us into thinking that a walk is "linear." Ask Richard Long. On the surface, his life's work is making circles and lines through walking. It's not so much his poetic geometry that fascinates as what happens to us all when we walk outdoors. By putting one foot in front of another, I hope in some small way to prove that time, is indeed, a dodo.

miles: **1**
seeds: **26**
longs: **gangster rabbits, write dryly under bridge, a gale broods, magic of the moonlit teasel**

Thalking already. This is what landscape does to us – begs the brain to take a delta of walks simultaneously. The Harry Hill of rambling. Translating thalking into writing is a hazard. The telepathic ether from land-to-foot-to-head-to-hand is, at its most lucid, a bovine mode of dictation. Keep noting. Words are restless, hungry to the point of mute, from being born on a many-too-many-mile trek through ground that cried every acupunctural step of the way. Start a walk 98 per cent man. End it 98 per cent land.

O S M O S I S   O F   W A L K I N G

ROCK – BOOT – SOCK – SKIN – BLOOD – BONE – SOUL
⟨

⟩
Distance loves direction. As the kittiwake flies, the most southerly north coast of mainland Britain lies 26 miles from the most southerly south coast of mainland Britain. With January daylight, at a modest pace and no knee jip, it's doable. Just. Hurl in a force 8 SW gale and a reservoir of rain per hour, then the distance doubles. Walking into weather that got out of the sky the wrong side is, well, fun. But weather changes the gender of land. Nursery slopes grow muscles with the up of a gust. Rain saturates the pores of a moor that will limpet a trespasser's boot. "BABAM!BABAM!BABAM!" says the sun as it dries out the moisture cushion so that the heels absorb the daddy of all upper cuts. And finally, beware, the seven fatal interferences of terrain. Sleet. Snow. Frost. Ice. Dew. Dung. And duff shoes. All of which are simply land's way of playing hard to get.   *miles: 2*
seeds: 25
longs: giant concrete cruet, monkey-puzzle
cacophony, parachuting Santa cruci-
fied to chimneybreast

I write about a walk, while paradoxically, I sit. Still. My memory orienteers through thick skull-fog for eidetic paths. These paths, mown by foot, will fade unless followed. Keep ferreting. Kinetics is a law of Long. Movement is his medium, just as my fingers meander with their own delicious spirit, governed only by the law of QWERTY. Even the finest laptop words are genetically modified. CUT. EDIT. PASTE. Yet, if I channel my thoughts through a single point of pencil lead that was itself once land, my free-range free-will erupts.   *miles: 3*
seeds: 24
longs: panzer of seven
conifers, two
human mornings,

one canine hello,
public byway verses
private myway

People once belonged to land. Now land belongs to people. Blame the Benedictine monk, Fra Luca Bartolomeo and his double entry bookkeeping that gave rise to capitalism and the owning of everything. As the sea nibbles away at the cliffs, the notion of common land for the common man shrinks. I see it now ... "Mother Ocean v Mother Earth ... cannibalistic tussle of oestrogen ... refereed by Old Father Time ... book now for your ringside seat ... with ever decreasing legroom ... at the Great Outdoor Super-Slow-Mo Reality Show."

miles: 4

seeds: 23

longs: head high footing for a tree house, drunk driver
remnants, tarmac stream races to the ford that flirts
a fortnight a year

Impermanence appeals to Long.

miles: 5

seeds: 22

longs: confrontations of a bull, "rifle shots ring out in a
ballroom night ..."

He sings with his feet. The landscape mucks in as his orchestra.

miles: 6

seeds: 21

longs: dolphin stair lifts
of Gurlyn Farm
where they grow
operatic ladies

The hills play Sigur Ros to me. I hear a "landguage" I pray I'll never understand, for fear of its beauty waning. A waft of wind turns a dying weed into a reed, and blows its last gasp of philharmonic joy. How the fields can sing.

miles: 7

seeds: 20

longs: malachite moss, apish swings over iron oxide
swamp, thumb gash gapes open, make-life-up-on-
the-hoof-and-it-smiles

Walk a Dogme walk. Take only a skeletal script: to plant a shrine at every mile. Tiny stacks of sunflower seeds hand-grown in urban SE1 to be hand-sewn in tundra TR12. These Lilliputian cairns mark the passing of a point. The walk is a wake. The seeds are my ashes. Head south with my DIY crematorium.

miles: **8**

seeds: **19**

longs: **the Shawshank tree, Dr Gilly's mucus-coated energy bar, apartheid of daffs**

Smell the shape of the land. Contours are 50 per cent concave, 50 per cent convex, 50 per cent confusion. With every season, altitudes grow a size, then slim a size. Terra firma is a fib. Nature taught fashion how to move, baby.

miles: **9**

seeds: **18**

longs: **lost, went the way the map said no, serendipity, Yorkshire couple contra-Sherpa one another over cup of tea they never offer as I stand there shivering**

Long's precision is my suck-it-and-see. His stride invigilates Ordnance Survey. This disentwined crop-circle-of-a-man is forever in sync with the wild canvas he walks upon. Nature looks forward to Long.

miles: **10**

seeds: **17**

longs: **rainbow's end, sunbow's start, plant seeds at Rocky Lane nursery and sting forehead**

A mountain launders the head of a thousand dilemmas. The air alone sifts the gunk, allowing the heart to think and the lungs to sprint. Psychotherapists should listen to us at the top of a hill if they are ever to sell us happiness. Conquering a peak, whatever the height, can wipe the sulk from a teenager or assuage the grief of a widow. It can unite the most hated of enemies and still make an accountant strip naked. Mountains move men, women and at a push, IT consultants. They offer the peace money can't buy. Serenity is the freeholder of all summits, so go climb even when the weather's beating down the door for the rent.

miles: **11**

seeds: **16**

longs: **school song sung into oblique wind on top of Godolphin hill, Turkish power-lifter holly tree wee**

Only when we stop do we sense the random interconnectedness of the world about us. Ground is gravity's lawyer. Tide is sea's lung. Cloud is sky's belly button fluff. That is this there. Me is the geology of I. Every thing is related; all we have to do is unpick the lineage. Keep weaving. We are as much mineral or vegetable as we are animal.

miles: **12**

seeds: **15**

longs: **Castle Pencaire, many stone circles, a Scott-gazumped-by-Amundsen feeling, stab seeds in sword-of-remembrance sand so the wind won't blow them all away**

Writing outdoors floods our veins with chlorophyll, and strips away that veneer of cosy domesticity. It anchors us deep in dialogue with the land and serves up a 4,600,000,000-year conversation, which may, or may not, include "the weather." Stand up while writing and our relationship with the page alters again. With both feet firmly rooted to the ground, the earth's primordial energy and urgency surge up from the core to the crust in half a yoctosecond. The writer who stands knows how to boot a benign phrase up the backside. Ask any biped.

miles: **13**

seeds: **14**

longs: **194 metres, Tregonning Hill, I love you text from Kate, prayer out loud for Tony**

The Bible, rumour has it, was written by a penguin, stood starkers, on a small hillock, in rural Greenland. Keep believing.

miles: 14

seeds: 13

longs: seeds sewn and flown, Culdrose clones, camera dies, dead animals run free

Outprisonment is the future for crime. If we sentence the guilty to do time in the open, we remove subordination and their carrot of escape. A one-year walk across "all that nature can throw at him" will redirect the morals of a man much deeper in his gut than serving twenty years inside. For solitary confinement, read solitary exposure.

miles: 15

seeds: 12

longs: San Andreas Fault in crust of Queens Arms pie, cycling vicar brags of brass tombs

As the body tires, we try death's dress on. Call me bleak, but I'll be happy to die today, providing it's outdoors, beside a stream, after a full day's fatigue, with a bird in song, a tree in bloom and a butterfly in flight.

miles: 16

seeds: 11

longs: Breage olde morgue, teasel-lapelled pallbearers lay a football team of seeds to rest

Shadows are shy.

miles: 17

seeds: 10

longs: Rinsey road chemical blackberries, hedge is a mile long brolly

Horizons fidget.

miles: 18

seeds: 9

longs: medusa snake climbs Kate's hair tree, Tremeane schtum beach, sea

carves granite
Buddha for
meditating
seals

Every journey by foot is a pilgrimage, even if its reason is never to be known. Richard Long teaches us to trust a walk. The land always delivers, even in its most barren moments. Dragging a foot, bead upon bead of cascading sweat, a hermit cloud. He is not precious how he creates his pieces, only that the method is easy and appropriate. Often, the paucity of materials can force the land to declare its composition, as if by chance. This faith in fate gives roots to his work. Every single word of text has to fight for its place in our world, and once we become witness, it holds us to ransom.

miles: **19**
seeds: **8**
longs: **Gaza Strip**
stile,
Hamas
gusts, cow
parsley
gymnastics

See the wall not as an obstacle, but as an element, and all the pieces will fall right into place.

M A R A T H O N
MILES **26** LETTERS
A L P H A B E T

Start to feel the lean of the loop. The centrifugal pull of home. Despite all attempts to walk a line from A to B, I am now convinced that the sequence is not that logical. Fibonacci was onto something. Keep going forward but never dismiss what you leave behind. Destination is overrated and admits as much in its ontology class. All that matters is place.

miles: **20**
seeds: **7**
longs: **thrift duvet warren, down below 10 ft barrels of salty**
insomnia avalanche in, under, up 'n' over

Grass gets springier the closer you get to the sea to help sui-
cides jump. Keep breathing.
miles: 21

seeds: 6

longs: the wrestling fields,
tamarisk boulevard,
wind freewheels me
like a child

Bottle the sensation of writing downhill. Release the breaks of
doubt, the screen goes black and the uninhibited me can feel
what darkness does to the written word. Hit the chiaroscuro
key. The silhouette skyline clings to the rind of the emerging
moon. I sense the odd punctuation of light, an electric bush,
palsied sheep with neon eyes. Gulls play crows at aerial chess.
The crows cheat. Keep plotting. My route waltzes with civi-
lization; a wavy line that marries then divorces then remarries
then adulterates then celibates. A river slurs its reflection. Sad
tapered tears of light dagger their way into the flickering
ripples of an alcoholic alter ego and make me gag for dense,
red wine. Is this why sleeping under stars rams 40,000 volts
though our soul? Keep camping.
miles: 22

seeds: 5

longs: chips with every-
thing, deed fried
in sunflower oil,
potatoes must
grow ready-
battered

Space. Inner, Outer, Third, Fourth, Absolute. Why do we try so
hard to put space in a box? Its beauty is its borderless blankness.

See. Keep pausing.   *miles: 23*
                      seeds: 4
                      longs: hate usurps spite, Morrissey
                      misery piggybacks me,
                      Gunwalloe 3¾
Nature is innumerate, thank God, as I am too. Yes sure, there are patterns and rhythms, but every single blade of grass is its own size, shape and colour. Try as they might, plants cannot grow metronomically. Some are social, some solitary, some sow themselves a land mass away. But come autumn and a zealous prevailing wind, they may just park side by side again, such is the freedom of propagation. Keep blowing.

miles: 24
seeds: 3
longs: macabre Loe Bar, shout punk anthem against
        elements
The weather is having a complete nervous breakdown and I am no Samaritan. I fight thunder with thunder. Angry symmetry. Feel like naming a band after this reaction and immediately soothe. Wondering if Long's stoic calm ever simmers over. Return aptly, to symmetry. Recall a forty-foot face I made nine years ago in the camber of a cliff at Gurnard's Head and how, one year on, the sculpture was lost to the unshaven land. When Long does return to his work, it is not to admire or record it, but to dismantle it.

miles: 25
seeds: 2
longs: empty words in fertile mouths, tell the age of
        a bench by the depth of scuff beneath it
My haggard hands are now caked in Avon mud to feel the phenomenon with which Long makes his installation murals in galleries across the world. Despite two weeks in a bag, the mud has no stench. Yet it retains a viscosity, which with water, allows him to paint by hand using the land. Another beautiful circle completes. Time throws in the towel. I raise my mudded paws,

shattered but happy, and expend my last few joules in search of a title.

3. "AN ENCYCLOPEDIA OF TENACITY." Kind of true, but kind of bloated.
2. "OF." Immense little filler of a word. Poignant, powerful and wedded to landscape, just like Long himself. As is: to, at, in, up, he, me. So no go.
1. "FOOTNOTES." First word I wrote prepping for this project. It stuck with me. Intuition says I told you so.

miles: 26
seeds: 1
longs: darkness mugs dayness, right knee sighs & sings
        "oh coastal path ... take me home ... to the place ...
        where I belong ..."

DYLAN THOMAS
KEITH
EDWARD THOMAS
JASPER
FFORDE
RICHARD LONG
HW TILMAN
THOMAS HARDY
MARY
BUTTS

Salt Calling Home to Salt

HW Tilman in Falmouth

by Penelope Williams

For me, it's all about the sea. It's where we came from. The mix of salts in the ancient oceans still echoes in our blood, whether you take this as a scientific fact or feel it in your marrow.

Growing up aboard a wooden ketch in Falmouth Harbour, the sea and its moods were my chief concerns. My hopes hung on every syllable of the shipping forecast. Would we be seasick? Would the anchor drag? Would we get ashore to school? My head, when not buried in a book from Falmouth library, was popping out of the hatch on the foredeck to see what other boats had most recently arrived from the shores of America, Australia, South Africa or the West Indies. Did they need fresh milk, fresh bread? My sister and I would be rowing ashore to fetch these delectable prizes, and back to gaze, speechless, at the bronzed faces, bleached locks and crinkled eyes of our local heroes.

We saw hands of bananas hanging from the cabin beams. We saw beads from Canada, carvings from St Helena, scrimshaw from the Azores, and we sipped, surreptitiously, from mugs of local rum (local to the Bahamas). We sat, quiet as sea-mice, in the corners of these cabins, hoping to remain unobserved and unsent-to-bed, while our parents exchanged tales, charts and weather reports with the newly arrived. Bottled dorado, Barbadian molasses and biltong from Port Elizabeth were eagerly traded for tins whose soggy labels had slipped into bilges, but whose attraction for sailors on monotonous shoestrings lay in the "surprise."

Perched on the granite steps of the dinghy basin at the Prince of Wales Pier, where I was dropped ashore to school every day, and picked up at half past four, I smiled earnestly at every landing sailor and dreamed of stowing away. *Pomona, Xlendi, Armorel, Romadi, Pegasus, Morgana* ... for me, the visiting yachts offered all the solemn promise of wave-leaping unicorns. Over the years, some of these yachts would return with news of yachts we had met before. Others sailed never to be heard of again, leaving rumours floating like wreckage in the doldrums. The stories went on into the small hours, wreathing with tobacco smoke and the flicker of Tilley lamps, giving me a lifelong fascination with tales tall and small.

The main reason for living on a boat in the seventies, I discovered, was to "escape the rat race." My visions of giant rodents on the West Way, where we went to visit grandma in Ealing, were crystal clear. Myth and reality mingled perfectly in my life afloat. They still do. It's what makes me write.

In the breezy May of 1976, *Baroque* arrived, to excitement in the harbour. The skipper was Bill (Major HW) Tilman, a notoriously grumpy, living legend whose books about voyages in his first boat, *Mischief,* were on the cramped wooden shelves of every yacht I'd ever been aboard. *Mischief in Greenland, Mischief in Patagonia, Mischief Among the Penguins.* I hadn't read them then. Their damp-curled pages ranked, with Slocum, Chichester, Hiscock, and *Reed's Nautical Almanac,* amongst the bibles of the world's sailing population. "See if you can get aboard" grinned my father. He might as well have suggested I invite myself to tea with the Ancient Mariner.

But I was a lot braver then. I simply rowed circles around *Baroque,* singing sea shanties, until his crew finally let me aboard. I sat chirruping nonsense in the cabin, dark and damp as church and almost as awe-inspiring, until Major Tilman, somewhat surprisingly, offered me a can of coke. He asked my name, but couldn't catch it: "Benny?" "No, *Penny*. I'm a girl!" I might as well have said "duchess." In the disconcerted silence that followed Tilman growled at his crew, "Well, fetch her a glass!" Ladies drank from glasses, even if they were only ten years old. He signed our new copy of *Ice with Everything* and subsided into his bunk, staring up at the deck beams as if he could see right through them. I'd seen that look before. It was the thousand mile stare of men stuck in port, waiting for the wind. I knew he wanted to be back at sea, and I knew, without having the words yet, why.

Thirty years later, the mere idea of writing about Tilman has me nervously splashing my oars and singing off-key. Few outside the sailing or mountaineering communities will ever have heard of him. How to do justice to the man's deeds, let alone his words?

Tim Madge's excellent biography of Tilman, *The Last Hero*, is an insightful and inspiring account of a man whose life was spent compensating in heroic effort and achievement for all the lives Tilman he saw lost in the mud of the Somme, before he was twenty years old. It was as if he was trying to do everything he thought that they, "so many better men, some of them friends,"[1] could have done, or *would* have done, if they had not been killed. In *Two Mountains and a River* he alludes to his distress by quoting Coleridge: "And a thousand, thousand slimy things/Lived on and so did I."[2]

Tilman was fond of quoting. It absolved him from more personal revelations that he found uncomfortable. After winning a Military Cross in the First World War, still aged only twenty, he went to Africa to carve a coffee plantation from the jungle, where isolation and his own unsociability left him to read the whole of Dent's *Everyman* in his spare time. Carving completed, and library exhausted, he grew bored and switched to prospecting for gold. Prospects unimproved, he then cycled across Africa, east to west, living for two months on bananas. This exploit inspired his first book, *Snow on the Equator*. Real readers can't help but dream of being writers.

While in Africa, Tilman met and climbed with another exceptional writer–explorer, Eric Shipton. The two became known as the "terrible twins" of their generation, pioneering the oxygen and climbing techniques that eventually helped Tensing and Hillary reach the summit of Everest. Tilman wrote seven books about mountaineering, recording an era, and a sense of endeavour, that is lost forever.

Already into middle age, he then decided to sail to his mountains, and wrote a further eight books. In language as plain and wiry as a salt-rimed length of hemp, he carries the reader safely through icebergs, williwaws, kelp, storms, mutinies, and uncharted islands. His style is consistently understated. "On a voyage to Iceland in *Mischief* we once watched the eruption and formation of a volcanic island where the successive explosions under the sea and the uprush of steam, smoke and ash to a great height were sufficiently awe-inspiring."[3] Sufficiently!

The only romance he ever refers to was the sea itself. On the trip from Las Palmas to Montevideo, en route for his first adventure in Patagonia, he writes: "For the next seven days we ran in the full swing of the trades. These were days of glorious sailing. The sun blazed down till the pitch in the seams bubbled, the dazzling white twins swayed and curtsied until their booms kissed the water, while the ship rolled lazily along her run of more than a hundred miles every day. … We even had flying fish for breakfast every morning with no exertion at all."[4]

Tilman's love of nature was more than gastronomic. Sighting polar bears in Arctic waters made one whole voyage worthwhile. He frequently identifies wild flowers and plants, noting the "pleasing" scent of wild ylang-ylang, or the fact that Kerguelen cabbage must be boiled for three hours to make it edible. In the Patagonian Channels, he blends admiration with a dry, self-deprecating humour, and a rare reference to his experience in the trenches. "Several more floes of fantastic shape and delicate blue colouring, now drifted by close to the ship and were greeted with pleased cries, much as some ignorant clown might greet the first few ranging shots of a hostile battery."[5] Securing a safer anchorage, Tilman left half the crew in charge of the ship, and went ashore with the rest to make the first-ever crossing of the Patagonian ice cap, from Chile to Argentina.

The restraint in his prose makes Tilman's honesty all the more poignant. *In Mischief's Wake* includes his obituary for his first yacht. *Mischief* struck a rock on someone else's watch, and, after days of painful rescue efforts, while she was battered by sea and ice on a beach, she sank as she was being towed to harbour. "For me it was the loss of more than a yacht. I felt like one who had first betrayed and then deserted a stricken friend; a friend with whom for the past fourteen years I had spent more time at sea than on land, and who, when not at sea, had seldom been out of my thoughts ... I shall never forget her." His final reference to Milton's *Paradise Lost* says it all: "The world was all before her, where to choose / Her place of rest, and Providence her guide."[6]

Tilman sailed and climbed without any of the technology or corporate sponsorships that insure the modern hero. Not for him the weeping on camera in a cockpit dwarfed by mighty seas. When they sailed, Tilman and his crew knew that they might not come back. In trouble, the only ones to save them would be themselves. He would not have wanted it any other way.

Writing for a stunt-hungry publisher was the last thing on his mind. He was lucky enough not to have to earn a living, or rely on a sponsor, but worked harder than most labourers at sea or on the mountains. The only solace he could find ashore was in painstakingly trekking ink across pages as empty, white and defiant as unexplored glaciers. For this alone, he is my hero. His favourite word on the map of Patagonia, was "inesplorado." Unexplored. As a woman who loves the sea, the ice and occasional degrees of solitude, I believe this was not, as Freudians might have it, the desire to penetrate the unbroken, but the desire to be alone with the purity of creation: "to seek those first experiences and try to feel as felt the earlier man in a happier time, to see the world as they saw it." (Tilman quoting Belloc.)[7]

Was Tilman a man driven, or drawn? Hard on others, he was harder on himself. Was he driven by survivor's guilt, a heavy-handed father, or a Victorian work ethic? He steadfastly refused to comment on his own motivation for doing anything, this time resorting to Stevenson: "In the joy of the actors lies the sense of any action. That is the explanation, that the excuse."[8]

I don't believe any man could be driven to do what he did, given that he had a choice, and could have retired on an independent income to sit on his war laurels. Tilman *chose* to sail and climb.

So what is it that draws a man to spend most of his years at sea, with companions he hardly knows?

Space. Ice. Waves. Wind. The unexpected. The unknown. The primeval pull of the sea in the blood, salt calling home to salt. Even on the glaciers, or in the ice, Tilman was treading frozen water, frozen sea. My sense is that Tilman went back there because that's where he felt he belonged.

The feeling of belonging, whether to a lover or a family, a group of friends or a country or, ultimately, in the world, is essential to human happiness. Belonging is the antidote to loneliness. Tilman, a self-confessed hermit, found it hard to "belong" with most people, but perhaps even harder to be totally alone. The fact that he never took the single-handed sailor's route was not because it was impossible to do so in icy waters, but because he didn't want to. There is an undeniable satisfaction in putting together a crew of men who might walk past each other in the street, but who, when crisis comes, will pull together and survive. Tilman learned the value, and the vulnerability, of human bonds in the trenches. He never lost it. He was much more human, in that sense, than he is generally given credit for.

Between 1954 and 1977, Bill Tilman sailed over 160,000 miles across the world's oceans. In 2002, I crewed a paltry 500 miles on a steel ketch from Ushuaia to Antarctica. The month we spent cruising the Antarctic Peninsula showed me a beauty I felt was holy. Magnificent icebergs lured and appalled me in equal measure. The sense of awe was overwhelming. No wonder Tilman was drawn.

Down below in the cabin, I felt as much at home in the frozen south as I did as a child in Falmouth Harbour. I lay in my bunk, listening to the water burbling along the hull, while the "bergy bits" scrabbled past, and imagined the molecules of unfrozen ocean, each linking to the next, all the way back to Falmouth on the other side of the world. Home on the water, is home, anywhere.

Incorrigible as always, and wishing to celebrate his eightieth birthday in Antarctica, Tilman sailed as crew on a converted tug, *En Avant*. The voyage to Rio de Janeiro was very happy. *En Avant* sailed for Port Stanley in November 1977. She never arrived. The old man of the sea, and his brave companions, had gone.

I can't leave him there. In honour of his underestimated humour, and his kindness, I'd rather leave you with his views on elephant seals, as he met them in the Crozet Islands. "Should an aggressive old fellow decide to shuffle forwards one has to step back pretty smartly. The youngsters have better manners. They just lie with one eye open and the other half shut as one approaches, and if one begins stroking them they shut both and go to sleep again."[9] Imagine this fierce old mariner sitting quietly down by a young seal, and stroking it to sleep.

It's lonely at a keyboard, for any writer. Humdrum, tap-tap, on a voyage across the unknown, in search of the extraordinary. I'm a copywriter these days. It's an artisan's job, managing language for people who can't, the way a shipwright handles timber. It's still about telling stories. That's how I grew up: listening out for the fabulous thread that spins into a narrative spell.

Living on the water taught me to observe the world from its margin: the quiet, unregarded space in which some of the most sincere thoughts are often noted. My marginal life was a gift to me from my parents. Tilman's was a brave and remarkable choice.

My next adventure will no doubt be on paper, that daunting voyage across the wilderness of my novel. Like the icebergs, this lures and appals.

But "To the brave all things are possible."[10] That's me, quoting Tilman.

Notes

1 HW Tilman, "Two Mountains and a River," *The Seven Mountain-Travel Books,* Mountaineers Books, 2003, p. 517.

2 Ibid.

3 HW Tilman, "In Mischief's Wake," *The Eight Sailing/Mountain-Exploration Books,* Diadem Books, 1993, p. 651.

4 Tilman, "Mischief in Patagonia," op. cit., p. 42.

5 Ibid, p. 81.

6 Tilman, "In Mischief's Wake," op. cit., p. 658.

7 Tilman, "Mischief in Patagonia," op. cit., p. 21.

8 Tilman, "Mischief in Greenland," op. cit., p. 263.

9 Tilman, "Mischief Among the Penguins," op. cit., p. 191.

10 Ibid, p. 203.

The Diadem Books collection includes an introduction by Colin Putt, one of Tilman's crew, and a more comprehensive bibliography. For anyone seeking a Tilman first edition that might have been to sea on someone else's boat, these notes might help.

Mischief in Patagonia first published by Cambridge University Press, 1957.
Mischief Among the Penguins first published by Rupert Hart-Davis, 1961.
Mischief in Greenland first published by Hollis & Carter Ltd, 1964.
Mostly Mischief first published by Hollis & Carter Ltd, 1966.
Mischief Goes South first published by Hollis & Carter Ltd, 1968.
In Mischief's Wake first published by Hollis & Carter Ltd, 1971.
Ice With Everything first published by Nautical Publishing Company,
in association with George G. Harrap & Co. Ltd, 1974.
Triumph and Tribulation first published by Nautical Publishing Company, 1977.

Diadem Books also published HW Tilman, *The Seven Mountain-Travel Books.*
The collection is also published by Mountaineers Books. It comprises:
Snow on the Equator, The Ascent of Nanda Devi, When Men and Mountains Meet, Everest, 1938, Two Mountains and a River, China to Chitral, Nepal Himalaya.

Tim Madge's biography, *The Last Hero,* is published by Hodder & Stoughton.

Bob Comlay, another of Tilman's crew, runs a fascinating website with some beautiful photographs at www.comlay.net/tilman

PAUL AUSTER

ABBOTT

KEITH

WATERH[OUSE]

ALAN GARNER

DAVID LODGE

DYLAN THOMAS

WILLIAM SHAKESPEARE

WILL S

EDWARD THOMAS

REV W AWDRY

JULIAN H

JOHN

PAT

BARNES

IL

HILA

JASPER FFORDE

VIRGINIA

MARY BUTTS

WOOLF

RICHARD LONG

HW TILMAN

THOMAS HARDY

A Nameless Luminous

Dorset, Word-tunes and Mary Butts

by Molly Mackey

"What's your name and where do you come from?" screeched Cilla Black every Saturday night as she stage-managed a *Blind Date* for two well-rehearsed singletons – her own accent threading back years to the city in which she grew up. Names and places: important first questions. They lead somewhere; start a trail; plant clues. Finding out where a stranger hails from gives acquaintanceship direction. From the Queen of England to a stadium of football fans, places add definition to identity.

Take the Bloomsbury Group, for example. Writers and artists in the early twentieth century bound together by a place, originally a house in Gordon Square, London. The names are familiar: Virginia Woolf, Vanessa Bell, Roger Fry, EM Forster. Not, however, Mary Butts. Born in 1890, Butts hovered on the periphery of this literary set. She knew, and was close to, many of the group's major players, but she was not one of them. Butts's bohemian lifestyle and her determined pursuit of the spiritual set her apart. In addition, Butts's brother, Anthony, a friend of the Bloomsbury group, shared his dislike of Mary with those who would listen. Virginia Woolf described Tony

Butts as being "ashamed" of his sister, who features in Woolf's diaries as "the malignant Mary."[1] Woolf also refused to publish Butts's first novel, *Ashe of Rings*, under the Hogarth Press, describing it as "an indecent book, about the Greeks and the Downs."[2] Butts herself realised that she was "some sort of observer, some sort of witness, who [after a brief time spent in the company of Roger Fry] was never again so far as Bloomsbury *personalities* were concerned, to be wholly in or wholly out of touch."[3]

Butts didn't belong in – or to – London, despite living there on-and-off for many years from 1909. Even with her literary friends, numerous lovers and swirling city social life, Mary Butts was not "town-tuned." She belonged instead to Dorset. Born in Poole, Butts grew up by the coast, in the twenty-one acres surrounding Salterns, the family home near Parkstone, East Dorset. In an unpublished poem, Butts described herself as not just from Dorset, but of it: "A Child come out of the sea."[4]

For Butts, Dorset was not simply the answer to "Where are you from?" It was more than a scattering of scenery and beautiful views. Dorset defined her. It was a presence and a powerful force, both throughout her life and within her writing. Butts's novels, *Ashe of Rings*, *Armed with Madness* and *Death of Felicity Taverner* all take place in the county. But the coastal landscape isn't just a stage on which events unfold. In Butts's work, Dorset is centre stage. As Carston, the American visitor to the house in *Armed with Madness* observes, "Here, the scenery seemed to be the play."[5]

He's right. At the beginning of *Armed with Madness*, we meet the house, the wood and the sea before we encounter any of the characters. In the first few pages, Scylla, Felix, Clarence, Ross, and Picus remain an anonymous group known only as "they." "They belonged to the house and the wood and the turf."[6] The land owns *them*. The scenery lives, breathes and grabs the reader before anything, or anyone, else. It's a place that giggles, sighs, cackles and gossips. It needs appeasing. Here, silence is "Marvellously noisy … a complicated production of stone rooms, the natural silence of empty grass, and the equivocal, personal silence of the wood."[7] Carston, the house's guest – rather than the people's – is uncomfortable in this world. He finds the silence "intolerable" and notices "too much scenery that called for a too high quality of attention."[8] Bewildered, he longs for "a human scene."[9]

The scene however, *is* human. It's an agent, a character wrapped into the fabric of the text, pushing, prodding and directing the narrative. Places do this beyond the realm of fiction. They become involved in our lives as much as the people we meet within them. Intertwined. To know a place, Butts wrote, "One must have a private map of one's own in one's mind. A magic map …"[10] My own visits to the Dorset coast involve walks, friends, pub lunches, twisted ankles, air as fresh as mint, wild sea winds and, after noticing her unusual name on a bookshelf, the novels of Mary Butts. For me, the word Dorset sparks a private map of moments, images and faces. Much of this, of course, is the place's role as a memory carrier: a shared space in my head of scenery, action and people. Where events, personalities and emotions seep into the landscape, and vice versa.

I'm from Leicester in the East Midlands. It is not Dorset. I live in Finsbury Park, London. It is neither Dorset, nor Bloomsbury (alas!). I holiday in Dorset. Leicester, Dorset and Finsbury Park have entirely different roles in my life, but they each play a part. Each place has its own DNA and a particular story to tell. When the journalist AA Gill was asked by his editor what he wanted from his profession, he replied "I'd like to interview places. To treat a place as if it were a person, to go and listen to it, ask it questions, observe it the way you would interview a politician or a popstar."[11]

The landscape of Butts's childhood always had its own personality – independent and unique. In her autobiographical novel, *The Crystal Cabinet*, Butts describes how as a child at Salterns she played games around the base of a tree, which she called The Stump. This tree was "Alive with personality, the character proper to a large, worn, wise hump of old oak."[12] From an early age Mary Butts realised that "a place can be more than its assembly of wood and leaf and stone visible to us; more than the atomic structure common to all things."[13]

Butts's first novel, *Ashe of Rings*, explores this observation. The story takes place at Badbury Rings, the Iron Age earthworks near Wimborne Minster in Dorset – now in the grounds of a National Trust property. The Rings had a profound effect on Butts during her childhood. In *The Crystal Cabinet* she describes the "abnormal sleep" that took place after she visited them as a child. She dreamt that the earthworks "were the same and not the same as the Rings awake and by day. Another version, taller and stronger, their loveliness and power, as it were, extended to other terms, not to be described."[14] In *Ashe of Rings*, the three concentric circles of earth – "the triple crown and the wood" – and the house that lies in their shadow, also called Rings, are powerful forces, sources of agency at work in the narrative, as they were in Butts's life. "*The house has a thousand eyes*"[15] and it protects Anthony Ashe and other initiates of Rings, guarding them from those who do not feel its magic. Anthony's wife Melitta, an Ashe by marriage only, cannot understand the place's power, so the house treats her as a trespasser. Her daughter, Vanna, however, takes possession of Rings at birth. It is her lifeblood.

In Butts's work people and place merge until it's difficult to tell the difference between the two. Often, characters are defined and determined only by their relationship with the landscape. When Carston watches Scylla in *Armed with Madness* he notices that "The wood and the woman might be interchangeable."[16] And they are. Scylla lies "on the wood's roof: translating the stick and leaf that upheld her into herself: into sea: into sky. Sky back again into wood, flesh and sea."[17] She and her brother are "limbs of the same tree." Similarly, in Ashe of Rings, Vanna breathes the earth, communicates "with the chill fingers of the trees," until, lying on a stone at the top of the earthworks, she is saved from rape by "becom[ing] part of this place, [until they] only find a stone."[18] Rings absorbs and protects her.

The polarisation between the Rings' initiates and those excluded from their mystery powers the action. There are those like Vanna and the housekeeper, Clavel, who understand the setting's "spell," pitched against those who find it "vile." Poised between these two conflicting groups is Serge, a Russian exile whom Vanna Ashe befriends and to whom she wants to reveal the power of Rings. But Serge is detached. For him, Rings remains only "wet grass and high trees ... a cold place."[19]

On one level, Mary Butts herself had "never seen anything but the trees and grass and wind and their accompaniments" on Badbury Rings, but in another sense she had "felt" their magic. For her the place is "enchanted – technically – concretely – if there is such a thing – by reputation, by experience, by tradition." *Ashe of Rings* is her attempt to convey this feeling. Yet Butts acknowledges that this "mystical experience ... is extraordinarily hard to write about, to examine, to describe. Language wasn't invented to deal with it; so it mostly gets out by indirections, obliquely, something like the knight's move in chess."[20] Describing the magical powers of place in the fixed terms of reality is a struggle. It parallels what Butts described as the artist's "problem" – the need to "express an unknown in terms of the known."[21] Places are complex characters, difficult to translate into human terms. So each of Butts's novels introduces an "outsider," somebody new to the setting who is trying to get to grips with its power – somebody like the reader.

Butts also uses the classical world to express landscape's magic, mythic and mystic properties. Fascinated as a child by the Greek myths she acted out with her father, she found within them "a hidden source of loveliness and power." Using the same terms, she described Salterns as the place where "Power and Loveliness walked naked over East Dorset, side by side." The world of the ancients and the Dorset landscape are inextricably linked. "Rings is different. It is a precinct, like Eleusis." And Salterns is Butts's sacred enclosure, her temenos in "the county where ... the secret of England is implicit, concealed, yet continually giving out the stored forces of its genius."[22] Where is Dorset from? Hellas, would be Mary Butts's answer. It is both ancient Greece and English landscape. Certain places are sacred, "a trap for more worlds than one."[23]

These other worlds seep out when Butts writes about landscape. The text gestures, often lyrically, to a world beyond that in which the scene is set. Place takes charge – and is charged. In *Armed with Madness*, Carston notices as a storm brews that "it was like the place to leap up from its equivocal quiet into an orgy of cracking and banging." And then the landscape takes over:

> "For an hour it rained, through sheet lightning, and thunder like a departing train, the hills calling to one another. The gutters of the roof rushed and sang and leaked, single notes from which the ear eventually picked out a tune. Syncopation, magic, nature imitating Mozart? Carston came to hear it as an overture, for some private-earth life, mercifully and tiresomely apart from his.
>
> Things going on singing, not to him. Escaping also, not finishing, or finishing somewhere else. Beginning again, to enchant him with fragments. He admitted that he was enchanted – when would Scylla wind up the charm by coming through the wood?
>
> The storm tuned up again, the rain striking in rods, filling the air with fine spray. The others were enjoying it, the first row of the stalls for a nature-play."[24]

Carston becomes invisible. The storm takes place in front of him and somewhere else at the same time. It does not sing to, or for, him. Once again, the scenery is the play. The novel's characters are passive observers, watching a powerful, active landscape that lives on elsewhere. As Vera in *Ashe of Rings* remarks, "We are spectators of a situation which is the mask for another situation, that existed perhaps some remote age, or in a world that is outside time."[25] In Butts's work, Dorset is "magic, whatever magic is."[26]

"You get out of it what you put in," says Vanna when talking about Rings in *Ashe of Rings*. That, she says, "is the first rule of magic."[27] My recent visits to Dorset have been an attempt to access what Mary Butts felt there. To get out what she put in, to see the magic, to watch Dorset live. While doing so I pour in my own experiences of the seascape and walks along the three-tiered wedding cake that is Badbury Rings. But Dorset and I have a different relationship. Influenced, no doubt by Mary Butts and her "seven ways of looking at a piece of jade," but also by my own experiences there. And as someone who is clearly town-tuned, I'm exactly the kind of person Butts advises to steer clear of the countryside in her pamphlet *Warning to Hikers* "because there threatens soon to be no country-side left ... to discover."[28] I sometimes wonder whether, when cast into Butts's world, I would be one of the initiates, or if I would hover between two worlds, like Serge in *Ashe of Rings*. Mary Butts probably wouldn't care. She knew that Dorset will always be "real by itself, without any reference to us."

Butts didn't need Bloomsbury and its personalities. She had Dorset – real by itself. The county lives and breathes in her novels more intensely than any other character. Dorset speaks of another world. Its woods and waters spark the beginning of a ritual, present the complex relations "between things of a different order: the moon and a stone, the sea and a piece of wood, women and fish."[29] It's a setting in which people become leaves and leaves become people, where place is the true protagonist. Like Mary Butts's novels, Dorset is "equivocal and exquisite." It talks in "word-tunes" and it speaks of magic.

Notes

1 Anne Olivier Bell (ed.), *The Diary of Virginia Woolf: Volume Five, 1936–1941,* Harvest/HBJ Book, 1985, 16 June 1937 entry.

2 Nigel Nicolson and Joanne Trautmann (eds), *The Letters of Virginia Woolf: Volume Two, 1912–1922,* Harvest/HBJ Book, 1982, no. 1307, 29 October 1922.

3 From the essay "Bloomsbury" (1936) cited in Nathalie Blondel, *Mary Butts: Scenes from the Life,* McPherson & Company, 1998, pp. 401–402.

4 "To Drakonti," written in 1909 cited in Nathalie Blondel (ed.), *The Journals of Mary Butts,* Yale University Press, 2003, p. 6.

5 Mary Butts, *The Taverner Novels: Armed with Madness/Death of Felicity Taverner,* McPherson & Company, 1992, p. 12.

6 Ibid., p. 4.

7 Ibid., p. 3.

8 Ibid., p. 18.

9 Ibid., p. 13.

10 "The Magic of Person and Place," *The Bookman,* December 1933 cited in *Mary Butts: Scenes from the Life,* p. 291.

11 AA Gill, *AA Gill is Away,* Orion, 2003, back cover.

12 Mary Butts, *The Crystal Cabinet: My Childhood at Salterns,* 2nd edition, Carnacet Press, 1988, p. 84.

13 Mary Butts, "Ghosties and Ghoulies: The uses of the supernatural in English fiction" in *Ashe of Rings and Other Writings,* McPherson & Company, 1998, p. 350.

14 Butts, *The Crystal Cabinet,* op. cit., p. 278.

15 Butts, "Ashe of Rings" in *Ashe of Rings and Other Writings,* op. cit., p. 5.

16 Butts, *Armed with Madness,* op. cit., p. 12.

17 Ibid., pp. 67–8.

18 Butts, *Ashe of Rings and Other Writings,* op. cit., p. 188.

19 Ibid., p. 214.

20 Letter to Hugh Ross Williamson in the 1930s cited in Christopher Wagstaff (ed.), *A Sacred Quest: The Life and Writings of Mary Butts,* McPherson & Company, 1995, p. 149.

21 Butts's diary entry, early November 1926 cited in Blondel, *Mary Butts: Scenes from the Life,* op. cit., p. 174.

22 "Mr Powys's Dorset," The Sunday Times, 18 February 1934, 11 in Blondel (ed.), *The Journals of Mary Butts,* op. cit., p. 7.

23   Butts's diary entry, September 1933 cited in Blondel, *Mary Butts: Scenes from the Life,* op. cit., p. 289.

24   Butts, *Armed with Madness,* p. 36.

25   Butts, *Ashe of Rings and Other Writings,* op. cit., p. 44.

26   Ibid., p. 169.

27   Ibid., p. 86.

28   Mary Butts, "Warning to Hikers," in *Ashe of Rings and Other Writings,* p. 269.

29   Mary Butts, "Traps for Unbelievers," in *Ashe of Rings and Other Writings,* p. 312.

PAUL

ABBOT

KEITH

WAT

ALAN GARNER

LODGE

WILLA

SHAKES

DYLAN THOMAS

EDWARD THOMAS

REYN AWDRY

JU

BA

JASPER FFORDE

VIRGINIA WOO

RICHARD LONG

HW TILMAN

MARY BUTTS

THOMAS HARDY

Growing Pains

Living with Thomas Hardy and Dorset

by Sarah Burnett

North Dorset in the 1970s felt like the end of the earth. There were farmers who tied up their coats with string and had never left the county. Car journeys often included a lengthy wait as a herd of cows was driven along the road. While the rest of Britain was riding around on Choppers and playing Scalextric, those of us growing up in Dorset were doing things like throwing stones at farm rats. In the entire decade, the only thing that happened was a rumour that Princess Anne might buy a house in a nearby village. She didn't.

When you live in a county so obscure that even the people in neighbouring counties are vague about its whereabouts, evidence of external recognition becomes important. So when I read Thomas Hardy's *Far From the Madding Crowd* at the age of fourteen, it seemed momentous: I felt validated, as if I had grown in stature because my surroundings were worth writing about. Best of all was the page at the beginning of the book: "Key to Place Names." It was like the topography of my life: Shottsford Forum was Blandford Forum, the town where I went to school; Stourcastle was Sturminster Newton, where we went to the weekly livestock market; Marlott was Marnhull, the village where we were dragged to church. Some of these places hardly earned an appearance in a guidebook to Dorset, but here they were in Literature, with a capital L. It did not matter that they were barely mentioned in the novel, it was enough that they appeared in print at all.

After the initial excitement, I found large parts of *Far From the Madding Crowd* tedious – the dialect dialogues of the rustics, the agricultural detail, the moralising. The shepherd Gabriel Oak, with his felt hat and ruddy cheeks, is hardly Mr Darcy. And though we were pleased that someone was writing about Dorset, we were unmoved by Hardy's ability to evoke the landscape itself: we don't want to read long descriptions of the countryside, we shrugged, because it's already right there in front of us. But the deficiencies were balanced by some amazingly vivid scenes, like Gabriel Oak's young sheepdog chasing hundreds of sheep over the edge of a cliff in a storm, and Sergeant Troy demonstrating his swordsmanship to Bathsheba. These scenes helped close my eyes to the hints of what lay in store with Hardy. I glossed over the humiliation of Bathsheba, and the fact that she is reduced to a shadow of the bold, scarlet-jacketed woman she was at the beginning. I thought the novel's heavy-handed signposting of the disasters and gloom to come might be unique to this book.

It was a year or two later, the first year of English A-level, that I realised the full implications of living in Hardy country. First, we read *The Mayor of Casterbridge*, then we went straight into *Tess of the D'Urbervilles*, supplemented by spending free afternoons on field trips to places like Hardy's Cottage and Casterbridge (Dorchester). There we would find coach-loads of literary tourists (mostly American), novels in hand, en route to a Dorset cream tea and inevitably marvelling at the quaintness of it all. Teachers and tourists alike were constantly reminding us how lucky we were to be almost inside the pages of his books.

Back in the classroom, we were feeling the full weight of Hardy's view of the world: the precariousness of agricultural life; the doomed love triangles; the slow descents into poverty; the fatalism about people, society, the world in general. In French A-level classes we'd talk about existential-ism, freedom and God's irrelevance to man; back in Hardy country, God was alive, intolerant and opposed to change.

Our resentment of Hardy was heightened by the fact that his tragedies were so dreary. We'd studied our Shakespeare and our Greek tragedy, and we expected crash-and-burn, catharsis. Hardy gave us none of that, just the slow process of people being ground down by society, financial hardship and the accumulated misfortunes of everyday life. What we wanted to read were dramas like those we'd already studied in *Macbeth* and *King Lear* – storms, madness, blindness; what *Tess of the D'Urbervilles* gave us was the bathos of the Durbeyfields' horse dying, or Tess losing her boots in a hedge, all accompanied by Hardy's irritating commentary of "If only Tess hadn't done that" and "If only Tess had known this ..."

It was those aspects of *Tess of the D'Urbervilles* that helped to change my exasperation with Hardy into loathing. I read much of the book with fists clenched, furious that the character of Tess seemed so accepting of the way men and society mistreated her. I was impatient with her "purity" and unimpressed by her "tender" eyes and "mobile, peony" mouth. Angel Clare inspired me with even greater contempt, with his self-indulgence and his prudish, inadequate response to the truth about Tess's background. The book's filmic climax – with Tess asleep on the sacrificial slabs of rock at Stonehenge as the sun rises and the law closes in on her – seemed melodramatic. Its ending – with Angel Clare and Tess's sister Liza-Lu ("half girl, half woman") standing hand-in-hand, looking down at Wintonchester (Winchester) cathedral and the uplands of Wiltshire, and the scene of Tess's execution – is simply distasteful (though beautifully described).

Looking back, it seems odd that my relationship with Thomas Hardy became so personal. There were other books I disliked – *Wuthering Heights*, *The Mill on the Floss* – but I never felt the same anger against their long-dead authors. It must have been the proximity – particularly with *Tess*, which is set in exactly the part of Dorset where I lived. I looked at the same landscapes, listened to the same dialects, and compared my own life to those of Hardy's characters. When Tess walked through the "long and broken village" of Marlott to fetch her father from the inn, I knew the road she walked along. When she leaves the village and stops on the curve of the hill to look back at her parents' home and the "Vale of the Little Dairies," I knew the view she was looking at. I was so immersed in these places that when Hardy thwarted his characters' lives, it felt like he was telling me that my own life and aspirations would be thwarted. In the red corner, there was I, sixteen or seventeen years old, fully confident that I would escape Dorset, and be free to love or live exactly as I wanted to. In the blue corner was Hardy, a morose old man lecturing that I didn't understand, that I wasn't free, that we're all doomed. It somehow seems symptomatic of the isolation of Dorset in the late 1970s that, while the youth of the Home Counties were busy turning to punk, I was fighting the world-view of Thomas Hardy.

* * *

For the next twenty or so years, Hardy and I had nothing to do with each other. I left school, left Dorset, and the only time I came into contact with any of his work was packing and unpacking my books when moving from London to Brussels to Scotland. But then it happened, by chance, that I needed to re-read *Far From the Madding Crowd* for a work project. The approach of my fortieth birthday meant I was already thinking about the past, and where I had come to, and it seemed that re-reading Hardy fitted in with that. To my own surprise, I decided that I wanted to go back to Hardy, to read the novels again, and to revisit Hardy country from the safety of 500 miles and twenty years away.

The beginning was painful. Not because of nostalgia or memory, but because it was just so laborious. Two pages of Hardy's moralising and circumlocutions were enough to send me to sleep regardless of the time of day. No longer excited by the "Key to Place Names," it was even harder to engage with Dorset agricultural life than it had been years previously.

To the immense irritation of those around me, who had to listen day after day to my complaining, I read five Hardy novels over the course of a month. And slowly, surreptitiously, I began to enjoy them. Someone once said about

Hardy that he is terrible at writing sentences and paragraphs but great at writing books, and certainly I found myself being drawn in. Far from falling asleep after a page, I was reading chapter after chapter late into the night. And, of course, I responded differently from the first time around.

I still loathe Hardy's moroseness and moralising, I'm still exasperated by the "if only" sentences and I still want to punch Angel Clare, but I no longer dismiss the books or their characters on the grounds of their fatalism. As a teenager, I thought that Tess accepted her fate too willingly: she is ruined by Alex D'Urberville, and then lets herself be ruined again – though in a different way – by Angel Clare. Instead of fighting against his treatment of her, she waits patiently for him to come to terms with her past, while sinking further into poverty and desperation. But what I never appreciated as a teenager is that Tess manages to achieve her period of greatest happiness and vitality *after* her "ruin" and after the death of her child. Far from giving up, she continues to hope that society and fate might permit her happiness and a future. Unlike some of her peers in the novel, she does not attempt suicide, turn to drink, or lapse into self-pity.

My teenage self thought that Hardy's characters were passive because they did not protest loudly enough against their misfortunes. I expected them to go mad on a heath or to do the nineteenth-century equivalent of forming a punk band. What I failed to understand is that by carrying on their daily lives and struggles, they *are* fighting back and even showing a type of heroism. It's merely the type of heroism and resilience that is appreciated more by the middle-aged than by the young.

* * *

The other change I notice is that reading Hardy twenty years on has renewed my relationship with Dorset and my youth. There is a scene in Tess where she returns to the Blackmore Vale, the "Vale of the Little Dairies," after her disastrous few months on The Chase (Cranborne Chase) with the D'Urbervilles. She reaches the edge of the chalk escarpment that bounds the vale and looks down at the "familiar green world beyond, now half-veiled in mist." It's a vivid and pivotal moment in the book, very typically Hardyesque as he combines a description of place with something more portentous: "It was always beautiful from here; it was terribly beautiful to Tess today for since her eyes last fell upon it she had learnt that the serpent hisses where the sweet birds sing, and her views of life had been totally changed for her by the lesson."[1]

As I reread the description, I feel like Tess standing on the chalk ridge (though happier), looking down at the vale and my own childhood. It's more than twenty years since I have lived there, but the view suddenly seems intensely real. As I read further into the book, more and more images from my childhood resurface. In his evocation of Dorset, Hardy also evokes for me my own childhood. I can picture the muddy banks of the river Stour where we played or swam; the lushness of the grass and weeds in the early morning, damp with dew and cuckoo-spit; the smell and sound of cows in the stagnant heat of August "following the shadow of the smallest tree"; the slight sense of dislocation when I visited parts of Dorset where the landscape was bigger or bleaker than my own.

As I think about the woods, fields and riverbanks where I grew up, I realise that I will never again be connected so strongly to any landscape. However long I live in Scotland, and however wonderful I find the landscape here, I will never have the same relationship with it. Though I do not find the landscape in Dorset particularly beautiful, I'm beginning to see that it matters to me – and it probably influences many of my reactions to other landscapes. I am also reminded that the childhood experiences that contribute to your adult personality are not just events and people, but place and landscape as well.

Where that leaves me or what it adds to my life now, I am not quite sure. I've certainly no desire to re-engage with Shottsford Forum, Stourcastle or the Vale of the Little Dairies – indeed, many of the places I remember are probably buried beneath new housing developments. I feel no nostalgia for lost youth, and have no Hardyesque inclinations to look back at what might have been. But I do have a new sense that I did not leave Dorset behind as completely as I thought I had.

And I also know that I've started a dangerous journey: twenty-five years hence, newly retired, I'll be on a literary coach-tour of Wessex, standing on the chalk ridge that skirts the Blackmore Vale, novels in hand, telling an angry teenager how lucky they are to live in Hardy country.

Note

1   From the opening page of the second section of *Tess of the D'Urbervilles*, "Maiden No More."

PAUL KISTER
ABBOTT
KEITH
WATERHOUSE
ALAN GARNER
DAVID LODGE
DYLAN THOMAS
WILLIAM SHAKESPEARE
WILL SELF
EDWARD THOMAS
JULIAN BARNES
JOHN
PATRICK HAM
MILTON
REV W AWDRY
HILAIRE
JASPER FFORDE
RICHARD
H W TILMAN LONG
MARY BUTTS
VIRGINIA WOOLF
THOMAS HARDY

Through the Looking Glass in Wiltshire

Jasper Fforde's Swindon

by Maja Pawinska Sims

"I handed her the *SpecOps Gazette*; it outlined postings around the country. Paige looked at the entry I had circled in red ink.

'Swindon?'

'Why not? It's home.'

'Home it might be,' replied Turner, 'but weird it definitely is.'"[1]

Swindon, or at least Swindon in a parallel universe, is the setting for Jasper Fforde's first four published novels about literary detective Thursday Next's adventures: *The Eyre Affair*, *Lost in a Good Book*, *The Well of Lost Plots*, and *Something Rotten*.

In this alternative Swindon of 1985, croquet is played at the County Ground, the town boasts an underground train, skyrail, an airship port, and cloned dodos are favourite pets. The all-powerful Goliath Corporation pervades daily life, a mysterious agency called Jurisfiction keeps characters in order within books, and the country is policed by Special

Operations, or SpecOps, teams. Woolly mammoths migrate through Devizes every year, and time travel is commonplace.

Trying to categorise Fforde's novels must have made publisher Hodder & Stoughton's marketing squirrels cross-eyed with effort, since the books defy any attempt at being placed within a genre. No sooner has the reader decided the stories are comic fantasies or literary parody, than they give a sly wink and nip off to the science fiction or detective thriller shelves.

At the start of *The Eyre Affair*, our fearless heroine Thursday returns to her family home of Swindon in a move to SpecOps 5, the literary detectives, or LiteraTecs. She is on the trail of the villain Acheron Hades, who is kidnapping characters from works of fiction and holding them to ransom, including Jane Eyre. It's up to Thursday to reinstate her, while still finding time to rescue her aunt from inside a Wordsworth poem (where she is trapped thanks to uncle Mycroft's invention of a Prose Portal through which it is possible to pass from reality into fiction, and vice versa), resolve the ongoing Crimean War, and figure out who wrote Shakespeare's plays:

> "There was a knock at the door and Buckett instinctively reached for his handgun. He was more on edge than I had thought ...
>
> 'Who's there?' I said without opening the door.
>
> 'Hello!' replied a voice. 'My name's Edmund Capillary. Have you ever stopped to wonder whether it was really William Shakespeare who penned all those wonderful plays?'
>
> We both briefed a sign of relief and Buckett put the safety back on his automatic, muttering under his breath:
>
> 'Bloody Baconians!'"[2]

Silly books for smart people

I discovered Fforde by accident, a good couple of years after *The Eyre Affair* and *Lost in a Good Book* were published, and they immediately became two of my most-loved novels. I wanted to be Thursday, just as I wanted to be Alice falling through the looking glass, and it was no surprise to me when I found out that Fforde's favourite book is *Alice in Wonderland*.

The world he has created for Thursday shares the same gleeful, mischievous tone as Lewis Carroll's most famous creation, and the Cheshire Cat even makes a guest appearance in Thursday's stories. He is now known as the "Unitary Authority of Warrington Cat," however, after the county boundaries were moved (or more commonly, "The Cat formerly known as Cheshire").

Fforde's Swindon is not exactly surreal: it's subtler than that, as he melts the extraordinary and the ordinary together into an absurd, intricate world that is clearly related to reality, but probably no closer than a second cousin. In *Lost in a Good Book*, for example, Thursday describes how she spent some downtime before her next assignment:

"I spent the afternoon surreptitiously reading the Jurisfiction instruction manual, which felt a little like flicking through *Bunty* during school. I was tempted to have a go at entering a work of fiction to try out a few of their 'handy book jumping tips' but Havisham had roundly forbidden me from doing anything of the sort 'until I was more experienced.' By the time I was ready to go home I had learned a few tricks about emergency book evacuation procedures, read about the aims of the Bowdlerizers, a group of well-meaning yet censorious individuals hell-bent on removing obscenities from fiction. I also read about Healthcliff's unexpected three-year career in Hollywood under the name of Buck Stallion and his eventual return to the pages of *Wuthering Heights*, the forty-six abortive attempts to illegally save Beth from dying in *Little Women*, details of the Character Exchange Program ... and how to use spelling mistakes, misprints and double negatives to signal to other Prose Resource Operatives in case emergency book evacuation procedures failed."[3]

We first see Thursday's Swindon in *The Eyre Affair*, when she arrives from London to take up her new post: "I took a small 20-seater airship to Swindon ... The airfield lounge was empty when I came out. It was bigger than was required for the amount of traffic that came to town: an off-white elephant that reflected the dashed hopes of Swindon's town planners."[4]

This forlorn view of Swindon is not a million miles away from reality: the town is not especially attractive, and if you were to spend some time doing an audit of the relative merits of Wiltshire's urban areas, Swindon would fare rather badly in comparison with the beautiful cathedral city of Salisbury. The target of similar jokes to those directed at Slough even before David Brent started playing office, Swindon even appeared as one of the 50 worst places to live in the UK in a book elegantly titled *Crap Towns*.

I managed to pin down Fforde down for a chat about Thursday and Swindon between drafts of his new novel. He looks and sounds as distinctive as his name: he's enthusiastic, twinkly, and well-spoken, with a slightly perplexed undertone to his voice, and chiselled features. When I asked him why he chose Swindon as the setting for his "silly books for smart people" as one reviewer put it, he told me: "Why not? Setting a story in London, Edinburgh or Bristol would have been too easy, and too obvious. I always set my stories somewhere that people don't expect. I think you have to take the less travelled path in writing to retain any originality or quirkiness. I lived nearby in Marlborough for twelve years, so there is a personal connection. Thursday's Swindon is not the Swindon I know, but it is still recognisable."[5]

For me, the pell-mell plots and subplots of the novels just wouldn't seem so extraordinary if they were set in a buzzing metropolis where anything goes, instead of a provincial town (population: 180,000) formerly regarded, by non-residents at least, as rather dull. The playful juxtaposition of the real Swindon with the gently hallucinogenic quality of Thursday's town all adds to the ffun.

The Tower of Brunel and other wonders

Many of Swindon's real landmarks make an appearance in Thursday country, including the infamous Magic Roundabout, a town planner's challenge to motorists, with five mini roundabouts around one central roundabout, and the County Ground, the home of Swindon Town FC in the real world. The road layouts are accurate, as is the description of the countryside and towns around Swindon. Not wishing to limit himself to the real town's charms, however, Fforde has created the Seven Wonders of Swindon as something of an affectionate, tongue-in-cheek tribute.

The Seven Wonders are the Tower of Brunel ("This 88-storey colossus is not only the highest building in Wessex but it also has a very reasonably priced cafeteria"); the Hanging Baskets of Babbington; the Double Helix of Carfax ("Not only the first stressed spiral concrete construction in the world, but also the inspiration for Frank Lloyd Wright's clearly inferior Guggenheim museum in New York"); the lighthouse on Alexandra Road ("Constructed during the Great Global Warming Scare of 1832, this famous Swindon landmark is unique for being the only lighthouse in the world invisible from any navigable waterway"); the statue of local celebrity Lola Vavoom at the bus station; the Cathedral of St Zvlkx (site of); and the Elgin Llamas, which graze to the north of Swindon.

Fforde's boisterous celebration of literature and the written word[6] has developed something of a cult following, and Fforde has a loyal community of "ffans" who discuss all things Nextian, in his lively online Fforum.

Fforde uses the internet to give a fuller, interactive overview of his fabulous world, and the Seven Wonders have their own page, along with DVD-style "special features" sections for all his books. These include a "making-of wordumentary and deleted scenes," a Swindon photo album, and a list of famous people who come from Swindon, with the not-quite-A-list James Dyson at the top, followed by model Melinda Messenger and actress Billie Piper.

Throughout his labyrinth of websites, Fforde has scattered photos of the Seven Wonders and other notable sights such as dodo road signs and airships flying over the town, created with the use of Photoshop software. These doctored photos have also been used as souvenir "postcards from Swindon" inserted into the hardback editions of his novels.

Fforde's pre-literary career was as a focus-puller in the film industry, working on films such as *Quills*, *Goldeneye*, *Entrapment* and the *Mask of Zorro*. There is a strong visual, Technicolor quality to Thursday Next's Swindon, including hand-drawn "advertisements" for Pete and Dave's Dodo Emporium in the back of the books, and he agrees his movie-making background has contributed to the content and feel of the books and the websites.

"All writers are the product of everything they have experienced," he says. "I like the merging of reality and imagination, and using Photoshop to create that look for Swindon is a good joke. It throws a question mark over what is real and what isn't, and I think the blurring of those bound-aries is fun. I love the idea of the Seven Wonders of Swindon – it's perfect. At first there were three genuine wonders on the list but the other ones got more and more weird and pushed out the real ones."[7]

Ffans and ffestivals

Until Fforde and Thursday Next came along, few creative endeavours had championed Swindon. In Mark Haddon's bestseller *The Curious Incident of the Dog in the Night Time*, Swindon is described by one character as "the arsehole of the world." Sherlock Holmes ate lunch in the town in *The Boscombe Valley Mystery* and the town has apparently been used for a couple of scenes in James Bond movies, but that was pretty much it.

After Next, the town's literary ambitions have blossomed. The Swindon literary fringe, with Fforde's patronage, became bigger than Swindon's original literary festival (no, I didn't know there was one, either), and in 2005 the town went one step further to host the first Fforde Ffestival, bringing the setting of the Thursday Next books to life with an open-topped bus tour of the "sights" in the novels and two days of activities for ffans from around the world, including a World Croquet Challenge.

The burghers of Swindon council were slow to cotton on to Fforde's lively vision of their town, but are now active supporters of all things Nextian, and are even in the process of naming six new roads after characters in the books in developments to the north of Swindon, including Thursday Street. "The council planning department have sent me a map," says Fforde. "They've been threatening to do this for years. We don't have road signs up yet, though I am hoping to be cutting some ribbons. It is extraordinary."[8]

Fforde is not a Swindon resident. He was born in London and now lives in Wales (which in Thursday's world is a Sovietesque no-go area: the People's Republic of Wales). He suffered 76 rejections before getting a publisher for *The Eyre Affair*, the fifth novel he had written. By the time the third Thursday Next book, *The Well of Lost Plots*, was published, Fforde had enough clout to get his early novels published too. *The Big Easy* (a whodunit about who killed Humpty Dumpty), was followed by *The Fourth Bear*, exploring some strange events concerning Goldilocks and the three bears. Both novels star a new hero, detective inspector Jack Spratt, and are unmistakeably from the same mould as the Thursday Next stories.

The Jack Spratt novels are set in Reading, so will the people of Reading take Fforde to their hearts as much as Swindonians? "Well, they haven't so far," says Fforde. "I did a talk in Reading last year and they were chuffed but they seem more busy and serious. The book also uses Reading as more of a backdrop, whereas in the Thursday Next books, Swindon is an integral part of the story."[9]

Ambassador for hire

Swindonians have embraced Fforde and Next, and he is now something of a local hero. In 2004 he was even named "Mayor for an Hour":

> "At the Swindon civic centre on 26 January, presiding Swindon Mayor Mr Derek Benfield welcomed Fforde to Swindon, thanked him for writing about the town and bestowed upon him the honour of wearing the mayoral robes for a photocall. Fforde was delighted and accepted the offer gratefully, posing for pictures and generally wondering if he hadn't fallen into one of his own books. The meeting closed with Fforde proclaiming a 'Lola Vavoom' national holiday, the establishment of Swindon as an independent City-State and for the language of the town to be Welsh. All proclamations were wisely rejected, and the afternoon finished with some excellent carrot cake."[10]

Fforde is modest about his status in the town: "I suppose I am vaguely a hero to people who have read the books. It's quite nice really. The thing about Swindon is that no one has really written about it in a fictional way, except in passing or as a joke. The good people of Swindon are very sensitive about being the butt of jokes, and a lot of people there feel like they should be given a fairer crack of the whip, because Swindon is a lot better than many provincial towns. When they found someone who was using Swindon but not as a joke, they loved it."[11]

The team behind the lively, unofficial Swindon Web internet site[12] clearly adores being associated with Fforde's eccentric humour, and even based an April Fool's Day story on his Nextian Swindon, claiming that the council had approved plans for a monorail around the town.

The Swindon Tourist board has noticed the Fforde ffactor, and often gets calls from tourists who want to know where the Seven Wonders are. Thursday is particularly popular with Americans, many of whom have expressed surprise that

Swindon exists, and have started including the town on their tours of the UK. "I am doing my bit to raise the profile of Swindon," says Fforde. "The tourist office, by the way, sells Magic Roundabout metal key rings and calendars with pictures of Swindon's roundabouts – now if that's not a sense of humour, I don't know what is."[13]

Next time you find yourself racing down the M4 between London and Wales, or even vice versa, give some thought to the town nestled between junctions 15 and 16, where, despite appearances, anything could happen Next.

Notes

1   Jasper Fforde, *The Eyre Affair,* Hodder & Stoughton, 2001.

2   Ibid.

3   Jasper Fforde, *Lost in a Good Book,* Hodder & Stoughton, 2002.

4   Jasper Fforde, *The Eyre Affair,* op. cit.

5   Jasper Fforde, interview with Maja Pawinska Sims, 28 February 2006.

6   Some characters in *Lost in a Good Book* speak to Thursday in footnotes that other characters can't hear.

7   Jasper Fforde, interview with Maja Pawinska Sims, 28 February 2006.

8   Ibid.

9   Ibid.

10   Fforde Fflash Archive, www.jasperfforde.com

11   Jasper Fforde, interview with Maja Pawinska Sims, 28 February 2006.

12   www.swindonweb.com

PAUL AUSTER
ABBOTT
KEITH WATERHOUSE
ALAN GARNER
DYLAN THOMAS
GEORGE
DAVID LODGE
WILLIAM SHAKESPEARE
WILL SELF
EDWARD THOMAS
JULIAN BARNES
JOHN MI...
PATRICK HAM ILTON
T.S.
REV W AWDRY
JASPER FFORDE
HILAIRE BE...
RICHARD LONG
WILLIAM
THOMAS WARD Y
MARY BUTTS
VIRGINIA WOOLF
CHAB...

Tunnel Vision

The Rev. W. Awdry's Box

by Will Awdry

Set it up. Set it up. Set it up.

It is extraordinary what you find in tomato sauce. Elements of British character are revealed in its translucent, orange glory as nowhere else.

We're not talking about ketchup. The world and his wife dip their chips into tomato ketchup the planet over with numbing similarity. It's the British take on tomato *sauce* that is so particular. A sweet and salty film, it coats the feature presentations of some very British cuisine. You won't find a baked bean in anything else. Pilchards and faggots squat in the stuff in supermarket aisles. Few other countries would touch tuna fish in tomato sauce, but we do. Occasional curiosities crop up, such as sweet corn – or French beans the French would never eat – swimming in its saucy puddles. You could assume that, as a British foodstuff, you've really arrived if you've made it to tomato sauce. Consider tinned pasta. Myriad variations stretch along the shelves, a whole West End of aluminium theatres in which casts of letters, shapes and characters are currently appearing.

Among these, one owes its contents to a story. It was first told to a two year-old boy with measles by his father. Within the tin, in light tomato sauce, are pasta tracks, trains, signals and even Fat Controllers. These are the sticky hallmarks of a very specific branch of English literature. The father was

Wilbert Awdry, a country parson. The stories he cooked up were to become, eventually, twenty-six much-loved books, best known as the Thomas the Tank Engine series. Thomas and his colleagues steam about the mythical island of Sodor, which is tucked between Barrow-in-Furness and the Isle of Man.

The Reverend Wilbert was my second cousin, once removed. Where did an idea that encourages thousands of children to eat Fat Controllers for tea actually start?

* * *

How d'you do. How d'you do. How d'you do.

When I first met Wilbert, he had a mane of white hair and the mellifluous voice of a clarinet. His glasses framed a kindly gaze of stubborn humility. Fifty years apart, we shared the same initial and surname. I was fascinated. His presence was, unsurprisingly, that of a vicar meeting his wider family. There was an air of formality, a precision and strength but no sense of self-importance. In the few times I saw him, always at Awdry weddings, funerals or significant birthdays, he was entirely approachable, even to a squit like me.

He may have been modest, but he was already famous. School friends asked shyly for copies of their favourite story to be signed "by your uncle." (I gave up correcting them.) The fame grew. Prince Charles had enjoyed the books as a boy. When his son, Prince William, first went to school, he was clutching a Thomas the Tank Engine lunchbox. Today, typing "the Rev. W. Awdry" into *Google* produces 2,700,000 replies. Something approaching 1,000 Thomas "And Friends" products have been developed, pasta shapes included. More than 100 episodes of a television series have been screened and an additional 200 titles published beyond the original twenty-six. Wilbert's son, Christopher, has continued the writing. Brit Alcroft bought the rights and, through her company, has catapulted the enterprise into a success story worth millions, most of them apparently hers.

Wilbert and I always came across each other in Wiltshire. It is a county with a pivotal role in both Wilbert's life and that of our entire family. The Awdry name traces back to the early seventeenth century. (Echoing a brand of holiday resorts, we are a One-And-Only outfit. Anyone who shares the surname is related.) In the 1870s, the diarist Frances Kilvert remarks on the profusion of Awdrys in Wiltshire in his rambles round the West Country. A prototype presenter for "Down Your Way," he refers to us as "the weeds of Wiltshire." Since then, county records have us popping up like groundsel as mayors of Chippenham (my grandfather and his brother), doctors, solicitors and an MP, Daniel Awdry of Melksham. I am blessed with a writer father – a Wiltshire escapee – whose existence is part fuelled by inexhaustible family anecdotes. I grew up with as many local stories as there are trains that run through Swindon. Never having lived there, save brief boarding school years, I still see the county as my spiritual home. As an actual inhabitant, Wilbert's imagination was properly forged and tempered there.

Pin it down. Pin it down. Pin it down.

The bald facts about the leonine Wilbert are relatively straightforward. He was born in 1911 in Ampfield in Hampshire. His father Vere was 57. His mother, Lucy, was the third Mrs Awdry after a succession of health tragedies, sadly typical of the times. (There were grim trials to come too: Wilbert's half-brother, Carol, was killed in action early in the Great War. Wilbert later became a conscientious objector.) Lucy was a tough cookie who bequeathed Wilbert a fierce determination. The family moved to Box in Wiltshire and his childhood was spent in three different houses in the village.

After a sort of "gap" year teaching in the Holy Land, he was married to Margaret and ordained in Winchester. They produced three children, Christopher, Veronica and Hilary. Following a smattering of curacies, the family settled in King's Norton, Birmingham for Wilbert's first job as vicar. It was there that he told poor Christopher, suffering from measles with the curtains tightly drawn, the stories that were to emerge as the Railway Series. In 1946, the Awdrys left for Elsworth, in Cambridgeshire and, in 1953, Emneth, near Wisbech. His final years were spent in Stroud, preaching postally rather than via the pulpit. Having read his stories to their children, parents wrote seeking his spiritual advice to pass on as well. He accepted the role of a liturgical Marge Proops enthusiastically.

It was Wilbert's father, Vere, who nurtured the boy's life-long love of railways. A vicar too, he was obsessed by steam driven locomotives. There was, for instance, an elaborate, fully working model railway in the back garden in Hampshire. The fascination passed to both Wilbert and his brother George. As adults, both devoted countless hours to setting up similarly epic model railways in the attic. In the end, George never really moved much beyond this hobby. He failed to leave home altogether, remaining with his mother for life. His magnificent beard matched an equally magnificent lack of ambition. That obituary euphemism, "He never married," doesn't seem quite appropriate. George simply never developed a relationship beyond his immediate family and railway trains. He was, however, a valuable muse for his brother, encouraging him in all his works.

Wilbert died in 1997. The broadsheets carried obituaries both lengthy and affectionate. Our family mourned.

Find the heart. Find the heart. Find the heart.

The key to Wilbert's sense of place is Box, poised between Bath and Chippenham. As an amateur literary detective on his case, it's impossible not to draw chalk marks around the village. Box is, emphatically, Wilbert's centre of gravity.

During his childhood there, daily events provided the inspiration for the later stories. The name "Box" itself suggests neat, straight lines. This tallies with Wilbert's writing style, which has a squared-off, prosaic quality, albeit not without wit. The most apposite straight line is Isambard Kingdom Brunel's tunnel, constructed in 1841. This was, for some time, the longest rail tunnel in the country at one mile and seven furlongs. From Vere's dressing room in the family's first house in the village, father and son would train-spot with a telescope. The Great Western Railway trains ploughed up the hill towards the tunnel, often assisted by an extra locomotive. After listing them by day, Wilbert would listen to them by night, shunting and panting up the steep gradient. He imagined the trains talking to each other. The notion stuck.

Today, Box still makes something of Wilbert's resident years. He is well charted by local historians on the village website. Other points of interest are the Bath stone quarry and a famous resident in musician Peter Gabriel. Mrs Bowdler is buried in the churchyard. Mother of the censorious Thomas, who removed those chunks from Shakespeare he considered indecent, she takes dubious credit for spawning the notion of Bowdlerising. Wilbert consistently refused any hint of censure or editorial input to any of his work, changing editors more readily than he would change a paragraph.

What of the books? What of the books? What of the books?

Reading the books again, the stories emerge fully-fledged on the page. Like the locomotives that would shoot out of Brunel's tunnel, the tales of Edward, Thomas, Henry, Gordon *et al* steam straight into action. There is little set up. "Soft" elements of the story are the responsibility of the illustrations, left to the heavy lifting of background detail. The prose is the locomotive, pulling readers along sharply defined tracks.

Wilbert wrote each book within a week. Much plot is executed through dialogue, characters vividly etched by their speech. The books certainly come to life when read aloud. I never heard a Wilbert sermon, but clues allow one to speculate about the likely tone. In the introduction to *Troublesome Engines* (1950), he worries that Gordon and James "have been Getting Above Themselves." In the same piece, he tells us the Fat Controller has "kindly but very firmly, put them In Their Place." The capital letters are instructive. In Box, the trains were either in the tunnel or out of them. In Sodor, the trains are either on the rails or off them. It's a black and white world of Right or Wrong. When asked by young readers whether the Fat Controller, later Sir Topham Hat, represented God, Wilbert was happy to accept that he could, if it gave them "an idea of there being someone who is in control of the world."[1]

Wilbert was writing at a time of great optimism, immediately after the Second War. People craved order after chaos. Simplistic morality tales of anthropomorphic trains, running through an idealised, English landscape could not have better matched the mood.

Of course, Wilbert's was by no means the first talking train book to be published. There were many character train stories in the 1930s and 1940s, but none has endured as powerfully. That he was published at all is down to Margaret's persistence as well as his skill as a story-maker. It was she who steered him to a literary agent that led to the printing of *The Three Railway Engines* in 1945. The enduring fascination with Thomas and Co. beyond that of all other fictional trains has a parallel in Wilbert's day job. The Christianity we know today and that Wilbert practised as a clergyman – creationist, resurrection-dependent – was just one of 300 similar cults identified in the centuries around the birth of Christ. All the others have fallen away.

Over the years, Wilbert has also come in for a lot of flak. There are accusations of pedantry, sexism, racism and being just plain dull. Knowing him a little, the criticisms come across as mean spirited. For balance, Brian Sibley's *The Thomas the Tank Engine Man* (Heinemann, 1995) is a highly readable chronology of Wilbert's life.

How does it look? How does it look? How does it look?

It wasn't just Wilbert's writing that built the Railway Series into a global phenomenon. The illustrations in the books play a huge part in the appeal. He did submit his own sketches (with faces), but professional illustrators were commissioned for publication. Wilbert's instructions were then explicit. The steam trains were to be rendered realistically. (Even though railway buffs loved them, the results were never quite accurate enough to his eyes.) There were at least five different illustrators, all of whom he kept pretty much at arm's length. C. Reginald Dalby, the most influential, only met Wilbert twice. Relations were cool, if not tetchy.

The actual pictures are wonders to behold. Despite Wilbert's exasperation about wheel sizes and piston alignments, the engines appear meticulously detailed. (Perspectives elsewhere are a little ropey.) Life depicted beyond the tracks is a revelation. If not exactly Wiltshire, it is definitely shire England. Neat and symmetrical, fields are more vacuumed than ploughed. Think Box boxed. Farm animals are perfectly spaced. Postmen collect post. Policemen police. In fact, all the people seen fulfil their roles to the letter. (Wilbert, Margaret and the children are drawn in frequently.) So perfect is the overall vision, it verges on the propagandist. There is a whiff of Soviet social revision among the saturated colours and rich tones.

Back in the text, Wilbert displays a great ear for rhythm. The euphony of the prose is built on the time signature of rail tracks. He caught the patter of trains exactly. Onomatopoeic groans and *staccato* grumbles of coaches are beat-perfect. Metronomic, repeated phrases, they reflect the architecture of rail lengths in the steam age. Shorter than today, the rhythms are snappy; Trad jazz compared with the asymmetrical clicks and soundproofed plinks of the Railtrack age. Wilbert's rolling stock is sonically distinctive, and even those who never experienced steam travel are left yearning. For all their expression, however, I can't detect a hint of Wiltshire burr.

What does it mean? What does it mean? What does it mean?

Attempting to locate the epicentre of Wilbert's place, I enlisted my father's help. He chipped in with many details and a characteristic volley of stories, fizzing with life and colour.

Did I appreciate Wilbert's eccentric approach to money? For instance, as vicar in his Cambridgeshire village, he frequently invited guest preachers. One such was Graham Leonard, a future Bishop of London. Rather than the customary five pounds, Wilbert rewarded him with a live hamster – without a cage – that the visiting Leonard had to take home on the bus.

Or there was the time that my older sister and brother invited Wilbert to address the railway society at school. Of his allotted hour, he spent 55 minutes detailing the exact terrain of the bogus terrain of Sodor to an increasingly bemused group of students.

Before the television programmes so widely known were filmed, there were two hopeless attempts to bring Sodor to the small screen. In one, the scriptwriters, unbeknownst to Wilbert, renamed some of the engines to make them female. This was too much. He successfully sued the makers for bringing "inappropriate sex to a children's television programme." The undisclosed damages were believed to be around £15,000. The Bishop of Ely called a meeting with Wilbert to ask whether, as a result of his win and growing income from his writing, he would forgo his stipend. Wilbert replied that if that were the case, he would be obliged to resign. "Goodbye Awdry," the Bishop supposedly replied.

Wrap it up. Wrap it up. Wrap it up.

Wilbert's landscape – literary, illustrated, sonic and geographic – is fuzzily non-specific, yet unmistakeably English. It is one I have been visiting all my life. It may start in the imagination of a tall, thickly thatched and avuncular clergyman, but it has solid dimension to me. I know – or am convinced that I know – the places he had in his head. I'm eternally grateful he found time to steer them into my heart.

Note

1   Quoted by Brian Sibley in *The Thomas the Tank Engine Man,* Heinemann, 1995.

...ISTERHOUSE

ABBOTT

FLO...

KEITH

K WATERHOUSE

ALAN GARNER

THOMAS

DAVID LODGE

WILLIAM SHAKESPEARE

WILL SELF

JOHN MILTON

EDWARD

JULIAN

PATRICK

HAROLD PINTER

GILES

SMITH

THOMAS

REY W

BARNES

MILTON

T.S. ELIOT

JASPER

AWDRY

HILAIRE BELLOC

CHARLES DICKENS

FORDE

VIRGINIA WOOLF

BUTTS

26

Lost and Found

Looking for John Milton in Chalfont St Giles

by John Simmons

This is commuter country. Chalfont St Giles settles in the Chilterns just outside the M25 that encircles London and within a short drive of the nearest tube station at the end of the Metropolitan Line. But in 1665 it would have taken Milton a long, uncomfortable day's cart ride to reach here as he fled the plague in his native London.

The cottage he lived in for less than two years is not the oldest building in Chalfont St Giles. When I arrive at the village green, the air is cold but the pallid sun is shining. It's a pleasant place to walk, and the church, approached through a Tudor gateway off the high street, has an air of contemplative melancholy that we recognise from Gray's Elegy. The church, like many English churches, is a construction of various periods, dating back to Norman times. The tombstones ancient and modern, the scattered feathers of a startled perhaps slaughtered crow, the spongy grass beneath your feet, the clumps of snowdrops, all tell a story of life passing, being recorded, being renewed.

The cottage itself is a hundred yards further up the road. When Milton lived here it was the last house in the village, never a grand house, but pleasantly situated. In these little low-ceilinged rooms Milton sat in the dark of blindness and created pictures of heaven, earth and hell. A sense of awe lingers as the presence of Milton makes itself felt through the first editions that lie open in cabinets, through the portraits on the walls, through the timber beams that stripe the surfaces. How confined was this world of poky rooms. Even the upper storey was inaccessible to a blind man: it was reached by rope by those, the poor women in Milton's life, who slept in the space above. But even this could have been a metaphor that resonated with his constant composition on the theme of heaven and hell.

Milton seems perhaps the unlikeliest of influences on a modern writer for business. Writing epic poems in heroic verse, often with convoluted sentences and extended similes, Milton follows none of the advice of the Plain English Campaign. But that, in essence, is what Milton has to offer me and all of us. He had higher ambitions than to be plain. Through his ideas, language and verse he encourages us all to strive higher in our everyday writing. In *Paradise Lost* he sets out his ambition: "To justify the ways of God to men." So should we all not strive for an extraordinary ambition in our writing? In the business world, it's all too easy to accept "They'll never let me do that." Perhaps they will if you try:

> "The mind is its own place, and in itself
> Can make a heaven of hell, a hell of heaven."

You understand this a little more by visiting the cottage. In midwinter spring its glooming darkness is lit by occasional shafts of thin sunlight. This is the only surviving house in which Milton lived. The house survived and so did Milton. In London the plague had been suppurating all around him, the bells had been ringing to bring out the dead. Had he stayed *Paradise Lost* might never have seen the light of day, so he completed it during his time of refuge in Chalfont St Giles.

By 1665, the light of day had been long lost to Milton. He had gone blind in 1652, but his literary output never abated – he simply dictated his words to amanuenses. So he composed the thousands of lines of *Paradise Lost* and then *Paradise*

Regained by reciting them aloud; forming the words in his head but speaking them for the ears of his scribes and his readers. His other senses sharpened by the loss of vision, his power to create pictures in our imaginations increased. He used the sense of sound to add layers of meaning to his story-telling, and in doing so he shows us a fundamental principle of writing. Philip Pullman describes it in his own way of reading Milton: "So I begin with sound. I read *Paradise Lost* not only with my eyes, but with my mouth."[1]

The cottage is the place where Milton composed many of his words aloud and where he heard them read back to him:

> "He spake: and to confirm his words, outflew
> Millions of flaming swords, drawn from the thighs
> Of mighty cherubim; the sudden blaze
> Far round illumined hell: highly they raged
> Against the highest, and fierce with grasped arms
> Clashed on their sounding shields the din of war,
> Hurling defiance towards the vault of heaven."

The rolling momentum of the verse is glorious. Imagine Milton speaking these words here for the first time. But then, pulling back from this close clamour of sound, taking a more distant view of what Milton does, as if looking down from the heights of heaven, admire his ability to create striking visual images with words – and his ease in telling a story. When you read *Paradise Lost* you realise that, for example, most fantasy fiction owes Milton a huge debt. Indeed you wonder whether a film-maker like Peter Jackson might have been reading *Paradise Lost* before creating storyboards for the films of *Lord of the Rings*.

* * *

Eddie Dawson is your guide. As curator, he welcomes you to Milton's cottage, a genial figure unlike any of the grim gatekeepers in *Paradise Lost*. He is proud to show his latest electronic recruit, inviting me to press the button on the fireplace. A recorded voice speaks to the room, an actor who plays Thomas Ellwood, Milton's pupil and friend who found him this refuge from the plague. And so you listen to the description by Thomas Ellwood of his encounters with Milton in this "pretty box."[2]

The story is the nearest we have to a recorded conversation with Milton. In short, Milton gives Ellwood the manuscript of *Paradise Lost* to read. Ellwood reads the "excellent poem" and pays another visit. They chat and Ellwood remarks: "Thou hast said much here of *Paradise Lost,* but what hast thou to say of *Paradise Found?*" The question sends Milton into a muse. Some time later, after Milton's return to London, the two men meet again and Milton shows Ellwood a new poem called *Paradise Regained*, the direct result of the conversation in Chalfont St Giles.

There is much in this place that has been lost and found, but it seems hubristic to seek beyond Paradise. Yet Eddie Dawson has the Miltonic mission to educate and persuade. I had remembered earlier visits when he had rediscovered for me many aspects of Milton that have been effectively lost to general knowledge. Eddie will talk for as long as you wish about Milton as "foreign secretary," as a founding influence on the American constitution, as the writer of the *Areopagitica* that provided the intellectual muscle for Cromwell's English Revolution and the republican case for the execution of King Charles I. But Milton did this through essays and pamphlets that set out arguments in poetic prose that stiffened the sinews of Parliament – and that still moves our spirits today.

> "As good kill a Man as kill a good Book; who kills a Man kills a reasonable creature, God's Image; but he who destroys a good Book kills reason itself, kills the Image of God, as it were in the eye. Many a man lives a burden to the Earth; but a good Book is the precious life-blood of a master spirit, imbalm'd and treasur'd up on purpose to a life beyond life."

Milton's sight began to fail at the time of writing the *Areopagitica* in 1644. He was advised to rest his eyes and avoid stress, but he insisted that he had important work to do – writing – and that he must continue. Within eight years his blindness was complete but his work flowed on. On the restoration of the monarchy in 1660 many of Milton's colleagues received gruesome retribution by being hung, drawn and quartered. Milton endured a spell in prison but no harsher punishment, except that some of his works were burned by the hangman. His disaffected daughters removed many of his books from his house and sold them. People contemplate acts of cruelty and make judgements about which acts will hurt their victim most. Yet Milton survived to write his greatest work and his books remain his life-blood.

* * *

I have always loved books. I love the physical form of a book and can never bear to throw a book away, so I hoard them even when the paper thins and yellows. So it was an important moment for me when I held in my hand the first book published under my name That excitement has now been repeated many times since, most recently when my book *Dark Angels* appeared.[3] *Dark Angels,* as the title might suggest, owes something in its inspiration to Milton. The dark angels of my book are you and me, human beings who are neither the heavenly angels, nor those fallen angels cast down into hell. Humans touched by the knowledge of good and evil, yet able to choose, gifted with curiosity and creativity, but too little encouraged to make use of them. My belief is that we should all be given encouragement to express our personalities through writing, inside and outside the workplace. In effect we should all be given our wings to fly and for our words to transport us to other places, realising the potential of our humanity.

Milton might not argue for that, God might remain the great forbidder. But there is a difference between the purpose of Milton's rational argument and the effect of his emotional writing. Satan is the heroic figure of *Paradise Lost*, perhaps against Milton's intentions, but the power of characterisation and storytelling have taken over. And the power of sound. Satan simply has all the best speeches. Sometimes his words ring out, bouncing off the vault of heaven; sometimes they slide out smoothly, seducing Eve in the shade of a tree with the forbidden fruit of knowledge. But the dullest passages of writing in *Paradise Lost* are spoken by God (the Almighty rather than the Son) and by the archangel Michael. Both come across as unyielding and cold managers of a rather harsh old school. Their language reflects their absence of emotion. They do not connect in a human way because they are not human. There is a gulf of authority between these divine beings and the humans they have set up to fail. Satan, on the other hand, is all too recognisably one of us – which might just prove, in fundamental Christian eyes, how far we have fallen.

Satan, before his fall, was known in heaven as Lucifer, the bearer of light. But now he has lost his brightness. Yet it simply adds to the sense of identification we feel with him as a heroic figure. Heroes have their prime. Heroes pass their prime. We were all luminous in youth and now the glow is fading, has faded. There is a humanity in Satan as a result, a humanity that is easier to connect with than the injunctions of the heavenly angels for Adam to forsake curiosity. Raphael pats Adam on the head as if to say, "There, there, don't go worrying your head about astronomy – take God's ways on trust, admire, worship and sing hallelujah." Adam in turn seems to learn from the angels an unthinking patronisation in his behaviour towards Eve. How was this shaped by Milton's own life? Three times married, not happily, and cast into the darkness of blindness. No wonder he made Eve a figure of submission. No wonder he felt the loss of light. But still he could allow the description in Eve's mouth of God as "our great forbidder."

By the poem's close, coming to terms with expulsion from Eden, Adam debates with Eve and with himself all sides of his new situation. He concludes that he will have to make the best of the new place where he will live, the Earth. It forms an intriguing echo of Satan's argument in the earlier part of the poem as, cast down into hell, he concludes that he must make the most of his changed circumstances. The effect is curious. The humanity displayed by Adam and Eve, the indomitable spirit, is exactly that displayed by Satan. We see Satan as heroic because he is so recognisably human. God, its hard being angelic. It's easier to follow our instincts and be human.

So the devil gets all the best tunes and Milton was the musician. He would play the organ in this cottage and he would sing too. Part of his musicality is his ability to create memorable phrases. Other writers have so admired Milton's facility in turning a phrase that they have appropriated many for their own book titles. The extraction from the density of the poetic text makes them shine brightly. *In Dubious Battle*: John Steinbeck. *Eyeless in Gaza*: Aldous Huxley. *His Dark Materials*: Philip Pullman. *Darkness Visible*: William Golding. Stirring phrases that sometimes have sneaked their way into vernacular use: "Wherefore with thee came not all hell broke loose?" sends a shock of sudden recognition of the "modern" phrase. Yet, seeing it in its original context changes it entirely, recreates it with its primeval force, reviving in you, as a reader, the vitality of words.

"His stature reached the sky, and in his crest
Sat horror plumed."

We near an ending. Milton was a master of endings. In *Paradise Lost* he does it at least twelve times, closing each of the books on a note that is sometimes elevated, sometimes reflective, sometimes melodramatic, but always perfectly pitched. Again it is all to do with the sound of the words, and we take our lead for meaning from the sound that enters our ears, like the serpent himself. The words like water lap against the shore. They have inevitable motion, driving readers to a meaning that enters the brain through the senses. We understand without the need to explain, no need to translate. The heroic blank verse rolls resonant, you are transported on a wave of sound until you pause, allowing the sonorous metre to linger in your memory while watching the pictures created in your mind. And reflecting, reflecting on what you have just felt and heard. The verse enters your being, becomes a part of you, it's there and never will it leave.

So you leave Eden, so you leave the cottage.[4] Tear in eye perhaps, but better for having once been there.

"Some natural tears they dropped, but wiped them soon;
The world was all before them, where to choose
Their place of rest, and providence their guide:
They hand in hand with wandering steps and slow,
Through Eden took their solitary way."

Notes

1   From *Paradise Lost,* an illustrated edition with an introduction by Philip Pullman, published by Oxford University Press, 2005. All quotations from *Paradise Lost* are taken from this edition.

2   Extracts from Thomas Ellwood's Life, his autobiography, are taken from a leaflet available at John Milton's Cottage.

3   John Simmons, *Dark Angels*, Cyan Books, 2004.

4   Milton's Cottage in Chalfont St Giles is open daily except Mondays from 1 March to 31 October. See www.miltonscottage.org for details of the Society of Friends of Milton's Cottage.

(Notes for) (My) Manifest Promise

Me, Julian Barnes and *Metroland*[1]

by *Rishi Dastidar*

* Epigram added, when read on the plane back from Hong Kong, where first draft of this piece was written, pulling together the Post-it® notes on which I'd scribbled fragments in a midnight frenzy when visiting Stanmore before leaving for HK

"Still, Robert Towne had thought of *Chinatown* like a creator, or like a writer beginning to open up a private world, albeit one found in such public places that it had meaning for millions. And he could not get it out of his head. Those are conditions, or symptoms, of art or of the aspiration to make something we call art."[2]

* Prologue, preamble &c

Places and times of composition: Streatham Hill; on the 159 bus travelling up Brixton Hill; Stanmore; Hong Kong; Clapham; and Stanmore. Between November 2005 and April 2006; primarily 20–31 January 2006.

Here are some working titles† and first lines‡ you weren't meant to see:

‡Remember those letters you sent to me from Paris, nearly seven years ago now, when you were on the edge of the city? When life was happening elsewhere?

†Letters to the Viscountess Metroland
†Letters to Bunny
†Suburban knives harmless ribbon
‡Third we take Stanmore, Middlesex
‡Repine: to feel discontent, to fret, to yearn for something
†The Stanmore Syndrome

* "On author" (or, critical need-to-know about Julian Barnes [JB]):[3]

"He bathes mundane realities in a transfiguring light, recognising the extraordinary in the ordinary. He observes a boring landscape and endows it with fanciful, wishful patterns and symbols – to pedantic and poignant effect."[4]

* The bit about the book[5]

Edition used in reading for, and writing of, piece: Picador: London, 1990. Front cover straplines: "Winner of the Somerset Maugham Prize," "Now a major film."

Structure: part 1 – Chris and Toni growing up in Metroland; part 2 – Chris living and studying in Paris, having first romantic relationship, and meeting future wife, Marion; part 3 – Chris and Marion living in Metroland, Toni's re-entry into their lives.

Key relationship: between Chris and Toni, first as school friends, then adults. Chris is the "hero," and nominally straight man to Toni's more exotic and restless, rebellious intellectual.

Key term used: *épat* – demonstration of superiority of intellect in whimsical, absurd or farcical situations, to show up persons in/of authority.

* Notes and annotations made (on the back of an envelope) whilst re-reading *Metroland*

Orange on red: the colour of suburbia
Being as smug and bourgeois as the area that
spawned them
Schooled – expensively no doubt – in town
Pt 1: it's 1963 – where are The Beatles?
Tripartite arc mirroring my own choices of places to live?
p 31: J'habite Metroland – wilfully clever, and yet author
gently deflates wherever possible
59: sense that best/promise is before them: does it
materialise? And immortality through Art
65: ... for want of choice
67: waiting at Wembley Park[6]
80: Jubilee line: *grey*, not silver
81: escape – first flower
86: even in Paris May '68, life – as history remembers it – is
happening elsewhere. Growing up in suburbia does this
88: deferment of pleasure – still true
98: on writing
a tour of the places where the mind, interiority,
is trapped – and then liberated. Of course we go further
than Paris now; but somehow our liberation hasn't
increased exponentially
150: trading on resonances
Past I; Past II/Future I; Future II
184: geography I recognise

* The bit about Betjeman

Poet laureate and architectural scholar described Metroland and environs in various poems and fondly remembered eponymous TV series, fixing term (and becoming associated with it) in public consciousness. Mostly mourned yielding of rural "Bucks, Herts and Middlesex" to maw of Jazz Age and beyond.[7]

* The bit about geographical definitions

Strict geographical definition (i.e., those villages included in the Metroland guide to new developments, as quoted in *Metro-Land: British Empire Exhibition Number*): Amersham & Chesham Bois; Aylesbury; Chalfont & Latimer; Chesham; Chorley Wood & Chenies; Eastcote; Great Missenden; Harrow-on-the-Hill; Hillingdon; Ickenham; Moor Park & Sandy Lodge; Northwood; Northwick Park & Kenton; Pinner; Preston Road; Rickmansworth; Ruislip; Uxbridge; Wembley Park; Wendover.[8]

Concerns of residents of Metroland, if adverts in guide are anything to go by: golf links; season ticket prices; educational facilities; holiday tours; hotels; caterers; mortgages; estates; houses; land; labour savers; insurance.

Philip Davies: "These urban and suburban villages are a unique aspect of London's polynuclear development."[9]

Where we lived and now live: Kingsbury (further north, more salubrious than Wembley Park or Neasden), then more lengthily (and still) in Stanmore, close to Tube station and corner of Edgware branch of Roman road Watling Street, now the A5. Local history books show railway present in Stanmore before Tube, plus evidence seen that the 142 bus author travelled on when young was in existence c1918–20.[10, 11]

Stanmore's relationship to Metroland: Outlier of one of main tube lines through old Metroland country. Until recently, more affordable entry level living in Metroland a possibility. Recent house price boom now most likely excludes this for many families. Strong Jewish population over last twenty years in part displaced by sub-continental migration into area, of which we were one of first families in.

"'Metro-land' is a country with elastic borders which every visitor can draw for himself, as Stevenson drew his map of Treasure Island." JB, as quoted in *Metro-Land: British Empire Exhibition Number*.[12]

Stanmore's contribution to history (2): During World War II, RAF Bentley Priory was the HQ of Fighter Command. RAF Stanmore Park was the HQ of Balloon Command.[13]

The word "Metroland": actually creation of unsung copy-writers of the Metropolitan Railway, looking for handy term to describe the new estates all the way up from Neasden out to deepest Buckinghamshire. Estates did not meet with universal approval. Waugh excoriated them in *Decline and Fall*: "Metroland" decidedly undesirable – the title that Margot's inappropriate new husband takes upon his elevation to the House of Lords. Shorthand for vulgar, noveau riche attitude.[14]

* The bit that perhaps reveals Barnes' true feelings about the suburbs

Barnes describes the defenestration of Mrs Thatcher in *Letters from London* as being "hustled into suburban exile," managing to make it sound worse than being sent to Coventry.[15]

* The Big Themes, that *Metroland* Deals With, all of Which are So Weighty that it Feels Like This Subheading Should Mostly Be Capitalised

Friendship – Art. Life. Truth – Precocity – Love and Betrayal – Ambition and Betrayal – Domesticity – Settling and Settling Down – Contentment

* Questions inspired by artists Richard Wentworth and Francis Alÿs[16]

If the city is theatre, what is suburbia?

The city is a set, thin and shallow; does this make the suburbs "thicker"?

* My Chris (or was I Chris, and he Toni?)

Matt and I met first at primary school (briefly), then again at our Cub Scouts pack (he played a flashy right winger to my dependable right back). We became solid at secondary school. He was the first in what has proved to be a relatively short list of creative others/collaborators.

* Where *Metroland* and my life diverge

Education (1): Chris and Toni came into town for their education (National Gallery and expensive institution). I came into town for my education (Soho, and Berwick Street environs in particular) – in music and shopping.

A certain *coarseness*: My Metroland, while not rough, had a lack of smoothness, and serrated edges to it. When I go back, the area looks as genteel and protected as it did in the novel. I'm not close enough any more to look beneath its skirts, and check for fraying seams.

How violence comes between friends: When I was 17, I was racially attacked outside the (bottom) school gates. What sticks – the memory of the reaction when Matt and I staggered back into the common room: the instant split into those concerned, and having to be prevented from rounding up a posse to go and find the assailant; and those who looked at me, bleeding, in shock, mumbling and barely coherent, and said, "Well, it's not that bad."

Education (2): Girls were for us, as much as for Chris and Toni at the same stage of their scholastic careers, subjects of fear (roooination [possibly] by unrequited love was still to come, at university). Example: Mr Dawson, a brilliant teacher and an even better manipulator of young men's minds, had a particularly effective way of motivating Matt and me for third-year[17] English. He didn't make us sit on separate tables: instead he put us together with Karly, Emma and Laura T, three of the four most conventionally desirable/lusted after girls in our year. We survived this heaven/hell situation by smirking at our own private jokes, mumbling the lyrics to R.E.M.'s *Moral Kiosk*[18] and affecting a studied, "Naah, fancy *you*?" attitude. Try keeping *that* act up for a whole year.

* A memory, about escaping

It was an afternoon soon after we'd got our A-level results but before we'd left for good, and we were still drifting in and around the common room, drinking up the last moments of our childish institution before reality kicked in. I was back in having a quick confab with my economics teacher. As we were finishing up, Laura C------- (occasional classmate [A-level history?] and cause of one moment of mutual embarrassment in lower sixth, when I ended up in a local restaurant where she was working one Saturday night) put her head round the door, and expressed surprise when she saw me there. "What are you doing back? I thought you'd be gone for good. If I was you, I would be. You've managed it. There's no need to hang around." I said I was just in to say my thanks and my goodbyes.

"No real need for that," she countered. "You've pretty much done it yourself. Don't forget it."

It's taken me nearly ten years to remember. That the work and the effort and the solitude and the sacrifice were actually worth it.

* The answer to a Big Question, as influenced by the novel and my own digressions

I wanted to achieve an elegant homage, or at least a smooth parody of Barnes' style. Instead all I've got is gobbets and fragments and shards and thoughts and Post-its® and ramblings. And yet, I think I've got an answer.

But I've always wanted to live in somewhere else. I don't want to come back, like Chris, I don't need to come back, like Chris. I have something still to prove, but elsewhere. I don't have anything to prove here. I didn't fuck up here. I left here. That was the right thing to do.

Once a place to aspire to, now a place to escape from.

Trouble is I think I have to answer it again. And again. And again. And no one tells you that you have to keep answering it correctly.

* Some thoughts while drafting (4)

I am at Heathrow, waiting to get on a plane to Hong Kong. I am listening to the Arctic Monkeys whose lyricist, Alex Turner, has done expertly, and first time out, the bastard, what I'm trying to do at the moment, what Barnes did first time out as well – finding some truth, humour, pathos, maybe even beauty in and about the surroundings where he has grown up.

And I keep fixating on the word "manifest" for some reason. The manifest, a/k/a the passenger list that I need to be checked off against before I can board. Manifesto, and a call to arms, a statement of principle. Manifest destiny. As in the conquering of the West beyond the Mississippi.

But I'm about to go east.

Also as in ambition. Will I fulfil it? The promise of this piece? My promise? My manifest promise.

Ah, I think that's the title.

* Afterword

Growing up in the suburbs now. As reported in the *Observer*:

> "What we have to accept is that we might be seeing a new breed of adolescent, a totally different kind of teenage tribe. A tribe so different they probably should not be called teenagers any more – a better term might be Metrolescents, the defining characteristic of the Metrolescent being that, in the age of the internet and the all-powerful teen media, they are united, bonded, on the same page like never before. It used to be that kids in suburbia, or in villages or small towns, used to feel left out; you had to make an effort to be part of the action, to fight and scrabble your way in."[19]

So: you don't *have* to escape any more.

Notes

1   (but mostly me)

2   David Thomson, *The Whole Equation*, Abacus, 2005, p. 11.

3   Term taken from introduction to *Letters from London*, which in turn is taken from *New Yorker* copy editors' marginalia for when writer will take responsibility/blame for a fact in a piece that cannot be corroborated.

4   Mira Stout, "Chameleon Novelist," *The New York Times*, 22 November 1992. Downloaded from http://www.nytimes.com/books/01/02/25/specials/barnes-chameleon.html on 18 November 2005.

5   Hopefully goes without saying that large chunks of book, especially Pt 1, broadly acknowledged to be autobiographical, as debut novels tend to be (Barnes grew up in Northwood, in heart of Metroland).

6   This is a reference to a joke I make to myself, and certain others, wherein I claim that the second chapter in any putative autobiography will be entitled "Waiting at Wembley Park," due to the amount of time that I have spent on the platforms of that station waiting for a Metropolitan line train to Baker Street.

7   John Betjeman, "Metro-land: A script for television, written and narrated by ...," in John Guest (ed), *The Best of Betjeman*, Penguin, 1978, p. 217.

8   *Metro-land: British Empire Exhibition Number* (1924 edn), Southbank Publishing, 2004, p. 5.

9   Philip Davies in foreword to Andrew Saint (ed), *London Suburbs*, Merrell Holberton, in association with English Heritage, 1999, p. 7.

10   Alfred E. Porter, *Edgware & The Stanmores in Camera: A Nostalgic Record,* Saint Michael's Abbey Press, 1984, p. 12.

11   Author did not travel on actual c1918–20 bus when journeying on 142 route.

12   *Metro-land: British Empire Exhibition Number*, op. cit., p. v.

13   John F Hamlin, *The History of Royal Air Force Bentley Priory and Stanmore Park,* London Borough of Harrow, 1997, p. 8.

14   Evelyn Waugh, *Decline and Fall,* Penguin, 1938, pp. 246, 254–5.

15   Julian Barnes, "Mrs Thatcher Discovers It's a Funny Old World," in *Letters from London: 1990–1995*, Picador, 1995, p. 45.

16   Questions set while initial attempts to answer the brief were proving fruitless, and it was thought a diversion into visual/installation/modern art might prove fruitful, which in a way it did, but not necessarily useful to this enterprise.

17 Modern currency: year 9.

18 Mumbled in part because lyrics almost indecipherable, mainly due to Michael Stipe's singing, and absence of lyric sheet on cassette. Lyrics can now be found at http://www.retroweb.com/rem/lyrics/song_MoralKiosk.html.

19 Barbara Ellen, "Meet the Metrolescents," *Observer*, 6 November 2005. Downloaded from http://www.guardian.co.uk/britain/article/0,,1635481,00.html on 25 March 2006.

PAUL AUSTER
ABBOTT ELIOT
KEITH
WATERHOUSE
ALAN GARNER
DAVID LODGE
THOMAS
WILLIAM SHAKESPEARE
WILL SELF
JOHN MILTON
HAROLD PINTER
GILES SMITH
EDWARD JULIAN BARNES
THOMAS
REYN AWDRY
PATRICK HAMILTON
T.S. ELIOT
JASPER
HILAIRE BELLOC
GAFFORDE
VIRGINIA WOOLF
CHARLES DICKENS
ARY BUTTS
DY

26

This Train Calls at Earl's Court, Hangover Square and Maidenhead

Stalking commuters with Patrick Hamilton

by Laura Forman

Loneliness comes in stylish packaging these days. Stalk the most forlorn of the homebound commuters, as they get off the tube at Earl's Court, and you'll soon see what I mean. Follow them to the Earl's Court Road exit. Make a mental note of The Courtfield pub (I'll meet you there later), and then track them through the everywhere-and-nowhereness of this metropolitan equivalent of motorway services.

They're on a pilgrimage to the altar of pre-packed single portions: Marks & Spencer Simply Food. They'll either forget or try not to buy anything to drink. Perhaps the twinkly clink-iness of Oddbins, a bit further down the road, will lure them in. "To those whom God has forsaken is given a gas-fire in Earl's Court"[1] wrote Patrick Hamilton in his 1941 novel, *Hangover Square*. Sixty-five years on, it's a microwave and a ready-meal.

As sprawlingly melancholic as the shabby streets it's set in, *Hangover Square* chronicles the gin-fuelled meanderings of George Harvey Bone. On a good day, he finds himself "going to the Kensington movie of an evening without consulting anybody, and walking back down the Earl's Court Road and having a cup of tea at the coffee-stall and going to bed."[2] After a succession of very bad days indeed, he commits the least malicious double-murder you'll ever read about.

Don't assume that gin-fuelled meanderings are best transcribed by a gin-fuelled meanderer; Hamilton was more of a wistful workaholic. He once said "the difference between failures or half-failures and the successes in this life is the difference between mild self-control and something partially fanatical."[3] While whisky and wayward women had more than cameo roles, you get the sense that his entanglements were more literary research than real-life encounters. For him, writing verged on being a religious calling, with vows to observe revelry, vitality and experience rather than poverty, chastity and obedience.

Shortly after telling his father he must be free to "follow my own career in my own way, without hindrance or help, standing or falling by myself,"[4] he was incredibly committed. He got up at half past six each morning, going to bed at half past nine. He hardly ever went out. If he did, he'd try to limit himself to three drinks, sometimes resorting to a strategy christened the "Hamilton Drop,"[5] making drinks last longer by topping them up with water.

Born on St Patrick's day, Hamilton grew up in a slightly shambolic, fairly well-to-do family with literary leanings. He was riddled with anxieties and eccentricities, later comparing the supposedly cheery noise of children playing with the unhappy clamour of the cocktail party. He had something of a phobia about doing *anything* – not just the usual behind-closed-doors activities – in a room, unless completely confident the door was firmly closed. At the risk of sounding like a quack psychologist, this might have been the first manifestation of a tendency to compartmentalise his life, going to some lengths to keep friends (not that there were that many) from different spheres completely separate. In a way, Hamilton *is* Earl's Court: all those boxy flats in relentless stacks, inhabitants rarely having much to do with each other. Thinking about it, though, that phenomenon is London-wide. I've lived in my current flat for seven or eight months now, and have only just managed to meet the neighbours.

In 1920, when he was 16, Hamilton left home to lodge in The White House Hotel on Earl's Court Square. He renamed it The Fauconberg Hotel in his first novel and *Hangover Square*, his eighth. The building is still there, but the closest I got to communing with Hamiltonian ghosts was staring at a head appearing and disappearing in a nearby window. It belonged to a woman bouncing on a trampoline and babbling on a mobile. Impressive multi-tasking.

Who knows what Hamilton's first impressions of Earl's Court were? When I first arrived in the city, and didn't realise an 0208 number was social suicide, my flat was just beyond the southernmost reaches of the District line. For a long time, Earl's Court meant nothing more than one thing: loitering on the platform, willing malevolent retro gameshow arrows to announce the glittering prize of a Wimbledon train. I now know that feeling of waiting for direction extends beyond the station. Earl's Court is known for its transient population of students and Australians. Hamilton didn't stay long either, lurching from one rented room to another, with occasional long-stay visits back to wherever his family had got to.

One of these moves, to New Cavendish Street, meant that he was within walking distance of his research ground: Soho. Fired up with alcohol, "the neurotic's microscope,"[6] he searched for and catalogued all the "stored observation"[7] he needed for *The Siege of Pleasure*. The second novel in his great trilogy, *Twenty Thousand Streets Under the Sky*, it focuses on the transformation of a servant girl to prostitute.

He had mentioned in a letter to his brother that he'd decided to work on this theme, and soon set about doing some research. Hamilton's dealings with women had never been straightforward. He tended to idolise those he found beautiful to the extent that he couldn't interact with them easily. But he couldn't really be bothered with those who didn't inspire this idolatry. He was often so paralysed by his own imagined ideal version of a woman that he couldn't actually do anything about getting close to her. Hamilton admitted that he enjoyed the feeling of yearning as much as anything else. He was only able to report his first experience of "unequivocal love-making"[8] in his mid-forties, with the aristocratic author who would become his second wife.

His research involved a number of prostitutes, most notably one called Lily. He claimed to be infatuated, yet all the while despising and mocking her for, amongst other things, thinking her surname, Connolly, was written "Connerlly."[9] His friends pressed him to pay his money and leave it at that, instead of mooning and yearning. But it was a long while before he could bring himself to do this – about long enough to furnish *The Siege of Pleasure* with accurate characters and details.

Hamilton revisited the theme of desperate infatuation in *Hangover Square*. George Harvey Bone is well and truly snagged on the beauty of Netta, a girl who wears her looks like magnetic barbed wire. "The fact that he was crazy about her physically, that he worshipped the ground she trod on and the air she breathed, that he could think of nothing else in the world all day long, had nothing to do with the underlying stream of scorn he bore towards her as a character. You might say he wasn't really "in love" with her: he was "in hate" with her. It was the same thing – just looking at his obsession from the other side."[10]

George often used to stroll around Earl's Court, apparently without a purpose, but usually to look up at Netta's flat and divine some knowledge about her from the configuration of curtains and lights. The point where George always stopped to look up was the exact point where, in 1932, Hamilton was almost killed by a car. You can navigate much of Hamilton's writing by his autobiographical signposts. This is the one where fact and fiction collide most violently. According to one of his biographers, Sean French, his "left leg and arm were so severely broken that the bone was projecting through the skin. Both bones in the wrist were broken, and he suffered a number of severe flesh wounds. His nose was virtually ripped off."[11] It left him unable to write for two years.

JB Priestley believed the accident was the main reason Hamilton never achieved the following he deserved, noting that, at the time, "his public were rapidly growing; the reviewers were waiting to praise the final novel of his trilogy; and he himself was obviously in a fine creative vein, a young artist quickly maturing. Few novelists can have had a more bitter stroke of bad luck."[12] Hamilton developed a hatred of the fast-car set. Disastrous road accidents and their consequences became a recurrent motif in his work.

Of course, London isn't a place where you can stand still, except in queues, for very long. And Hamilton knew that people become vulnerable when they stop. The city isn't set up for reflection or contemplation. Diaries are force-fed social events until they yield an oozing *foie gras* of busyness. Colleagues in lifts no longer open a conversation with "How are you?" but "Are you busy?". New-build flats are marketed as havens from the hectic pace of modern life – yet when they're next to thundering urban thoroughfares, the chances of any peace (even on that aspirational sofa) are slim. The noughties soundtrack is the white noise of relentless, often pointless, activity.

No wonder we're starting to see a backlash, with movements like Slow Food and Slow City – ideas that originate on the continent, which have found an English accent with farmers' markets and cycle paths. They're all about taking time to notice things: flavours, experiences and, crucially, other people. Maybe, today, Hamilton would subscribe to *The Idler* magazine. And not just because he developed a taste for afternoon drinking.

Still, we shouldn't get carried away with skipping through what George Harvey Bone called the "violets and primroses"[13] version of life. The seamy side of Earl's Court that Hamilton chronicled so well is still very present. Last time I was wandering around the area, I noticed a giant metal container on the pavement. Painted in an inappropriately innocent shade of baby blue, it sported the most depressingly catchy copywriting I've ever seen, "Get a life – bin that knife." It was an amnesty box for lethal weapons. George could've used it to deposit the golf club he used to dispatch one of Netta's lovers. Telling Netta "It's all right. Don't be frightened!",[14] he'd drowned her in her own bathtub, the only time he ever got to see her naked, seconds before.

So why did a fundamentally kindly man (look out for the scenes with the cat if you don't believe me) kill two people? When in a normal mood, George spent most of his time trying to engineer pathetically platonic and ruinously expensive encounters at Netta's preferred restaurants. But things changed whenever he sensed a click in his head "as though a shutter had fallen."[15]

George then felt that other people had "no valid existence; they were not creatures experiencing pleasure or pain. There was, in fact, no sensation, no pleasure or pain at all in this world: there was only himself – his dreary, numbed, dead self."[16] It's easy enough to slip into feeling like this in the city. How can you fully appreciate people when faced with so many of them every day? With George, this feeling is taken to extremes. When his mood is numb and dead, he is controlled by a overwhelming urge to kill Netta. Though the literary device isn't medically accurate or genuinely convincing, it does allow guilt-free sympathy for George: he does not know what he is doing.

George realised Netta wasn't the "fireside"[17] girl she pretended to be in the early days. He knew she'd "hoot with laughter"[18] if she found out what he really wanted: a "good old cottage in the country" and "to live happily and quietly ever afterwards." But George couldn't help wanting it, even though it reduced him to being a "sad, ungainly man with beer-shot eyes who loved a girl in Earl's Court."[19] A somewhat more successful dreamer, Hamilton got his country cottage, in

Norfolk's Overy Staithe. But the grass wasn't any greener there, and he was soon trying to escape back to London for his old adventures. Hamilton's first wife, Loïs, was described by his brother as playing "her usual part, patient, kind and sadly tolerant."[20]

Throughout *Hangover Square*, George longs to escape, at least for a while, and Maidenhead (a deliberately sexual pun?) becomes a destination where rowing boats and redemption are gift-wrapped in sunshine. But he soon realises he can never escape himself, the idealised women or the murders, and writes "I am taking my life, as coming to Maidenhead was not of any use."[21]

So let's head back down Earl's Court Road, and to The Courtfield pub. In the novel, it masquerades as The Rockingham, and it's there where George and Netta first met. "It happened in the big bar of the 'Rockingham,' opposite Earl's Court station," Hamilton writes. For Netta and her "theatrical gang," the drinks were on George that night. He "buttered in and paid. He was as tight as they were. He paid again and again, amidst their laughing and incredulous applause."[22]

In Hamilton's later years, workaholism gave way to alcoholism. Booze blotted out the white noise that had seeped into his head and drowned his authorial voice. He even dropped the pretence of the Hamilton Drop, needing whisky "as a car needs petrol."[23] When Hamilton died in 1962, his second wife, whose breathless novels he'd given up reading, described the "silence of snow"[24] filling the house.

Notes

1   Patrick Hamilton, *Hangover Square,* Penguin Classics, 2001, p. 38.

2   Ibid., p. 119.

3   Letter (Patrick Hamilton to Bruce Hamilton, 10 March 1927) quoted in Sean French, *Patrick Hamilton: A Life,* Faber and Faber, 1993, p. 66.

4   Letter (Patrick Hamilton to Bernard Hamilton, 28 August 1924), ibid., p. 51.

5   *Patrick – A Tragedy* (second version of Patrick Hamilton's memoir), p. 257, ibid., p 65.

6   Letter (Patrick Hamilton to Bruce Hamilton, 22 June 1934), ibid., p. 137.

7   Letter (Patrick Hamilton to Bruce Hamilton, undated, probably December 1928), ibid., p. 93.

8   Ibid., p. 203.

9   Letter (Patrick Hamilton to Bruce Hamilton, undated, probably December, 1928), ibid., p. 93.

10   Hamilton, *Hangover Square,* op. cit., p. 29.

11   French, *Patrick Hamilton: A Life ,* op. cit., p. 124.

12   JB Priestley's introduction to *Twenty Thousand Streets Under the Sky,* Craven, 1935, quoted in French, *Patrick Hamilton: A Life ,* op. cit., p. 125.

13   Hamilton, *Hangover Square,* op. cit., p. 68.

14   Ibid., p. 273.

15   Ibid., p. 15.

16   Ibid., p. 17.

17   Ibid., p. 51.

18   Ibid., p. 28.

19   Ibid., p. 146.

20   *Patrick – A Tragedy* (first version of Patrick Hamilton's memoir), p. 167 quoted in French, *Patrick Hamilton: A Life ,* op. cit., p. 144.

21   Hamilton, *Hangover Square,* op. cit., p. 280.

22   Ibid., p. 49.

23   Ibid., p. 7 (JB Priestley's introduction).

24   Letter (Ursula Hamilton to Bruce Hamilton, 27 September 1962) from *Patrick – A Tragedy* (second version of Patrick Hamilton's memoir) quoted in French, *Patrick Hamilton: A Life ,* op. cit., p. 279.

...STERHOUSE

KEITH WATERHOUSE

ALAN GARNER

DAVID LODGE

WILLIAM SHAKESPEARE

WILL SELF

JOHN MILTON

HAROLD PINTER

GILES SMITH

EDWARD

JULIAN

PATRICK HAMILTON

THOMAS

BARNES

REYN

HILAIRE BELLOC

JASPER

VIRGINIA WOOLF

CHARLES DICKENS

T.S. ELIOT

Considering Phlebas

TS Eliot and the City of London

by Jonathan Holt

April may be the cruellest month, but any month counts as cruel when you're stuck somewhere you don't want to be. For me in my mid-20s that place was the City, London's financial district and my idea of a waste land.

The City, so my thinking went, was dead space for the creatively inclined, about as far away in spirit from the artistic London of readings, galleries and Soho gadabouts as London was from the part of rural America I had grown up in. Furthermore, having come of age in the 1980s and 90s with no real wars to be conscripted into or rail against, I had embraced the one obvious rallying cry for an idealist of my generation. I held big business in contempt.

Yet here I was, my fate hanging on a corporate job, my long days spent in an open-plan Atwoodian prison, with electronic access points at the ends of space-centre bridges. The building's glass doors looked out onto the City morgue. I can't remember a day there when I didn't feel at least a little bit sorry for myself.

TS Eliot would not have approved. For the record, that's the stern and stuffy TS Eliot of lore. Who knows what the real TS Eliot would have thought about an upstart's career obstinacy. He'd been dead for 35 years. But a dead poet of Eliot's calibre has already said quite a lot. After all, Eliot wrote the book – or at least the definitive twentieth-century poem – on angst, even as his own life seemed to take a professional path more travelled by.

In 1917, Eliot joined Lloyds Bank as a clerk, working right in the heart of the City. Europe was at war and neither freelancing income nor Eliot's well-received first collection of poems had done wonders for his bank balance. Eliot called the new job a "stop-gap."

Five years later and still on the bank's payroll, he published *The Waste Land*, which would make him the most famous English-language poet alive. And still he did not leave the bank. He would stay for another four years. Printing poems is not the same as printing money, granted, but if you read *The Waste Land* as an indictment of London's dark financial heart, a portrayal of The City of London as a Dante's Inferno of the then modern world, Eliot's choice to remain there does look a bit masochistic.

"Under the brown fog of a winter dawn,
A crowd flowed over London Bridge, so many,
I had not thought death had undone so many."

Five lines later the crowds reach Saint Mary Woolnoth's Church, next door to Eliot's office, and her clock makes "a dead sound on the final stroke of nine."

Anyone now familiar with London Bridge at rush hour might recognise the Living Dead effect of several thousand black-clad commuters marching as to work. It's a disturbing scene, especially if you picture the poet's piercing eyes among the dead. That's just how Ezra Pound saw it. (He called his friend's bank job "the greatest waste in ang-sax letters at the moment.") And that was how I saw things too when I arrived in London in 1996, looking for the kind of literary-grade life experiences a young American believes can only be had in the quainter parts of an "olde" country.

"I plan to spend as little time as possible getting to know the City of London," I boldly told the first person I met about a job here, an American woman who published magazines out of a muffled basement space in Bishopsgate. (That's in the City of London, you know – I didn't.) No job was offered, and for my precociousness I have spent most of the last ten years getting to know the City of London.

"How are you?" I cheerfully asked a stranger in the lift at my first City-based temporary assignment. "I'd be a lot better if I wasn't in this place!" he replied. Nothing in my North Carolina upbringing had prepared me for the droll martyrdom of the British workplace.

But London would capture me spiritually in the way that England had once captured Eliot. Unfortunately my visa was about to run out. "There are ways to stay here," I wrote cryptically to a friend in the States, "but they are not for the faint of heart." I must have meant an inconvenient marriage or prostitution, but the way that worked out in the end was work permit sponsorship from a large British corporation. I would buy my freedom to remain with my weekdays, which would now belong fully to the City, the one part of London I didn't think I could stomach.

Intellectually, it turned out, writing and editing for corporate ends was the same challenge as writing and editing for the love of it, but the surrounding politics were cut-throat. I was out of my depth, lost in an organisation whose only shared language was based in numbers, process and perhaps the weather. I could leave the job whenever I pleased, of course, as long as I also left the country.

If Eliot's City job served as a welcome shelter from the traumas of an unhappy marriage, my City job *was* my bad marriage. A line and half from *The Waste Land* summed up how I felt:

"My feet are at Moorgate, and my heart
Under my feet."

At the turning point in *The Waste Land*, a man named Phlebas floats dead in a stream. He has been there for two weeks, and his forgotten-ness is a warning to us all.

My own Phlebas moment came the day a middle-aged stranger from another department set himself up to work out of a meeting room near my desk. The room was windowless and soulless. What a place to die, and yet that's exactly what this man did. Those who heard it said they would never forget the strangled brook of the gasps as he collapsed. Yet within moments, the body not cold and the man's laptop still whirring beside it, the busy sounds of typing and chatter resumed along the floor.

> "Consider Phlebas, who was once handsome and
> young as you."

Perhaps eyeing his friend's own mortality, Pound pushed hard to liberate Eliot from the bank. He planned to do it through a utopian scheme that would match the bank's wages one £5 annual pledge at a time. Eliot kept his distance from "Bel Esprit," fearing it might embarrass him in the end (it did). Besides, who would pay for his pension?

In fact, Eliot had never approached the City with anything like Pound's disdain. "Perhaps it will surprise you to hear that I enjoy the work," he had written to his mother in St Louis not long after starting at Lloyds. He liked working with numbers, liked and was liked by his co-workers.

Most importantly, in the beginning at least, the work left him the energy he needed to make good literary progress on the side. No, not on the side. If anything the bank job was a sideline compared to an astonishingly full life as a classic man of letters. Not only did Eliot write poetry and essays during this period, but he also started a prominent literary journal and exchanged correspondence or company with everyone from Virginia Woolf to Lytton Strachey, James Joyce and André Gide.

In his biography of TS Eliot, Peter Ackroyd suggested that far from impeding Eliot's creative progress, the day job may have been crucial to it, "as if he needed the discipline, or protection, of a 'proper' occupation before he could feel at ease with his own creative instincts."

City work may also have appealed to two of Eliot's more fundamental instincts: an emigrant's love for England and a devotion to personal and social order. What part of London would have been more English than the City, the capital's staid and ancient core? And there were much worse places for a man who needed everything in its place than the City of the 1920s. Think of the typist pools, the formal correspondence, the sturdy mahogany desks.

Within the United Kingdom at that time, only the palace or Canterbury may have had a stronger sense of order, and the City pointed its landmarks firmly towards both.

"The earth is the Lord's and the fullness thereof" was and is carved above the thick stone columns of the Royal Exchange. If this lettering, so permanent in its intent, was nearly invisible when it was new – thanks to the commonplace of the senti-ment – it must be entirely decorative now that corporations derive their purpose from their own financial might and defer to committee-written codes of conduct. ("The earth is Lloyds TSB's, and the fullness thereof"?)

This is what it's like to look for TS Eliot's City today. Even the stuff that's stayed the same has profoundly changed. Fox's still sells umbrellas, but the shop is an antique miniature next to the stripey glass pod that's a 20-storey office building. The Rolls-Royce outside Mansion House is a fine symbol of old-fashioned pomp, swarmed as it is by iPod-listening temps. "Gentlemen are requested to remove their hats," says a sign in the foyer at St Bartholomew's Church. The words were printed with a laser printer.

Peel back the synthetic layer of fluorescent-lit sameness that characterises business life almost everywhere now, and the underlying City is anything but barren. Where else could a short stroll take you past a soaring Richard Serra sculpture, an excavated chunk of Roman wall, an iconic Norman Foster building, tight alleyways lined with Victorian tiles and an artist installing a new work in a refurbished 1980s lobby?

Buildings overlay the ghosts of buildings past in a cityscape that's as disconcerting and full of energy as the shifting settings of *The Waste Land*.

Was the poem prophetic? Did the deconstruction of poetry into a jazz-like dissonance foreshadow the deconstruction of the City by Germany's bombs and America's consultants? It's certainly possible to see the flow of walking dead across London Bridge as a macabre vision of the coming World War's toll. Tellingly, Eliot had a nervous breakdown midway through his banking years. Only then did a finished version of *The Waste Land* emerge.

Luckily the creative process is not always quite so devastating. I picture a wry, private grin at the moment when Eliot saw that he could set the streets he walked as a dispassionate commuter into a work with literary spark. Just like that, Queen Victoria Street and Cannon Street became arteries in the "Unreal City" of a writer's imagination.

The City is not the waste land. The waste land is a figurative space in the interior lives of some people who just don't get it. Like the person in the poem who is blind to the "Inexplicable splendour of Ionian white and gold" just inside a church on Lower Thames Street, I had averted my eyes from the City's splendours – the real ones and also those that might take flight in my imagination.

My morning commute is not the forlorn journey it once was. On King William Street a young woman winks at me, her long hair disguised beneath a cap. We both know the roles we are playing. Two sullen extras in Mr Eliot's crowd scene.

The boards in the floors at St Michael's Church are of the same grey oak that made my Aunt Mary's porch a child's smell of dust to dust. In another nearby churchyard, Mother Goose is sprouting buttercups next to Pepys.

At the gigantic bronze doors in the wall on Princes Street, I pause to admire the elegant lions. Somewhere beneath my feet there's enough gold to pave the City's streets (and still keep a kingdom in credit cards).

Standing in Finsbury Circus, I'm inclined to take the long view of the City's character. Financial today, and almost nobody's home, but who's to say in another 50 or 100 years the curved neo-classical façades of Salisbury House and Britannic House won't front flats instead of corporate offices, the circus garden filled with homeworkers' children?

Hurrying now, I collide with a poem of sorts.

OBEY
CONFORM
CONSUME

Three simple words sprayed onto a concrete pillar, with the power to flood doubt or anger into minds full of not-yet-sent emails. Suppose that in his other role this vandalising Anonymous is a suit-wearing systems analyst for an insurance firm in Cheapside. Now who's calling who a cog in the capitalist works?

Between the banker and the poet, the office manager and the short story writer, the web editor and the novelist, who wins? There may be as many answers as there are bankers, poets and office managers. Walter de la Mare (poet, novelist, statistician) left his job at Standard Oil in 1908 the moment he got onto the civil list. Roy Fuller (poet, solicitor) stayed at The Woolwich right up to his retirement in 1987.

When Eliot finally left his job at Lloyds he moved up the road to Faber in Bloomsbury, where instead of vetting numbers for a living he would vet up-and-coming poets. And he never gave up the security of having a day job.

Time has made that security more elusive. Now that the corporation is both the Church and the coffeehouse; now that the panelled walls of City firms are felt-flimsy partitions; now that the Pugin screens of Victorian monasteries have been chopped up and buried, exposing three geriatric monks to an absent congregation, commercial companies have taken up the meaning-of-life stuff.

The modern City needs its poets, script writers and other wordsmiths almost as much as it needs its project managers and Starbucks-serving itinerants. "Poetry is a dark art, a form of magic," the poet Don Patterson said in a TS Eliot memorial lecture, "because it tries to change the way we perceive the world." Who else would big business call on to make their brands believable, day by day?

In all this, some see the promising rise of a new creative class, but for the writer just trying to stay solvent while getting his own stuff published, it creates a far trickier course to be manoeuvred. Giving us four jobs to do for the price of one, globalisation has democratised the nervous breakdown, robbing literary biography of one of its finest motifs. But the modern workplace, even in the City of London, shows signs of flexibility too, with potential new paths for the writer/worker that wouldn't have been available in Eliot's day.

Between the City and me, I think I finally get it. I had looked upon a place that's as bountiful as it is begging and seen only the dismal waste land from my own imagination.

You might say the brown fog has finally lifted.

Notes

Quotations from "The Waste Land" are from *Collected Poems 1909–1962* by TS Eliot, published in the UK by Faber and Faber Ltd, and used by permission.

Peter Ackroyd wrote the latest and probably most definitive Eliot biography. *TS Eliot*, 1984, was published in paperback by Abacus.

References to TS Eliot's letters and the famous letter from Ezra Pound to TS Eliot may be found in *The Letters of TS Eliot*, Volume 1, 1898–1922, 1988, edited by Valerie Eliot and published by Faber and Faber.

The Don Paterson quotation is from "Rhyme and Reason," *Guardian Review*, 6 November 2004, an edited version of the TS Eliot memorial lecture which he delivered on London's South Bank in that year.

TWISTER
ABBOTT
KEITH WATERHOUSE
ALAN GARNER
DAVID LODGE
WILLIAM SHAKESPEARE
WILL SELF
JOHN MILTON
GILES SMITH
HAROLD PINTER
EDWARD THOMAS
JULIAN BARNES
PATRICK HAMILTON
T.S. ELIOT
HILAIRE BELLOC
VIRGINIA WOOLF
CHARLES DICKENS

Playing Polo with Pinter in Hackney

by *William Easton*

Take the word "home" and pop it into your mouth like a lozenge. See how it nestles comfortably on your tongue. Now, without making a spectacle of yourself, upsetting the neighbours or annoying the person sitting beside you on the bus, say the word out loud three times. Note how it resonates in your mouth, comforting and full of breathy expectation. Next, impersonating your best cockney accent, repeat the exercise. If you weren't actually born within the sound of Bow bells think of Eliza Doolittle, or as a last resort of Dick van Dyke in Mary Poppins. 'ome 'ome 'ome. It's become a mantra. It's creating sympathetic vibrations behind your teeth, an aspirate exhalation. The lozenge has become a Polo mint, unyieldingly British, all sweet and syrupy. Your tongue seeks out the hole in the middle, a perfect O. You keep on sucking until the ribbon of sugar is paper thin and just before it dissolves you crush it in your back teeth and the circle shatters into tiny shards.

If you were to attempt something similar on the borough of Hackney, you end up with spots. The sebum clogs your pores and your face is a rash. Now it might seem unfair to match a London borough with the torment of teenage angst, but to be honest, Hackney isn't that pretty. It's a gangling, awkward bollocks of a place. Try as I might to add the nostalgia of lost girlfriend memories it still comes off at best as ungainly. The Blitz redesigned Hackney, opened up spaces that were filled with low-rise estates called mansions and villas. The occasional lumps of Victorian gothic stick out of a street architecture of one-pound-or-less stores, all-purpose-all-culture-newsagent-grocer-off-licences, and the more recent plush estate agents. It is a borough of fiefdoms and turf wars where rivals vie for corners, a league of nations and nationalities. The occasional square pretends gentrification but they resemble curious pioneer outposts rather than a shift in demography. The huge signs at the museum that say I "heart-shape" Hackney reveals, the myopia of star-crossed lovers and that "familiar acts are beautiful through love":

> "What do you think of the room? Big, isn't it? It's a big house. I mean it's a fine room don't you think?"
>
> *(The Homecoming)*[1]

Number 19, Thistlewaite Road, the birthplace of Harold Pinter is a short walk to the shops. Turn left at the end and cut down Cricketfield Road and you're at the Downs where he went to school. But the school's gone of course. Described by Thatcher's Conservative government as "the worst school in Britain" Pinter's alma mater and that of Michael Caine, and Steven Berkoff succumbed to the Tory clean sweep. It's been replaced by the extraordinary Mossbourne Community Academy. Richard Rogers' wood and glass building in bright yellow and blue is like the massive embassy of an unloved foreign power. The high-tech of its design is definitely alien and somewhat big brother. Surrounded by a high security fence and heavily guarded, the new school boasts an organic kitchen garden designed by Jamie Oliver. It's a triumphant edifice of New Labour. But it's hard to imagine Harry picking organic fennel for a vegetable ragout. Instead, just after the war, a teenager with teenage dreams, his anorak hood pulled over his head against a February rain walking down Mare Street longing for summer and thinking of Len Hutton:

"What a remarkably pleasant room. I feel at peace here. Safe from all danger, Please don't be alarmed. I shan't stay long."

(No Man's Land)[2]

There are few direct references to Hackney in Pinter's works, the notable exception being his semi-autobiographical novel *The Dwarfs*. The sites of Pinter's plays and poems do however make a map of London, Paddington, Shoreditch, Hampstead Heath, Bethnal Green, the Scrubs and a particular favourite where Stanley in *The Birthday Party* played his famous piano concert, Lower Edmonton. The city that emerges is not the one of bright lights or the grandeur of monuments, even of the New Labour variety. It is an urban reach of chintz-curtained propriety, where antimacassars are draped over the decaying armchairs of bed sits and front parlours. Two up, two downs, basements, shared accommodation and rented rooms. Hackney is always present, but in his stage writing, places are presented without geographic embellishment – "a room in North London, a room in a large house, the kitchen of a small house in south London, clean and tidy." Place is reduced to a prop. When he rewrote *The Dwarfs* as a play, the Hackney references disappear, as does curiously the main female character. The East End of his youth is replaced with a theatrical backdrop and the character that induces the betrayal and who drives the story, vanishes. Its not that Pinter doesn't relish place, one only has to think of his delight at inserting names like Maidenhead and Sidcup into a dialogue. Or one can hear John Gielgud delivering a delicious line from *No Man's Land* "I wrote my Homage to Wessex in the summerhouse at West Upfield." He uses place for comic effect or as a framing device. The wider geography of his writing seems driven by fleeting attempts at getting away from London. The Bank Holiday trips out of The Smoke, the charabanc trips to seaside fish and chips, rendezvous for dirty weekends, in Eastbourne, Worthing and Canvey Island. Dull Saturdays staring at the rain from the bandstand and bracing walks on the front, the haunts of travelling salesmen, adulterers and landladies.

"It's a nice house, isn't it? Roomy."
(*The Room*)[3]

Number 19, Thistlewaite Road is for sale. At the time of writing, the attractive 3bdm, 2rcp, 2bth, 2wc, ample cupboard space, full of period charm has an asking price of £490,000. The advert in the estate agents doesn't even mention Pinter and Marko, the Serbian road cleaner sitting on the wall outside, has never heard of him. There is a small triangle of grass at the end of the road you couldn't call it a park, it's just the place where Lower Clapton road leads into the Lea Bridge Road roundabout. On the fence that surrounds it flowers have been tied to mark the spot of a recent teenage murder. Two hundred yards down the road another floral tribute, but this time browned with age. Hackney has a history of violence and is currently rated as the place where you are most likely to hear the sound of gunshots anywhere in Britain. Homerton Hospital has become expert at treating bullet wounds of rival "yardies." Harold, as a teenager, was chased down the Ridley Road Market by an anti-Semitic gang only escaping possible injury by jumping on a bus. When I lived in Hackney, twenty years ago, it was as it has always been, one of the poorest areas of London. The particular bit of squalor I rented was a single room on the Graham Road with a view of the bus stop. Upstairs lived a man I had been warned was a member of the IRA, although I doubt the special branch was particularly worried. If he was part of a flying column he must have been under deep cover because he spent most of his time sitting on his bed or on the one chair in my room, crying into his Special Brew. The house had a regular turnover of tenants mostly heroin addicts and no bath. I was working as a roofer in Tooting at the time, so Friday nights I would go up to the public baths for a wash. There was always a line of the orthodox preparing for Sabbath. Mr and Mrs Snow the old black couple that looked after the place gave you a towel and a short black rubber tube. The tube acted as a plug and ensured that you couldn't overfill the bath. It's hard to romanticise about eight inches of tepid water. The house I lived in, my old home, my room, has gone, or rather, the collection of bed sits have been converted into an attractive 5bdm, 2rcp, 2bth, 2wc, ample cupboard space, full of period charm, property sold!

> "The germ of my plays? I'll be as accurate as I can about that. I went into a room and saw one person standing up and one person sitting down, and a few weeks later I wrote *The Room*. I went into another room and saw two people sitting down, and a few years later I wrote *The Birthday Party*. I looked through a door into a third room and saw two people standing up and I wrote *The Caretaker*."
>
> (*Writing for Myself*)[4]

I remember listening to an interview with the identical twin filmmakers known as The Brothers Quay. They admitted that when they were younger, much younger, someone had described their often dark and brooding animations as Kafkaesque. They confessed to not knowing who he was and believing that Kafkaesque was a word that meant something a little like morbid. I must confess to something similar when I was younger, much younger. I am certain that I discovered Pinteresque long before I saw anything in the theatre. It was part of the vernacular and it had to do with the difficult bits on *Play for Today*. I am part of a blessed generation of television drama, doubly blessed with enlightened parents who let me stay up and watch. William Trevor, Mike Leigh, Dennis Potter, Trevor Griffiths, and Colin Welland. So I was already up to speed when I got my first real taste of Pinteresque. Actually that's a lie! I remember clearly seeing *The Go-Between* on telly but I don't think I had a clue that all that Alan Bates–Julie Christie haystack romping had anything to do with Pinter. It does however seem worth marking this grammatical shift. Pinter goes from proper noun (repeat proper) to adjective. Note, it's not Pinter-like or Pinter-ish or Pinter-ic but Pinter-esque. Linked with Arabs and pictures and burls whatever they are. I have read that -esque differs from -ish and -ic and -like, in that rather than just showing resemblance it expresses "the possibility for multiple alterity." Now that seems pretty good to me. Pinter is the *urform*, the master recipe from which countless dishes derive. So to find the Pinter-esque in Hackney I'm not looking for the essence but its facsimile. The tension in the newsagent between the Turkish owner, the Polish girl on the till and the gang of teenagers he suspects of shoplifting. The road where half the houses are boarded up and the other half under construction with one house totally burnt out. The Bagel shop on Ridley Road where the onion platzels and chopped herring have been replaced by ackee and saltfish patties, the girl who serves tea asks if I'm from around here:

MARK
Sure! I've got a home. I know where I live.

LEN
You mean you've got roots. Why haven't I got roots? My house is older than yours. My family lived here. Why haven't I got a home?

MARK
Move out.

LEN
Do you believe in God?

MARK
Who?

LEN
God

MARK
God?

LEN
Do you believe in God?

MARK
Do I believe in God?

LEN
Yes.

MARK
Would you say that again?"
(*The Dwarfs*)[5]

In 1994 Pinter co-edited an anthology of poetry translations for Greville Press. It is a stunning eclectic, spanning seven hundred years before Christ to now, and includes everything from Catullus and Li Po to Tzara, Neruda and Apollinaire. It would be easy to over-determine the selection but there is a sense of melancholy, sexual tension and pure bloody-mindedness about much of the work. In other words you can find Pinter there. The following snippet from Milosz's poem *Strophes* is one example of many:

"It will be as it is in this life, the same room,
Yes, the same!

... Terrible, terrible youth; and the heart empty.
Oh! It will be as it is in this life; poor voices,
The winter voices in the worn-out suburbs"[6]

Looking for Pinter in Hackney or Hackney in Pinter the same empty room returns. It is a theatrical space, and as much as he prefers the traditional theatre of stage and curtain he also likes the empty rooms that must be filled with characters, filled with writing. The East End of Pinter's youth, his Hackney, doesn't lie between the library and The Empire but in conversations in coffee shops from long ago, in old friendships and rivalries. "The past is a foreign country. They do things differently there." And we're all living abroad. As a close friend of mine, who like myself has spent most of his adult life away from Britain, puts it, "going home would mean going back in time." Finding Pinter's home from the forties or mine from the eighties is no different. Hackney a transitive verb. Past Sutton House where I saw The Fuck Pigs playing, the Barnados home that was a squat where I shared studio space, the night the tree house collapsed and glue sniffers fell from the branches like acorns, the old library where Harold and I both found sanctuary, the Turkish market where they sell sour cherry juice, the cemetery good for a walk on Sunday, the long bus ride into town. Hackneyed, to make trite, vulgar, commonplace or jaded.

On the south side of Stockholm, in an area that is traditionally working class, is The English Shop. It is tucked away on the second floor of what Americans call with appetite, a mall, but which seems more like an after thought in old Europe. It is proof, if proof were needed, that the English really do have a separate food culture. The shelves are lined with mint jelly, bread sauce mix, gravy browning, custard powder and piccalilli. It is a veritable home from home, a place for those living abroad needing an old country fix. The advertisement for the shop reads "Our aim is to meet the needs of the ever-growing expatriate population in Sweden, as well as to introduce our Swedish customers to the culinary delights of English foods." What dominates the shop, however, is a huge selection of junk food, which may say more about the great British diet than Jamie Oliver or anybody else would want to admit. Packets of crisps, quavers, pork scratchings, jelly babies, dolly mixture, love hearts, sherbet fountains and of course Polo mints. The Polo has a long and distinguished place in British confectionery history with its roots going back to the early eighteenth century. The modern mint was originally an American import from the beginning of the last century and it has been the subject of legal battles and a symbol of British independence. Polos also have a curious chemistry. When you crush them they give off a blue light known as triboluminescence. What happens is that the sugar crystals break along planes that are positively and negatively charged. The opposite charges want to recombine and light leaps across the gap. So now, if you happen to have a

Polo mint to hand, pop it in. Bring your teeth together with all the force you can muster – blue lightning in your mouth and the sweet taste of home.

Notes

1   Harold Pinter, *Plays Three: The Homecoming,* Faber and Faber, 1996, p. 29.

2   Harold Pinter, *Plays Three: No Man's Land,* Faber and Faber, 1996, p. 323.

3   Harold Pinter, *Plays One: The Room,* Faber and Faber, 1996, p. 99.

4   Harold Pinter, *Plays Two: Introduction, Writing for Myself,* Faber and Faber, 1996), p. ix.

5   Harold Pinter, *Plays Two: The Dwarfs,* Faber and Faber, 1996, p. 99.

6   OV de L. Milosz in Harold Pinter, Anthony Astbury and Geoffrey Godbert (eds), *99 Poems in Translation: An Anthology,* Greville Press, 1994, p. 77.

On a Monkey's Birthday

Into the heart of Belloc's Sussex

by Tim Rich

It started with cheese. Someone was paying tribute to Brie, that pudgy French "Queen of Cheeses." This led another to repeat Henry II's belief in the sovereignty of cheddar, a claim enhanced by the King's purchase of 10,000lbs of the stuff in 1170. I was rather hoping we might return to our earlier dispute on whether maize is corn or corn is maize. If they are the same, why didn't the Bible refer to "an ear of maize"? And would the Romans have called their goddess of agriculture Ceres, name-giver to cereal, if they'd had the option of Maizey?

At this point a gnarled old boy wandered over, leant in and muttered "Belloc." An insult, I thought. A High Wealden verbal slap for our under-age, under-the-influence joutering here in the Rose and Crown. This magical rookery, where the crouching oaks outside are forever insinuating their splinter-fingers between the weatherboards, through the thick sweet fug of logsmoke and hoptalk and dampdogpong, and down into the dark fabric of the pub.

I'd like to say there were four of us – a reflection of the book we were about to meet – but no. Three. A friend obsessive about privacy, so I'll refer to him simply as Alfie Catt of 2 Spiked Rampion Cottages, Old Forge Lane, Mayfield, East Sussex TN20 9TR. Mark Cross, the extraordinarily hairy lead singer with local super-group Tolkien Heads. And the Holy Ghost, who we can call "I".

Mark looked into the conker-brown eyes of our interrupter and said: "What on earth are you on about?" Alfie smiled in the man's direction, and winked. I blushed like Sussex Flame.

Soft, just above the crawks and caws of the pub crowd, the man replied: "Hilaire Belloc. Talked about a cheese argument in *The Four Men*. Wrote an essay on cheeses, in fact. It's called *On Cheeses*. Much better about Sussex matters than that gloompond Kipling over at Burrish. Frenchy. Liked a drop. Ar." Then he turned and melted into a swaying gang of old boys murdering *Hi Ho Silver Lining* a cappella.

Mark, extracting a Capstan Full Strength from its coffin, said: "Good grief, clearly insane." Alfie slurped his Harvey's, eyes shut. I felt a cold snake of excitement slither down my spine and wondered where I could learn more about this fascinating *femme écrivain*, Hilary Bullock.

* * *

Turns out "Hilary Bullock" wasn't such an original mistake. Tongue in cheek, Belloc suggested he might adopt the name. Even the family grave at Our Lady of Consolation and St Francis in West Grinstead says "Pray for the soul of Elodie Agnes Hogan, the wife of Hilary Belloc of this parish."

Searching for Hilary revealed Hilaire, via some hilarity for the ferrety man who ran the village library. A forest of books, articles, careers and events loomed. Born near Paris in a violent thunderstorm. Outbreak of Franco-Prussian war three days later. Family fled to England. Childhood in Sussex. Soldier. Land agent (failed). Journalist. Novelist. Poet. Member of Parliament. Biographer. Lecturer. Religious apologist. Curmudgeon. "How profuse and pure a genius," noted Evelyn Waugh.[1]

Belloc's *Cautionary Tales for Children* and its inflammatory star Matilda were what many people knew, along with a reference to his name in *The Two Ronnies* (a faulty newsroom typewriter swaps each "e" for an "o"). I – a tender and earnest reader – only wanted the sophisticated stuff and ordered *The Four Men: A Farrago*. I didn't know what a farrago was; something to do with opera? The book would join my next literary expedition. Wracked by late teenage ennui, I wandered in search of lonely sunlit spots where I might try to understand Camus or Sartre and generally inspire myself to feel alienated. I read *The Stranger* in a beach-dry field of straw; *Nausea* in the barky embrace of an apple tree. The fruit was sweet and local, the prose always from elsewhere. Sussex writing seemed stuck in a muddy rut of histrionic doggerel. There was Kipling, but I saw him as a children's writer (my mistake). Besides, Bateman's – his morose walled house and garden – was where on hay-scented summer nights I tested my ability to trespass, face blackened with cork soot.

While we're loitering without intent in Rudyard's backyard, I should explain that by "Sussex" I mean rural Sussex. To write both words – Sussex and rural – creates something of a tautology as Sussex is only properly Sussex when it is rural. A place must have the smell of wood about it. There are villages and towns in the heart of the county that are not in Sussex. Where are they? Everywhere and nowhere, perhaps. If this is unclear visit Horsham. Or Uckfield (where, writes Christopher Nye in *Maximum Diner*, the River Uck is "a site of relentless struggle between the council and the town's graffiti artists"[2]). They smell of nothing, those places. In contrast, Lewes and Hastings are very woody, and most definitely in Sussex. Brighton and Hove are marvellous metropolises near Sussex. Crawley should be returned to Surrey. And Bexhill is a Kent town that has wandered down the coast into our county and refuses to go home.

Back in the reading room of some sun-dappled spinney or camomile-speckled slonk, I opened *The Four Men* and discovered farrago meant hotchpotch. I've learned since that it's derived from the Latin word for mixed cattle fodder; a perfect root for Belloc's discursive ramble from the Sussex–Kent border to his neck of the woods near Chichester. As a recovering Catholic who had moved with scurrilous haste from sips of sweet communion wine to illicit nights of bitter, I was relieved to find that the Roman Belloc preferred bibulous debate to pontification. True, he uses drinking to signal a communion between his principal characters, and there's much breaking of bread to mark pledges, but everyone goes on to quarrel or sigh over very down-to-earth matters, from friendship, wealth and love to whether earache is worse than toothache.

* * *

Autumn

Immersing myself in excellent biographies by AN Wilson[3] and Joseph Pearce,[4] it strikes me that Belloc was always an unfashionable writer. His religious and social prejudices did for him, perhaps. And he's probably too prolific, uneven and outspoken to win posthumous renown in our world of unique selling propositions, brand reputation and political correctness.

Regardless, I'm drawn back by the verve and exuberance of his language. Belloc's best work is a counter-blast to current anxieties over readers' attention spans, to our timid aspiration to write "plain English" that gets to the point quickly. He wanders around his point like a farmer inspecting a cow at market; ruminating, prodding, prompting, proposing. He sets up rumbustious dialogues that stretch and strain his themes. Even his interior monologues have a sense of conversation and exchange; of opinion forming as the writing unfolds.

I find Belloc a particularly fine writer of paragraphs, rather than sentences. And long paragraphs at that. Here's just a section of a paragraph I love, from an essay called *The Mowing of a Field*:

"Good verse is best written on good paper with an easy pen, not with a lump of coal on a whitewashed wall. The pen thinks for you; and so does the scythe mow for you if you treat it honourably and in a manner that makes it recognise its service. The manner is this. You must regard the scythe as a pendulum that swings, not as a knife that cuts. A good mower puts no more strength into his stroke than into his lifting. Again, stand up to your work. The bad mower, eager and full of pain, leans forward and tries to force the scythe through the grass. The good mower, serene and able, stands as nearly straight as the shape of the scythe will let him, and follows up every stroke closely, moving his left foot forward. Then also let every stroke get well away. Mowing is a thing of ample gestures, like drawing a cartoon. Then, again, get yourself into a mechanical and repetitive mood: be thinking of anything at all but your mowing, and be anxious only when there seems some interruption to the monotony of the sound. In this mowing should be like one's prayers-all of a sort and always the same, and so made that you can establish a monotony and work them, as it were, with half your mind: that happier half, the half that does not bother."[5]

And here I am sitting in London trying to let my pen think for me about Belloc. The grass won't cut. Time to head south.

* * *

Shipley. The village he made home. Very Sussex. Very woody. It's 5 November. Stout-black clouds are brewing to the north, but here by his windmill and house – King's Land he called it – we have sunshine and short performances of rain. Electric air suggests thunderclaps to follow. Thrushes are singing with the joy of a wet worm feast. A dryad wobbles past on a bike mumbling "Weather," or "Whether." Sussex calls such climatic confusion a monkey's birthday.

For Belloc this territory was beyond compare, even locally. In *Sussex, The Resistant County* he writes:

"The lines of West Sussex are long lines, like those of
waves following on a wind. The lines of East Sussex are
sharp, pyramidal, isolated, pointed ... The men of West
Sussex will tell you, when they choose to be articulate
(and they can be articulate when they choose), that
their landscape is the most subtle in the world; but
the landscape of East Sussex is quite clearly apparent
and needs no mental digging to understand it ... It is
striking. West Sussex is not striking. It is revealing."[6]

An elegant report, but quite wrong, I think. The eastern part is
enigmatic. Kipling's "secret Weald."[7] The western ground is
open and inviting to the eye – long, leggy expanses of photo-
genic downland with chalk-teeth smiles.

Two Sussex men disagreeing. How very unusual. "We
Wunt Be Druv" goes our motto, a polished relic from the
drovers. If we had an emblem it would be an immovable pig
with mischievous eyes and a bunch of bluebells in its mouth.
Belloc adored this theme:

"The County of Sussex has this peculiarity among all
the Counties of England: That it is more resistant than
any ... It has always had this quality. It was a separate
kingdom much later than any other county ... [To this
day] one may talk a little fantastically but without too
much exaggeration of 'the Kingdom of Sussex'."[8]

I wonder whom he imagined as King? Later, he states: "Sussex
has been equally stubborn and tenacious in its resistance to
any other change, even those of our own time."[9]

I'm tempted to follow this line, but rural conservatism is a
dead-end lane. The past might be pleasurable to visit but you
can't expect people to live there. Besides, old Sussex was never
an Eden. Its beauty was formed by the seasonal pilgrimages of
swineherds, who drove their pigs into the wild woods to
munch acorns. By their settlement in farmsteads, creating
small, irregular fields to match tough, irregular land. By the
huge growth in iron foundries making cannon, which farmed

the woods and funded glorious houses.[10] By each new prosperous generation preserving these qualities. Yes, Sussex should be protected. From unthinking rurburbanisation. From ubiquity. From Leylandii culture. But Sussex needs new life as well as continuity. An appreciation of what is and what could be as great as what was.

Unfortunately, Belloc's flames burn low when he considers the future. He projects his own maudlin – Magdalene – pessimism onto the land rather than celebrates its potential. Death, dread and sentiment stalk his feelings. Here he is in the preface to *The Four Men*:

> " ... on this account does a man come to love with all his heart , that part of earth which nourished his boyhood. For it does not change, or if it changes, it changes very little, and finds in it the character of enduring things. In this love he remains content, until, perhaps, some sort of warning reaches him, that even his own County is approaching its doom."[11]

"Doom." How very Catholic. The personal as universal. But enough of all this, we have a public burning to attend.

* * *

A blazing star turns Lewes night to day. Bonfire Night. The oratorio of shrieks and bellows and wails begins. This humpy necropolis at the meeting point of Downs and Weald is shuddering its ghosts from the mortar. A wake. You are not welcome, however. Lewes Bonfire Council suggests "outsiders" stay away. Police issue health and safety warnings. Trains are cancelled. Parking is impossible. It rains. Seventy-five thousand people turn up.

I can't find reference to Bonfire in Belloc. Perhaps it offended his Catholicity, for tonight, as always on the fifth, an effigy of a Pope will burn. The infamous "No Popery" banner is already flying down by the Ouse. It's normally a gift shop area; I'd like to add a banner declaring "No Pot Pourri."

There is serious history at play, however. Bonfires burned across Sussex in the 1550s. According to John Foxe's *The Book of Martyrs*,[12] four Protestants went to the stake in my home village, Mayfield. Seventeen were burnt outside the Star Inn in Lewes. A memorial in Mayfield depicts logs and flames and declares "Thy Word is Truth." I think of *Matilda Who Told Lies, And Was Burned to Death*. Remembrance of the martyrs was introduced to Bonfire in the 1850s – a Protestant response to contemporary political and religious issues.[13]

Mark and Alfie meet me by the War Memorial, as arranged. "Good Lord, why are you hanging around here like a bad smell?" asks Mark, now with jazz-grunge experimentalists Horny Devil. Alfie has been helping one of the societies; he can't reveal which. I mention Belloc and Sussex and the Rose and Crown affair. "What on earth are you on about?", asks Mark. Alfie smiles in my direction, and winks.

Torches are lit, the procession begins, rook-scarers split cold hard air, and the bacchantes chant "Oi! Oi! Oi!". There are Cavaliers. Zulus. Mongolian warriors. Siamese dancers. American Indians. Pirates. Space aliens. A man dressed as Herne the Hunter. A long line of mixed metaphors.

Despite the anti-popery, there's something Bellocose about this combination of dark fuming and expressive zest, this farrago of black powders. Effigies of "Enemies of Bonfire" – usually local officials – are paraded on pikes, but there's also togetherness and vitality. Sectarian prejudice is a persistent but feint stain. For most, "Popery" has become shorthand for authoritarianism.

Following a Society to its firesite, we find ourselves mixed up in the ranks of torchbearers. A marshall dressed as a Wren screeches "Respect the procession! Respect the procession!" The pyre is lit. The Archbishop of Bonfire hollers his sermon into the wind … to blazes with identity cards … Bonfire prayers rumble. Guy's head explodes.

I raise a glass and a cheddar sandwich to Belloc. He would probably see all this as a memorial service for lost ways – a remembrance. But I think we can choose our fate. The real story of Sussex is one of resurgence not passive wistfulness.

All the energy stored in those woods; the budding promise in the earth; the enduring local passion for the land; the vibrant spirit that filled the alleys of this town tonight – Sussex still has what it takes to inspire exuberant feelings, exuberant words.

It may have ceded ground, but there is life in the old kingdom yet.

Notes

1   From "Here's Richness," Evelyn Waugh's review in *The Spectator*, 21 May 1954, of WN Roughead (ed), *The Verses of Hilaire Belloc,* Nonesuch Press.

2   Christopher Nye, *Maximum Diner: Making it Big in Uckfield*, Sort of Books, 2004.

3   AN Wilson, *Hilaire Belloc*, Gibson Square Books, 2003.

4. Joseph Pearce, *Old Thunder: A Life of Hilaire Belloc*, HarperCollins, 2002.

5. Hilaire Belloc, *The Mowing of a Field*, from *Hills and the Sea*, Methuen, 1906.

6. Hilaire Belloc, introduction to *Sussex: A Resistant County*, The Homeland Association, 1929, British Library shelf mark YA 1996 b.4884.

7   From *Puck's Song*, in Rudyard Kipling, *Puck of Pook's Hill*, Macmillan, 1906.

8   Belloc, introduction to *Sussex: A Resistant County*, op. cit.

9   Ibid.

10 For an excellent description of this human shaping of the Weald visit www.highweald.org

11 Hilaire Belloc, preface to *The Four Men: A Farrago*, first published by Thomas Nelson and Sons, 1911.

12 John Foxe, *The Book of Martyrs*, also known as *Foxe's Actes and Monuments of these Latter and Perillous Days, touching Matters of the Church*, John Day, 1563.

13 For a thorough analysis of bonfire and religion in Lewes see Jeremy Goring, *Burn Holy Fire: Religion in Lewes since the Reformation*, The Lutterworth Press, 2003.

PAUL ABBOTT

MISTER

ROBERT

KEITH

WATERHOUSE

ALAN GARNER

DYLAN THOMAS

DAVID LODGE

WILLIAM SHAKESPEARE

WILL SELF

JOHN MILTON

HAROLD PINTER

GILES

EDWARD THOMAS

JULIAN BARNES

PATRICK HAMILTON

T.S. ELIOT

REV W AWDRY

HILAIRE BELLOC

JASPER FFORDE

MA LONG

MARY BUTTS

HARDY

VIRGINIA WOOLF

CHARLES DICKE

2E

Unpretending Orlando

Virginia Woolf and the Downs

by Elise Valmorbida

Scratch the fine carpet of green and there is white. The horizon line is untroubled, smooth where it meets a clean glazed sky. Few trees take root here. The powdery downs roll, curvaceous as flesh, soft valleys interlacing. Wind, fresh in every season, sweeps across the tops, smoothing the smooth. The paths are springy underfoot. They vibrate.

I have walked here with Greg, whom I call Leonard sometimes, hoping he'll publish my mistresspieces. And Suna, who drove across America with me to research my last novel. And Bob (who is dead, but left me Suna), and Sam (who is dead, but left me with the memory of his speaking voice, and his writing voice) and Virginia (who drowned herself in a river here, but left us her deep-bright voice, clear and resonant against the clamour of the early twentieth century).

Leonard and Virginia Woolf bought Monk's House in 1919. It huddles into a slope in Rodmell, an unspoilt Sussex village of flint and moss, with narrow curving streets and sudden prospects of the downs. She wrote in her diary: "It is an unpretending house, long and low, a house of many doors."[1]

Life was unpretending here: "no bath, one servant and an earth closet down a winding glade."[2] But with income from Virginia's writing, the Woolfs spent years removing partitions and doors, installing modern conveniences such as heating and plumbing, painting the walls in wild colours, reviving the patchwork garden where "unexpected flowers sprouted among cabbages"[3] and fruit hung heavily from orchard trees. Virginia was writing *A Room of One's Own* while the builders were building it. But the new space became a bedroom instead. Leonard brought her breakfast on a tray and she wrote from bed when it was too cold for the place where a woman with means could write fiction: "The Lodge."

Of course the name is dry and Woolfish. Virginia's lover Vita Sackville-West inhabited castles with wings and courts and towers, if not lodges. She had lost her grand family property Knole because she was female. To get over the wrench, she created her own fairytale in the ruins of Sissinghurst. And Virginia created Orlando, the male protagonist who grows up in a literary version of Knole, gallivants through the centuries, writes, quests, becomes a she, and learns that property and power are everything to do with gender. Virginia started the novel "as a joke."[4]

The Lodge is a small clapboard shed at the end of the garden of Monk's House, by the churchyard wall. It has a roof of wood shingles, glass-paned doors to the front, and a window at the back. Two tall horse-chestnut trees lean in to each other by the entrance.

Inside is spare, bare boards, unvarnished. The ceiling is high-pitched to store apples, but I'm not sure if this lofty idea of Leonard's ever bore fruit. In the corners of the room there are objects that hint at stories: a stack of deck-chairs for the summer, a quaint electric heater, an old travelling trunk stamped "Ceylon." In the centre of the room is a plain inky desk of warped plywood. Here, Virginia sat with her notebooks, her pen, her tobacco and her spectacles. She sat and wrote, in her fine leaning hand, crossing out less than most, stopping to think and gaze at the view between her words.

I don't usually haunt the haunts of the famous. But when I come to Monk's House I feel inspired. It is intimate, informal, peaceful, colourful. I could happily live here. And Charleston Farmhouse is just a few miles away, up and down a down or two, where Virginia's sister and assorted Bloomsburys made love not war, and beautiful things with their hands. They are sister houses. Painting and writing.

Virginia wrote steel-sharp political essays and daring poetic fiction. She loved men and women and words. She was a modernist, a feminist, a pacifist. She was the one who pointed out to me that the world's news was full of men. Always pictures of men making decisions, governments, wars. Their pomp and circumstance, their robes and rituals, were lanced again and again by her mighty pen.

Many things have changed since Virginia Woolf's time, but her Sussex home is much as it was, and the world's news is still full of men making decisions, governments, wars. I notice this, fresh, every day.

The Lodge is small and bare, but the view is long. Expansive. Beyond the hedges and meadows there are great motionless waves of smoothest green, skinned to brilliant white in giant oblique patches. The South Downs. I can't think of a better place to be lost for words. Not that Virginia ever was.

She wrote through the distraction of church bells and the neighbours' dogs. She walked the downs every day, and she wrote as she walked, her long strides springing with the rhythms of her sentences. She found calm clarity here, away from fraying London. She wrote despite frequent illness, sometimes because of it.

For her character Orlando, writing was something of an affliction: "once the disease of reading has laid upon the system it weakens it so that it falls an easy prey to that other scourge which dwells in the inkpot and festers in the quill. The wretch takes to writing."[5] Typical Virginia: wretchedness is wrought until it becomes wry.

After penning a frenzied finale, Orlando "was almost felled to the ground by the extraordinary sight which now met her eyes. There was the garden and some birds. The world was going on as usual. All the time she was writing the world had continued. 'And if I were dead, it would be just the same!' she exclaimed."[6]

It's so unpretending.

And if she were dead.

Always close to this writer's hand, death never hides in brackets.

Virginia took to writing when she was very young. She wrote household newspapers and diaries. She wrote Victorian novels and Elizabethan compositions long before discovering her own voice. She devoured her father's library. "Gracious child," he said, "how you gobble."[7] He censored her reading supplies until he judged her fit to choose her own books. She was encouraged to think for herself, and not to be swayed by accepted opinion, no matter how authoritative it seemed to be. Critics and opinion-formers "made one feel … that one must always, always write like somebody else."[8] Orlando understood that "the transaction between a writer and the spirit of the age is one of infinite delicacy, and upon a nice arrangement between the two the whole fortune of his works depends."[9]

When Virginia was thirteen, her mother died, worn out like a fine bird in a folk tale. "Her death was the greatest disaster that could happen,"[10] said the daughter who soon discovered deep depression and breakdown. Her father filled the family house with years and years and years of self-pity and rage, demanding devoted surrender from his stepdaughter Stella (until she died), and then from his daughter Vanessa, who was too much of a painter to become fully his martyr.

"Virginia, who witnessed it all, was consumed with silent indignation," wrote Quentin Bell of his aunt. "How could her father behave with such brutality and why was it that he reserved these bellowings and screamings for his women? With men his conduct was invariably gentle, considerate and rational … But he needed and expected feminine sympathy."[11]

Virginia never went to school. She missed out on the expensive education her brothers took for granted. And

Cambridge was no place for a lady. Years later, she wrote in *Three Guineas*, "The very word 'society' sets tolling in memory the dismal bells of a harsh music: shall not, shall not, shall not. You shall not learn; you shall not earn; you shall not own."[12] It led her to imagine a new society for the daughters of educated men. The Outsiders' Society. Between two World Wars, she saw the unisex fight against Fascist tyranny as a mere extension of the female fight against patriarchal tyranny. She knew that it was a short hop, heavy-booted, from the crushing of gender to the crushing of race or creed. At the heart of her feminism was a love of liberty. And imagination. I love her for that.

While boys went to university and sharpened their wits, the girl Outsider stayed at home writing letters instead of essays, devouring more books than was ladylike, thirsting for the clever company of her brother's friends: Strachey, Sydney-Turner, Bell, Woolf.

Vanessa became a Bell.

Virginia became a Woolf.

And, later, Vita became Orlando – the boy, the Courtier, the Soldier, the Ambassador, the Gipsy, the Hermit, the girl in love with life, the Patroness of Letters.[13]

My dearest friends are intimately connected with Orlando. Dena gave me the book and wished me "lots of Orlando-ish adventures" some time before I left Australia for a new life in England. Sonia named her son Orlando, a darling baby who "laughs so heartily at the smallest things" it takes her breath away. Greg – whom I call Leonard sometimes, hoping he'll take up the publishing business, not just the breakfast tray – was born at the edge of the downs. Together we've sought out Knole, and Sissinghurst, and Charleston, and Rodmell. And we've returned with my mother to all these places. She's a fan of Vita's gardens and stories. In her emails, sometimes, she calls me Ginnie.

I get Vita and Orlando mixed up. One is life and one is art, but the two come together as one in Virginia's words. Her lover/protagonist has eyes like drenched violets, "the strength of a man and a woman's grace," a mixture of "Kentish or

Sussex … brown earth and blue blood."[14] She is restless, ambiguous and utterly literary. The novel *Orlando* is pointedly called "a biography" but its subject lives for centuries and switches gender. It's dedicated to V. Sackville-West, but she is inseparable from Knole. In the dream of fiction, she doesn't quite hand over her estate and title. In real life, her cousin inherits the earth simply because he is male.

Knole is as grand as Monk's House is not. Orlando brags about it to some gipsies:

"… she could not help with some pride describing the house where she was born, how it had 365 bedrooms and had been in the possession of her family for four or five hundred years. Her ancestors were earls, or even dukes, she added. At this she noticed again that the gipsies were uneasy … they were courteous, but concerned as people of fine breeding are when a stranger has been made to reveal his low birth or poverty."[15]

The gipsies' forebears, it turns out, helped to build the pyramids thousands of years before Christ. Against that backdrop, Knole is something of a parvenu. Who needs "nine acres of stone" with all those rooms, all those silver-lidded dishes and housemaids dusting?[16] Perhaps this is Virginia's attempt at consolation.

But Vita, like Orlando, could never quite detach herself from the place. Knole defined her, framed her childhood imagination, linked her to literary history. There were vital clues to Shakespeare here, and a Poets' Parlour where Pope, Dryden and other literary greats had dined with her poetic predecessors. Virginia has them dine with Orlando and she revels in unpretending: between their flashes of inspiration, men of genius are "much like other people," fond of tea, prone to jealousies, delighted by praise, and they collect "little bits of coloured glass."[17]

Virginia's fiction was published in 1928, the same year Vita's father died. Vita was dispossessed at her father's death, as arbitrarily as a Jane Austen heroine. She persuaded herself that she had "finally torn Knole out of my heart" but, when bombs hit in 1944, she wrote: "the moment anything touches it every nerve is *à vif* again. I cannot bear to think of Knole wounded, and me not there to look after it and be worried about it."[18] She created Sissinghurst with its legendary gardens and romantic towers, and yet it was Knole that Orlando returned to again and again.

Knole is gothic, fanciful, light. The parkland today is just as Orlando saw it, falling gently like a smooth green tide. Even the deer seem to have stepped off the page. The courtyards are pale and softly golden. The rooms are filled with painted faces, leopards, grotesques and deep silence. There's not much evidence of Vita, because she is hidden. But there is a clumsy wooden door-stop of Shakespeare – I can picture her hauling him about by the loop in his head. And there is the manuscript of *Orlando*, open to show Knole translated into words:

"There it lay in the early sunshine of spring. It looked a town rather than a house, but a town built, not hither and thither, as this man wished or that, but circumspectly, by a single architect with one idea in his head."[19]

Virginia crossed out more here than was usual for her. But it took her no time at all to see through the grandeur:

"This vast, yet ordered building, which could house a thousand men and perhaps two thousand horses, was built, Orlando thought, by workmen whose names are unknown. Here have lived, for more centuries than I can count, the obscure generations of my own obscure family. Not one of these Richards, Johns, Annes, Elizabeths has left a token of himself behind him, yet all, working together with their spades and their needles, their love-making and their child-bearing, have left this.

Never had the house looked more noble and humane."[20]

Just before her Second World War, unpretending Virginia wrote about the choice of evils faced by the daughters of educated men: the private house with its nullity and servility, and the public world that revolved around property. She probed the oppressions within society that led to war.

She asked: "Had we not better plunge off the bridge and into the river; give up the game; declare that the whole of human life is a mistake and so end it?"[21]

At this page in her life she answered no.

Notes

1 Anne Olivier Bell (ed.), *Diary of Virginia Woolf*, The Hogarth Press, 1977–84, published in Penguin Books 1977–85, entry from Vol. 1, July 1919.
2 Ibid., Vol. 2, 1 October 1920.
3 Ibid., Vol. 1, July 1919.
4 Quentin Bell, *Virginia Woolf A Biography*, Volume 2, Appendix A, The Hogarth Press, London, 1972, p. 239.
5 Virginia Woolf, *Orlando*, first published by The Hogarth Press, London, 1928, published by Granada Publishing Ltd, 1977, reprinted 1982, p. 47.
6 Ibid., p. 170.
7 Quentin Bell, *Virginia Woolf A Biography*, Vol. 1, The Hogarth Press, London, 1972, p. 51.
8 Woolf, *Orlando*, op. cit., p. 179.
9 Ibid., p. 167.
10 Bell, *Virginia Woolf A Biography*, Vol. 1, op. cit., p. 40.
11 Ibid., p. 63.
12 Virginia Woolf, *Three Guineas*, first published by The Hogarth Press, London, 1938, published in Penguin Books 1977, reprinted 1982, p. 121.
13 Woolf, *Orlando*, op. cit., p. 193.
14 Ibid., pp. 10, 18, 86.
15 Ibid., p. 92.
16 Ibid., p. 46.
17 Ibid., pp. 129–30.
18 Robert Sackville-West, *Knole*, The National Trust, Great Britain, 1998, reprinted 2003, p. 94.
19 *Orlando*, op. cit., p. 66.
20 Ibid., p. 66.
21 Woolf, *Three Guineas*, op. cit., p. 86.

Acknowledgments
My thanks to Jonathon Zoob and Caroline, Steven Dedman, Dottie Owens and Alma M. for helping so generously with my research.

KEITH WATERHOUSE

ABBS

KEITH

ALAN GARNER

DAVID LODGE

WILLIAM SHAKESPEARE

WILL SELF

JOHN MILTON

HAROLD PINTER

GILES SMITH

EDWARD

JULIAN

PATRICK HAMILTON

THOMAS

BARNES

T.S. ELIOT

HILAIRE BELLOC

VIRGINIA WOOLF

CHARLES DICKENS

Ours was the Marsh Country

In Darkest Kent with Dickens

by Robert Mighall

"One need not be a chamber to be haunted,
One need not be a house;
The brain has corridors surpassing
Material place."
(Emily Dickinson, "One Need Not Be a Chamber to be Haunted")

The phrase "Dickens's London" always strikes me as somewhat
meaningless. His unique ability to capture the sights, smells
and voices of the capital from centre to suburb, makes all of
London Dickens's. There *are* parts he once made his own; but
it now requires a psychogeographer to summon up his spirit
from the stones of these districts. The so-called "Old Curiosity
Shop" is nothing of the kind, and fools none but American
tourists. The Marshalsea obliterated. Bleeding Heart Yard a
bleeding disappointment, looking something like a small car
park. Try to retrace Fagin's passage through the "maze of mean
and dirty streets" from his lair in Saffron Hill to his favourite
boozer in Whitechapel, and reality and rival associations will
intervene. The only maze you will see is the Barbican, and
you would spend most of your time negotiating anonymous

council estates. It gets picturesquely promising as you reach Spitalfields and Whitechapel, but this is contested territory. Ripper tours or Kray walks have subsequently marked out this manor with more insistent proprietorial claims.

I realised If I wanted to find the Dickens of my imagination I had to go down river. To the north Kent marshes, the cradle of Pip's *Great Expectations* (1861), as well as of the nightmarish recollections that haunt him throughout the tale he tells.

One glance at the map told me this was a place apart. The Thames appeared to be forcing Kent and Essex asunder, like the gaping fissures made by Hollywood earthquakes. The (slowly eroding) differences between north and south of the river imagined in central London, are but nothing to those that confront you here. Basildon, Southend and Canvey Island are scary enough in their own rights. But cross the divide, and you find the Hoo Peninsula, a vast depopulated hinterland between the Thames and the Medway. Look closer and such names as Horrid Hill, Bedlams Bottom and Bishop Ooze explain this area's suitability for staging one of the most powerfully Gothic opening scenes in English fiction. Down river is still one of the dark places of the earth. And one Dickens has made indisputably his own.

It is Christmas Eve, the traditional time for telling and setting ghost stories. A cold, frightened young boy is in a remote graveyard on the marshes, contemplating the tombs of most of his family. It is not a ghost but a convict who materialises out of the marsh. Escaped from the hulks (prison ships moored in the lower reaches of the Thames), Magwich forces the terrified Pip to help him make good his escape. The next day, Pip rises early, steals some food and a file, and brings them to the convict, who is recaptured later that day. Many years later Magwich returns to reveal that it is he who has set Pip up as a gentleman, rewarding his help that misty Christmas morning. The marshes define Pip's destiny.

These opening pages have always left a powerful impression on me, largely due to the stark economy of Dickens's extraordinarily vivid descriptions of the territory. As night draws in on the frightened boy:

"The marshes were just a long black horizontal line then ... and the river was just another horizontal line, not nearly so broad nor yet so black; and the sky was just a row of long angry red lines and dense black lines intermixed. On the edge of the river I could faintly make out the only two black things in the whole prospect that seemed to be standing upright; one of these was a beacon ... the other, a gibbet with some chains hanging to it which had once held a pirate. The man was limping towards this latter, as if he were the pirate come to life, and come down, and going back to hook himself up again."[1]

These few broad strokes of black and red give this scene a painterly quality that has etched it on to my mind's eye. I picture a Whistler riverscape. But a Whistler of nightmare, depicting a scene from Henri Fuseli dipped in the apocalyptic colour palette of John Martin. Pip's terrified imaginings transform landscape into nightmarish mindscape, ensuring that this remote, desolate hinterland has haunted me long after other descriptions from the novel have receded. Like Wuthering Heights or the Grimpen Mire of Baskerville Hound fame, Dickens's Kent marshland occupies a conspicuous corner of my mind's Gothic geography.

"Atmosphere" is generally a pretty meaningless term, but I think it can be used precisely, even literally, here. Pip returns to the marshes "in summer time and lovely weather" (p. 127); yet it is under its original aspect that I always picture it. Pip recalls his "first most vivid and broad impressions"; that "the dark flat wilderness beyond the churchyard ... was the marshes; and that the low leaden line beyond was the river; and that the distant savage lair from which the wind was rushing was the sea; and that the small bundle of shivers growing afraid of it all and beginning to cry, was Pip" (pp. 3–4). You feel those shivers, as well as the loneliness and vulnerability of a small boy on that bleak hostile landscape. Like incidental music in a film, the weather underscores the key emotions of the passage. But the weather conveys meaning as well as mood, a trick Dickens used earlier in *Bleak House* (1854) another (literally) atmospheric opening:

> "LONDON. Michaelmas Term lately over ... implacable November weather ...
> Fog everywhere. Fog up the river, where it flows among the green aits and meadows; fog down the river, where it rolls defiled among the tiers of shipping, and the waterside pollutions of a great (and dirty) city. ... Gas looming through the fog in divers places in the streets ... Most of the shops lighted two hours before their time – as the gas seems to know, for it has a haggard unwilling look.
> [but] never can there come fog too thick, never can there come mud and mire too deep, to assort with the groping and floundering condition which this High Court of Chancery, most pestilent of hoary sinners, holds, this day, in the sight of heaven and earth."[2]

Dickens defines our abiding image of late-Victorian London, with the elements translated into a political allegory for the muddlement of Chancery. In *Great Expectations* they are internalised and psychologised. Pip rising early the next day to keep his appointment with Magwich, finds the marshes transformed by the weather:

> "It was a rimy morning, and very damp ... On every rail and gate, wet lay clammy, and the marsh mist was so thick, that the wooden finger on the post directing people to our village – a direction which they never accepted, for they never came there – was invisible to me until I was quite close under it. Then, as I looked up at it, while it dripped, it seemed to my oppressed conscience like a phantom devoting me to the Hulks. The mist was heavier yet when I got out upon the marshes, so that instead of my running at everything, everything seemed to run at me." (pp. 16–17)

Between land and water, river and sea, the marshes are a nebulous space at the best of times. In mist and fog they must be a positive labyrinth of confusion. Everything is unfamiliar, back to front, disorienting. But Pip's confusion is as much moral as navigational. Or if the latter, then it is the Road of Life on which we see him making his floundering Progress. Pip's disorientation points to the delusory nature of the Expectations that originate in his fateful meeting on the marsh. The glittering prize of gentility and status he imagines in the great world beyond the marshes, is but an *ignis fatuous*, the marsh light notorious for leading people astray. This "moral meteorology" is confirmed in the closing pages of the first book, as Pip finally leaves the marshes to realise his ambitions. A moment recollected in anything but tranquillity by the mature Pip, and one that never fails to tug at my emotions:

> "I whistled and made nothing of going. But the village was very peaceful and quiet, and the light mists were solemnly rising, as if to show me the world, and I had been so innocent and little there, and all beyond was so unknown and great, that in a moment with a strong heave and sob I broke into tears. It was by the finger-post at the end of the village, and I laid my hand upon it, and said, 'Good by, O my dear, dear friend!' ...
> [Later] We changed [coach] again, and yet again, and it was now too late and too far to go back, and I went on. And the mists had all solemnly risen now, and the world lay spread before me." (p. 159)

At first the mists rise to show him the world he is leaving, glimpsed clearly now, as plain as the finger post pointing back to the village he is forsaking. It is the world beyond that is fearful, unknown and confusing, and the familiar terrain seen in all its intrinsic value. But it is the mature Pip who acknowledges this, glancing back towards the village through a mist of tearful recollection. His younger self, now some way down the road to London, imagines that the great world of opportunity is revealed to him by the now risen mists.

One raw day in January I went in the opposite direction, from the heart of that great world to see the place Dickens had painted so vividly in my imagination. I took an early train to Higham. From Victoria, the station that had been my own gateway to the Capital when I had first ventured there (like Pip, abandoning an apprenticeship) twenty years before. From Higham I walked to the church at Cooling, where you still find the distinctive lozenge shape coffins (thirteen in a row). It is a lonely and desolate place indeed. I had come in search of the atmospheric, but the weather let me down. Russia was deep-frozen in its harshest winter for decades at the time, and there was talk of this coming West. Some flurries of snow in Soho the night before suggested that the next day might deliver some truly Dickensian weather. But for once the bright clear face of heaven was an unwelcome sight to me, with not a whiff of Pip's mist by the time I got there. It was however beastly raw, and I fancied I could smell the sea in the savage wind that whipped around the lonely graves bordering the marshes. I shivered with Pip for real this time, a solitary figure against a bleak landscape.

I spotted my first ship drifting past on the horizon and made off in that direction, following a vague path towards the Thames. Despite some industrial development, principally on the Essex side, and some gravel pits given over to bird sanctuaries, the terrain was much as Dickens described it: a "dark flat wilderness ... intersected with dykes and mounds and gates" (p. 3). A relentlessly horizontal realm, with the distant chimney of the oil refinery on the far bank providing the only vertical landmark for miles, standing in for Pip's grim gibbet. I had the marshes almost entirely to myself, seeing scarcely a soul (beyond a few furtive twitchers occasionally breaking cover) for hours. I fancied the cows to be the descendant of the "clerical" bovines that had troubled Pip's guilty senses that misty morning; and I imaginatively amplified the occasional gun shots from hunters somewhere in the vicinity into the signal from the hulks that another prisoner was on the loose. Such thoughts beguiled me as I trudged my lonely way towards the river. And increasingly other thoughts besides.

Mostly about Pip's expectations, and then about my own. My departure from Victoria that morning had already set me travelling into my own past. Assisted by Dickens's novel, which manages to point a lesson without quite sermonising. It drives you into yourself, forcing you to explore your own conscience, vanities, and delusions. This landscape was not unconducive in this respect too. As ascetics from the Desert Fathers onwards have demonstrated, desolate terrain promotes contemplation. The fact that I had turned thirty-nine a few days before might also have played its role in the fit of philosophical self-pity that took hold of me as I reached the river, and contemplated the widening sweep of the Thames as it embraces the sea. Some lines from Keats crept into my head.

"... then on the shore
Of the wide world I stand alone and think,
Till love and fame to nothingness do sink."
("When I have fears that I might cease to be")

For *Great Expectations* is about the pursuit of love and the pursuit of fame, and ultimately the realisation of the vanity of so many human wishes. Pip is truly an early case of what Alain de Botton has diagnosed as "status anxiety," a consequence of the bourgeois self-building that has become almost endemic in our society, and especially in that great glittering Babylon up river. This is the lesson Pip learns on his circular journey both from and back to the marshes, and the lesson I acknowledged as I stood in Pip's shoes, watching the ships beating ceaselessly onwards. Borne back into my past. There is nothing like a river pursuing its eternal course, solitary landscape and fragments of prose and verse to put things in perspective. I had set out in search of the specific, the local and the topographic, and had found the universal, the personal and the philosophic. Ultimately, Dickens doesn't so much evoke a landscape as an idea, and a universal one at that.

At day end and sunset I returned to the churchyard on my way home. Still empty, but for the winds. Before graveyards became the setting for Gothic tales, they served another function in literature. Like the skulls placed in still life paintings, or the skeletons brought to feasts, the contemplation of graves served as a reminder that all is vanity. This is the ultimate theme of Dickens's novel. And it is perhaps signalled in its opening pages as a grown man recalls a small boy staring at the relics of humanity, before he sets out on his own path towards the grave. Or so it struck me as night fell, the mists crept in, and I turned my steps back towards London.

Notes

1   Charles Dickens, *Great Expectations* (1861), David Trotter (ed.), Penguin, 1996, p. 7.
2   Charles Dickens, *Bleak House* (1854), Nicola Bradbury (ed.), Penguin, 1996, pp. 13–14.

WATERHOUSE

KEITH

ABBOT

ALAN
GARNER

DAVID LODGE

WILLIAM
SHAKESPEARE

WILL SELF

JOHN MILTON

HAROLD PINTER

GILES
SMITH

EDWARD
THOMAS
REY W

JULIAN
BARNES

PATRICK
HAMILTON

T.S. ELIOT

ASPER
DE
UTT

VIRGINIA
WOOLF

HILAIRE BELLOC

CHARLES DICKENS

2B

The Essex Factor

Rocking in Colchester with Giles Smith

by Tom Wilcox

"Once upon a time,
I don't remember when.
Caught in the vacuum between now and then.
Out on the road, phantom light lights to the East.
The forgotten land where no roads lead.

This is the Land That Time Forgot.
This is the Land That Time Forgot.
Call it Nowhere."
(Keith Godman, "The Land That Time Forgot," 1985)

I read Giles Smith's *Lost in Music* when I was twenty-one and quickly realised that my early adult life had been captured in words. Sort of. My joy was edged by irritation that Smith's "failed" musical career in Colchester – with The Cleaners from Venus – had been far more successful than my own with Maniac Squat. Such frustration is enough to make you want to write a punk song called "Fuck Off." Which I did, and then put it out on Maniac Squat's own label Heroin Dread. (Sales: 453.)

Having played music for a bit, Smith took to writing about it instead. *Lost in Music* is a chronicle of growing up with music – the nerdish obsession, the hero worship, the irrationality. He describes falling in love with Marc Bolan as a youth, and maturing to the well-crafted pop of XTC and Scritti Politti. I met him for a cup of tea recently and he said that the book was, amongst other things, a claim on behalf of all the obscure, unheralded, but adored records in people's collections. To be truly lost in music is to embrace the arcane.

Smith is probably correct in his implication[1] that Colchester is some way below Memphis, Liverpool and Bromley, Kent, in the pantheon of rock 'n' roll towns. Citing Pete Frame's *Rock Gazetteer of Great Britain*[2] as his authority, he represents Colchester's contribution as Modern English (early eighties new wave/post punk), Nik Kershaw (weird eighties pop), Sade (soulful eighties balladess), and Blur (nineties Brit pop, with arty pretensions).

I'm not sure if this appraisal somewhat underplays northeast Essex's musical heritage or whether I'm just more parochial than he is. Perhaps he can be forgiven for omitting to mention the wonderful Bum Gravy (military/industrial/complex), and their seminal single "Fat Digester," not to forget the execrable yet popular death metallers Cradle of Filth. Those bands' golden years came in the nineties after he'd left town for better things in the Smoke. But he could have mentioned that the legendary Jack Bruce of Cream lives in Alphamstone, just a few miles into the sticks. That John Cooper Clarke retreated to Colchester in the late eighties to escape the "habitual attractions" of Manchester and London. Or that Camulodonum, as the Romans called it, has always had a thriving bands scene; it's just that most have been completely unsuccessful.

One band that tried very hard to make it was Penny Arcade. Effete indie hopefuls of 1989, they turned down small record deals while they waited for the big one. Apparently, they can still be seen in Colchester's pubs, staring vacantly, as if wondering where it all went wrong.

* * *

"Britain's oldest recorded Town," Colchester is in flat, agrarian, coastal East Anglia. The grain belt of England. My thesis is that Essex, Suffolk, Norfolk and Cambridgeshire are culturally aligned with America's Confederate states; united by a common sense of rural secessionism and unfettered inbreeding. The analogy holds good until you start to analyse it. True to the naffness and vacuous core of provincial English town-life, Colchester is the land that time forgot, with every sub-culture lasting years longer than it should. There are still *bauhauses* of Goths to this day. The desire to bring an edge to this otherwise drab world is what has driven many young men into the pierced bosom of rock. Young men like Giles Smith. And me.

In towns such as Colchester there are no degrees of separation. *Lost in Music* conveys the feeling of living there so precisely because it takes time to explore the characters in the story and the connections between them. How important these details seem in the slow banality of a minor commuter-bation; how irrelevant they are once you've escaped.

Lost in Music gets beneath the clothes of Colchester, articulating more how it feels – or more precisely how it sounds – than what it looks like. The entire chapter dedicated to Nik Kershaw[3] gives deeper insight into the place than a census. Giles Smith's Colchester is defined more by who doesn't live there than by who does: "Marc Bolan was by no means the only pop star I hadn't seen in Colchester High Street. Others included Rod Stewart, Noddy Holder of Slade and that man with the sideburns out of Mungo Jerry … Colchester wasn't a good town for that. It wasn't the kind of place pop stars came to, or came from."[4]

* * *

Waveney Wilcox, or Waff, is an unconventional father figure. The son of a strict property-developing father (my grand-father), Waff balanced the conflicting demands of tree surgery, art, music and rampant alcoholism to assume legendary status across the north Essex/south Suffolk region.

As you might imagine, this had a few disadvantages for me, notably an acute fear of his imminent death or imprisonment. On a brighter note, his exceptional but largely unfulfilled musicianship and song writing were the primary influence on my youthful attempts at rock stardom. When I formed Maniac Squat with old friend Scott (Arsepiece) in late '91 my dad was the obvious candidate to play bass, not least because he was the only person I knew who actually could.

The early Maniac Squat sessions, gigs and a demo were characterised by clumsy playing, abject song writing, brazen plagiarism and, worst of all, my shockingly discordant singing. A demo recorded in 1992 is so bad I can't face ever hearing it again. Two of the four songs were "written" by Scott and me, and are poorly executed derivatives of Iggy Pop's "Dum Dum Boys" and "I Wanna Be Your Dog," unrespectively. The other two were written by Waff and had been first performed by his band Plasma in the late seventies. Auteurs we were not. As if in search of better musicians to play with, Dad moved to Germany after the demo and was replaced by Michael Giaquinto (Barnaby Wild) on bass, with Romford-born Chris Tate (who was too grown-up to adopt a pseudonym) coming in on drums.

Over in Smith's parallel universe, *Lost in Music* narrates the achingly familiar production and distribution of an early demo tape.[5] They never sound anything like a "proper record," and the only people who buy them are very good friends, relatives and other people in bands. Smith was fortunate enough to hand a tape of his first real band, *Orphans of Babylon*, directly into the car boot of the great John Peel,[6] with no more luck than if he had posted it, but better off by a fine anecdote. The piles of tapes to which Smith added his spoke more eloquently of the hopelessness of his musical aspirations than John Peel could ever have expressed in words.

When it comes to bands, everyone has an opinion. In two-bit Nowheresvilles the music journalist on the local paper can become a de facto John Peel. Coverage has its problems, however, as *Lost in Music* records: "The recognition, the pestering in the streets, the pressure of becoming a local 'face' overnight – none of these was a stake. But there was, instead, the chance of embarrassment, the grim likelihood of coming out of this venture ashen-faced with entirely the wrong result."[7] Smith then details the pain that results from the *Essex County Standard* augmenting its review of your band's latest gig with details of your age, occupation and the part of town you live in.

Although Maniac Squat's art was deficient, the live presentation of it was at least distinctive. I established the masochistic pre-gig ritual of guzzling a bottle of vodka. This process perpetuated the classic drug-genius myth to myself while absolving me of any personal responsibility for the fuck-awful music that came blaring out of the speakers. My band mates and I would play different songs at the same time, call the audience "cunts," trample on their drinks, and be sick mid-set. I'd also thrust my arse in their faces and wave my cock at them. If you were one of the few people who saw this, please note that it was very cold at the time.

Our compound of DaDa, punk and nihilism had been explored comprehensively by other artists – many times – but we had something distinct. Only a few people got it, however, and the punch I received from a biker at Wivenhoe May Fair in 1993 is perhaps representative of our public reception. There again, I did throw a can of Special Brew in his direction. At least no audience could ever have hated us more than we hated ourselves.

You are probably getting a sense that the rock odyssey that was Maniac Squat is broadly distinguished by disappoint-ment, but there were conspicuous highlights. We went into the studio in the summer of '93 and reproduced another one of dad's songs, "Total Annihilation," well enough for it to be played on a battle of the bands competition on Radio 1. We came last, yet this was progress. We were very pleased with ourselves, sickeningly so.

Then, like The Cleaners, we were asked to tour Europe. Or a bit of it. Drummer Chris couldn't come, so Damon (Did) – short, mad and straight out of Norwich prison where he'd been incarcerated for poll tax rioting – occupied the vacant stool. Did was a less metronomic drummer than Chris but he owned a van, which Giles Smith ranks justifiably as the most important qualification for being in a band.[8] So we set off in a matt black Ford Transit on the Harwich–Ostend ferry full of bright-eyed expectation. We returned two months later full of drugs and Slavic bodily fluids.

Our first gig was in Pilsen – famed for producing beer, and in retrospect an imprudent place to start, possibly. We got a wild reception in a packed club. One teenage boy was jumping about at the front of the stage the whole night, head-banging, smiling and generally digging it. I spoke to him after the set whereupon I discovered he was deaf. I didn't know whether to be walking on sunshine that our performance had communicated with him in such a special way or shot through the heart that you had to be deaf to like us that much.

Satisfaction at our Pilsen experience gave way to hubris as we rolled into Prague. The promoters at the Bunker Club greeted us warmly, took us out for a meal in an exquisite restaurant, then put us up in a flat near the venue. We thanked them by drinking two fridges full of beer and playing like complete wankers. Then we smashed up the flat.

If only we had been managed by Pete the Bastard, The Cleaners' manager, whose lush antics pepper *Lost in Music*. He was, at least, triumphant in getting them a record contract. Perversely, our managers never drank that much but failed to progress our career one notch.

For me, the best-written element of Smith's writing in *Lost in Music* is his portrayal of Martin Newell, The Cleaners from Venus front man and principal songwriter. Every interesting band needs at least one eccentric nutter. Although Smith's representation of Newell is affectionate and amusing, charac-terising him as a latter day Syd Barrett is rather disingenuous. Newell's refusal to undertake what could have been a career-defining follow up tour of Germany in 1988, he told me recently, had more to do with the economics of feeding his family than it being a danger to his "mental equilibrium,"[9] as Smith suggests.

Listening to The Cleaners from Venus today, it is hard to escape the conclusion that they could, and should, have achieved more. Unlike Maniac Squat they were good musicians, especially Nelson, the bassist. *Lost in Music* cites personality issues as the main reason they didn't supplant Sting. I put it to Giles Smith that poor production and the lack of one, truly great pop song in their repertoire created a glass ceiling for The Cleaners. He agreed, contrasting the high quality of production by Andy Partridge of XTC on Newell's first solo album "The Greatest Living Englishman"[10] and The Cleaners producer-less offerings.[11]

* * *

Scott and I simultaneously moved to London to go to university in late '94. We were still living the dream despite a couple of rough years in a musical hell that felt like a collaboration between Hieronymus Bosch and Jilted John. Combined student loans were utilised to cut a disk; the ultimate vanity purchase. We found a studio on an industrial estate in Maldon and "laid down" about ten tracks in two days. Something had changed. A few of them actually sounded good (ie not shit), so we hawked them round labels and distributors. Backs/RTM offered us a distribution deal and in early '95 "Fuck Off" backed with "Spit On Me" and "Hey Rude Boy" were released nationally to a glut of reviews including *NME, Melody Maker* and, best of all, "Single of the Week" in *Kerrang!* There were up to three gigs a week at this stage and for a few piss-golden months we were a passably competent rock band. I had never wanted more than that for my life. And I didn't get it.

Maniac Squat's "greatest hit" went like this:

"I always knew you was a little bugger
And now I caught you playing rugger
Fuck off, fuck off, fuck off

Yeah I caught you this time
And that's my only crime
Fuck off, fuck off, fuck off

FUCK
OFF
FUCK
OFF
FUCK
OFF
WHY DON'T YOU FUCK OFF YOU WANKER?"[12]

Good innit?

Our second single, "Aaaarghh!", was a case of flying too close to the sun with vinyl wings. We pressed too many, put on some poor tracks, chose the wrong A side and failed to promote it properly. At the same time it became increasingly difficult to get a domestically challenged Did to come up to London to do gigs. Consequently, Maniac Squat died a lingering death over the course of 1996. Unlike Giles Smith, I am not inclined to blame the "loony" in the band for its demise, we had actually all had enough. The thrill had gone. Once you realise that you will never be anything like as good at making music as your teenage heroes, it's harder and harder to keep doing it.

Giles Smith left music and has become a successful writer and award-winning journalist. He hasn't been able to leave the piano alone completely, however, making a guest appearance on a Martin Newell solo album. My self-delusion is sufficient to keep me rocking; I'm in a dirty blues/rock band called The Chavs, writing and recording with the exquisite Gillian Glover, and brilliant musicians Woody Woodmansey on drums and Rod Melvin on piano. I hide the dark truth of my Maniac Squat years from them like a priest hides evidence of an affair with an altar boy. There's no prospect of giving up the day job, but I'm happy to still be lost in music.

Notes

1   Giles Smith, *Lost in Music,* Picador, 1995, pp. 16–20.

2   Pete Frame, *Harp Beat Rock Gazetteer of Great Britain,* Banyan Books, 1989.

3   Giles Smith, *Lost in Music,* op. cit., pp. 120–32.

4   Ibid., pp. 16–17.

5   Ibid., pp. 110–11.

6   Ibid., pp. 103–4.

7   Ibid., p. 105.

8   Ibid., p. 34.

9   Ibid., p. 234.

10 Ibid., p. 264.

11 Ibid., pp. 196–205.

12 Maniac Squat, "*Fuck Off,*" 7" vinyl single, cat. HRN001.1995. Lyrics by Tom Wilcox.

PAUL ABBOTT

MISTER

KEITH WATERHOUSE

ALAN GARNER

DAVID LODGE

DYLAN THOMAS

WILLIAM SHAKESPEARE

@WILLSELF

JOHN MILTON

PATRICK HAMILTON

HAROLD PINTER

GILES SMITH

EDWARD THOMAS

JULIAN BARNES

REY W AND RY

JASPER FFORDE

HILAIRE BELLOC

T.S. ELIOT

NG

MARY BUTTS

VIRGINIA WOOLF

CHARLES DICKENS

HARDY

Ecstatic Boredom

Will Self and the Great British Motorway (with special reference to the M40)

by Justina Hart

> "Once you've acquired the habit of motorway driving, it's damned hard to kick it. You may set out on completely innocuous excursions, fully intending to take the scenic route, but yet again the slip-road will suck you in, a lobster-pot ingress to the virtual reality of motorway driving."[1]

Slip road

In 1996, Will Self described his London home as being sited "at the navel of the world, the absolute beginning of the M40."[2] I was born at its absolute end. The M40 is my backbone. My life's journey has followed its route down the middle of England from Birmingham to Oxford, back to

Birmingham and on to London. Raised in East Finchley, Self's journey has centred on the London to Oxford stretch.

Perhaps it is apt we should meet in the middle. When re-reading Self's short story collection, *Grey Area*, I discovered a connection that starts near Junction 8A (Thame, Aylesbury, Oxford), and encompasses a house, a car crash, a friend and a shoe.

A-road

At a loose end on a summer's day, with nowhere to live in my final year at Oxford and a desire to avoid the exam fever that would grip keener students, I spotted an ad for a room to rent in the countryside. That day in the champagne heat, the ad had a Bridesheady lure: share a gatehouse on a country estate with two trainee furniture makers and a teacher. Fancying a road trip, I unparked my ageing Toyota Corolla from the Iffley Road and set off down the dual carriageway towards the M40 and Thame.

The Red House, as it was called, lay off a fast, snaking A-road. Perfectly symmetrical, it was visible to the right of a flat, grassy track. Made of red brick with a red brick chimney and red tiled roof, it had huge Georgian windows which, on the ground floor, were partly swallowed by uncut grass. Apple trees hung about the building in an attempt at a wild orchard, and beyond spread fields. The roof sat inside the walls, as if planted on a smaller house which had since grown fat. It was love at first sight. I moved in and painted my room with the help of one of my house mates, David.

A month after the start of term (5 November, to be precise), I was indicating to turn right into the Red House driveway while waiting for a break in the traffic. A not unpleasant out-of-body spinning sensation followed. Tapes and burger boxes smashed against the dashboard; my forehead bounced against the steering wheel. When I came to, I was bemused at being parked neatly on a grass verge facing the opposite direction. It turned out that another car had careered into the back of me. A house mate tried to take me to A&E, but on bonfire night the queue went round the block and we gave up.

Having been shrunk to half its original size, the car had to be scrapped. It had been a lifeline with Oxford, with tutorials and friends. Stranded miles from town, I wandered round confused, sporting a purple bruise.

In Self's story, *Chest*, pollution in the form of a sulphurous fog chokes the characters. The protagonist, Simon-Arthur, drives along the A418 towards the village of Tiddington and "up the track to the Brown House."[3] Of course! I realised. The Brown House *is* the Red House; David told me just a couple of years ago that Self too had lived there. Self has taken the house and its environs and poisoned it – turned its red to brown, let its green fecundity rot:

> "The house stood about twenty yards back from the track, in an orchard of diseased apple trees; their branches were wreathed in some type of fungus that resembled Spanish moss. The impression the Brown House gave was of being absolutely four-square, like a child's drawing of a house. It had four twelve-paned windows on each side. As its name suggested, it was built from brown brick; atop the sloping brown-tiled roof was a brown brick chimney."[4]

Simon-Arthur later observes a pheasant shoot around the house which, apart from the fog and "sick trees,"[5] is exactly as I remember this intrusive winter activity. The shooters would stomp into our garden, point their guns and miss birds standing a couple of feet away. In *Chest*, they fire so close to the house that the shot hits the windows with a "sharp spatter."[6]

Contraflow

The purpose of motorway driving is to cut down the time it takes to get from A to B. Maybe it's hailing from suburbia, where a car symbolises the possibility of elsewhere, or being born near Spaghetti Junction (and loving those loopy lengths of 1960s fairground architecture), but long before reading

Will Self, I used to drive up and down A-roads and motorways for the sheer pleasure of it.

The completion of the Oxford to Birmingham stretch of the M40 coincided with my time at university. When it first opened, I had the road to myself. For a brief moment, British motorway driving took on something of the glamour of the freeway. Flat Warwickshire fields stretched out like prairies. You could weave from lane to lane as though splashing about in an empty swimming pool. I think this was what first sucked me in.

At university I was always the chauffeur. Spurred by reading Kerouac, we did extensive drives without necessarily having a destination in mind. On one occasion, two friends clambered into the back seat at pub closing time and woke up to find themselves on a mountain road in Snowdonia at sunrise. Going north on the M40 then west on the M54, I drove through the night on a couple of Pro Plus. My co-pilot swigged most of a bottle of tequila.

Later, living back home during the early 1990s, the recession contributed to my addiction. Whenever I was frustrated or bored, I'd head for the motorway and drive sometimes for hundreds of miles until I'd got my fix. Driving in a straight line seemed to re-align me internally. I loved the fact that everyone else was in a hurry to get somewhere while I obtained my pleasure by purposefully going nowhere. Since we were locked away from each other in our metal boxes, no one could know my inferior intent.

Self's own motorway interest was shunted into fifth gear one day when he was pootling along in the middle lane and realised that the other vehicles around him were static in relation to one another. "At that moment," he says, "you cannot be certain whether you are hurtling forward, or if, on the contrary, the great grass and concrete trough of the motorway is being reeled back behind you ... it was a profound epiphany. I was inside a synecdoche of society itself – a perfect figure of modern alienation."[7]

After that, like the protagonist of his short story, *Scale*, who is writing a motorway saga, *From Birmingham to London and Back Again Delivering Office Equipment, with Nary a Service Centre*

to Break the Monotony?,[8] Self was hooked: "I got a job that provided me with an utterly inconspicuous dark blue Ford Sierra
and a remit that allowed for plenty of motorway driving," he
says.[9] He became a service station connoisseur, a seeker after
complex gyratory systems,[10] a highbrow motorway geek.

Tailback

For years Self was ashamed of this obsession "because Britain
seemed so notably deficient in motorway culture."[11] Where
the US has Route 66, Cadillacs and the road movie, we have
short roads to divide a small country, snarl-ups and ugly
service stations. It's not surprising that our drizzly highways
have rarely made it into print.

My introduction to Self was a Penguin 60 of his short story,
Scale. The cover shows a dragon digging its claws into the
roofs of houses that feature in the story as the model village
of Beaconsfield. Pink, hallucinatory clouds float in the sky.
Scale put motorway driving on the map in a new way for
me. I'd always enjoyed my covert road adventures but had
allowed the motorway to flow past, not appreciating its
component parts.

Self pays homage by dissecting motorway architecture and
furniture (road fixtures and fittings) and using a specialised
vocabulary. Features that had been anonymous or shadowy
were now described with precision: instead of the triangular
box with stripy white lines, a no-go zone which had registered
subliminally, Self has "the curved wedge, adumbrated with ...
oblique white lines, that forms an interzone, an un-place,
between the slip road, as it pares away, and the inside carriageway of the motorway."[12]

In *Scale*, motorways filter into all aspects of the life and
work of the writer–junky who narrates the story. He writes
motorway novels, poetry and theses. He heads up the M40
to High Wycombe to buy kaolin and morphine supplies.
Knowing the make-up of the motorway as intimately as his
own body, he compares the history of his drug abuse to that
of the British thoroughfare. Injecting morphine laced with

193

kaolin chalk residue, he turns his veins "the tannish colour of drovers' paths."[13] Later, his body has become so scored by calcified deposits (underpasses and flyovers), that he sees a "route-planning image" when he stands naked in front of the mirror.[14] He has to be careful not miss an artery and "cause tailbacks right the way round the M25."[15]

Flyover

Self loves motorway driving not because it is exciting but because it is "ecstatically boring."[16] A long drive helps him to think. "It's very close to philosophising," he has said, arguing that thinking is taboo in England.[17] Driving for its own sake, he is free to enjoy all aspects of the journey, including traffic jams: "I love the frustration on the faces of people," he says.[18]

Like Self, I have always found the boredom of motorway driving exhilarating. My own epiphany came when I discovered that an extended drive led not only to feelings of freedom and abandonment, but that the movement allowed day dreams to knit into ideas. To enter this dream or hypnagogic state, you must be alone. Transcending tiredness you keep going until, finally, it's just you, the road and the machine travelling at what seems like no speed – 20mph and 80mph at the same time. Your hands feel welded to the wheel.

A car is a moving think-tank for one: unless you get so carried away that you career into the crash barrier, or have a narcoleptic fit, you're unlikely to be reprimanded for thinking inside this box. Driving is free time, freewheeling up-down-time for the mind. It's an amazing feature of motorway driving that you can be absorbed in two distinct tasks at once: driving blind in the fast lane while being plashed with lorry spray; and fantasising, plotting, jotting poems in the air.

I became particularly hooked on night driving. It's more dangerous and intoxicatingly beautiful in a lonely, drifting way. You enter an insomnious state, cutting through the night and road, charged with power while others sleep. It's poetry in motion, a journey to the end of the night. The intensity is magnified because there are so few drivers around. You alone are engaged in a romance with the road.

I once drove from Oxford to Birmingham at 4am, having not slept for two nights. The rhythm of the road conjured up a symphony which I could hear distinctly. Self poeticises this driving dream state in *Scale*. The protagonist writes "motorway verse" which arises from the way in which drivers subconsciously apprehend motorway furniture – signs, markings – and the physical sensations of travelling along different road surfaces:

> "F'tum. F'tum. F'tum.
> Kerchunk, kerchunk (Wat-ling-ton) ..."[19]

It's a brilliant conceit. The modernist American poet, Hart Crane, set out to create poetry which – by incorporating technological advances – would be a synthesis of modern America. This resulted in his epic poem in praise of Brooklyn Bridge, *The Bridge* (1930). Motorways, "these great works of twentieth-century monumentalism,"[20] are Self's equivalent of the nineteenth-century suspension bridge, and as such, ought to be celebrated artistically. His jokey, clunky motorway verse satirises our cultural refusal to take the motorway seriously.

Embankment

Self believes that motorways, not buildings, will be the grand testament to our age. They are "our pyramids ... our great collective earthworks."[21] In both *Scale* and *Chest*, characters have mystical visions of motorways as future archaeological sites. In *Chest*, Simon-Arthur, whose health is failing, gets out in a lay-by feeling "lost in time, ahistoric."[22] Turning away from the road, he feels "enclosed in his lay-by burial ship. A Sutton Hoo of the psyche."[23]

Scale pushes this idea further. The protagonist plans to be buried in "something in the manner of an ancient chamber tomb"[24] by Junction 5 of the M40 (Stokenchurch) where it bisects the ridgeway, described as "that neolithic drovers' path which was the motorway of Stone Age Britain."[25] When the M40 has become "a monument to a dead culture,"[26] he hopes that by linking his tomb with Avebury and Silbury Hill, future societies may posit the idea of "a continuous motorway culture, lasting some 7,000 years."[27] According to Self, motorways do not cut an ugly swathe through our green and pleasant land; they connect us down the centuries to our pre-historic past.

Loop

Mixing safety and danger, proximity and distance, anonymity and identity, motorways appear to separate us from one another but in fact connect us up. When the traffic stalls, we ram up against people but remain thankful for a tin veneer of separation. Feeling immune from normal rules, we don't expect to see these people again. We can be voyeuristic, extrapolating others' lives from a "support British farming" sticker on the back window, a plastic skeleton dangling from the rear view mirror.

As drivers, many of us go round angry with purpose, snobbishly hating everyone else, yet the odds are that we pass each other every few years. North and south, east and west, we go round the roundabout of a small island – and are all going to the same place in the end. The motorway is like the setting for a latter-day *Odyssey* in which we're all mundane mini-heroes travelling from obstacle to obstacle in the same democratic mode of transport, going everywhere and nowhere, bored out of our route-mapped minds. The least we can do is enjoy the journey.

Exit

I wasn't aware that Self had also lived in the Red/Brown House until shortly before my friend David died in 2004. After our year there, David moved into one of the nearby cottages. He recalled that during some sort of party at the Red House, one of Will Self's shoes shot through David's kitchen window:

I think he said it was an outsized brown brogue. Sadly, David took the shoe and the story to his grave.

Unfortunately, I have not been able to revisit the Red House to indulge in my own version of Simon-Arthur's lay-by nostalgia since, during the writing of this piece, someone drove into the back of my car and wrote it off.

Notes

1   Will Self, "Mad About Motorways," in *Junk Mail,* Bloomsbury, 1995, p. 129.

2   http://www.bostonphoenix.com/alt1/archive/books/reviews/03-96/WILL_SELF.html

3   Will Self, *Grey Area*, Penguin Books, 1996, p. 134.

4   Ibid.

5   Self, *Grey Area*, op. cit., p. 154.

6   Ibid., p. 153.

7   Self, *Junk Mail*, op. cit., pp. 130–31.

8   Will Self, *Scale*, Penguin Books, 1995, p. 26.

9   Self, *Junk Mail*, op. cit., p. 131.

10 Ibid.

11 Ibid., p. 132.

12 Self, *Scale*, op. cit., p. 3.

13 Ibid., p. 6.

14 Ibid., p. 7.

15 Ibid.

16 *The Idler*, issue 2, November 1993.
    http://www.idler.co.uk/archives/?page_id=2

17 Ibid.

18 Ibid.

19 Self, *Scale*, op. cit., p. 25.

20 Self, *Junk Mail*, op. cit., p. 130.

21 Ibid., p. 133.

22 Self, *Grey Area*, op. cit., p. 134.

23 Ibid.

24 Self, *Scale*, op. cit., p. 50.

25 Ibid.

26 Ibid.

27 Ibid, p. 51.

F.W.
PAUL
ABBOTT
LISTER
KEITH
WATERHOUSE
ALAN
GARNER
DYLAN
THOMAS
DAVID LODGE
WILLIAM
SHAKESPEARE
WILL SELF
JOHN MILTON
HAROLD PINTER
EDWARD
THOMAS
JULIAN
BARNES
PATRICK
HAMILTON
T.S. ELIOT
REYN...
JASPER FFORDE
VIRGINIA
HILAIRE
WOOLF
BELLOC
...AN LONG
MARY
THOMAS HARDY
BUTTS!
CHARLES
DICK

Your Time Starts Now

Questioning what's real in David Lodge's Birmingham

by Lorelei Mathias

QUESTION 3.b): "Rummidge is not Birmingham, though it owes something to popular prejudices about that city,"[1] David Lodge. Discuss.

Seven years ago, almost to the day. It was the middle of the afternoon, and the sun was just poking its head out over the green campus quadrangle. Inside Avanti, the half-empty campus diner, two people were perched high on stools, picking at cups of murky orange soup. One, a bespectacled middle-aged man named Don, turned to the other, a shy and awe-inspired girl of nineteen, and asked:

"Have you ever read any David Lodge?"

And that was my first whiff of Rummidge. In Edgbaston, just a year into my university education, sitting with Don Hughes –

who was and still is one of Random House Publishers' friendliest sales reps. Rummidge, as Don went on to explain, is an intriguing comic world created by David Lodge. Rummidge University in particular, is the main backdrop for the trilogy of "campus novels," *Changing Places*, *Small World* and *Nice Work*, written between1969 and 1989. In all these novels Rummidge is a version of Birmingham; a character in itself, born out of Lodge's learned satire. There is Birmingham, which belongs on the geographical map of England – in the belly of Britain, just past the perplexing spaghetti junction and Cadbury World. And then there is Rummidge, which resides firmly on the literary map of Lodge's comic imagination. But what do the two really have to do with each other?

Back in 1999, over lukewarm soup with Don, I had little idea of the significance I would later attach to Rummidge and its creator. Like most people in the last year of their teens, I didn't really know where I was going; what I wanted to do with my life. But I knew I loved reading, writing, and well, Birmingham – although as Lodge knows better than anyone, the latter is a statement that many people find hard to digest. The reason I was sitting there with Don was that I was at the mercy of an experimental scheme called the "Student Brand Manager" programme. This was a strange breed of pseudo-internship which entailed more free books landing on my doorstep than I could ever hope to find readers for, followed by a relentless stream of postcards, cardboard pig cut-outs, branded T-shirts, Noddy Holder masks and Captain Pugwash tattoos. Lamentably, many of these items lived their greatest years as house party decorations and dressing up materials, and not all of them found their way out of my filthy and almost certainly haunted cellar. But for those that did, the idea was that I, along with twelve other students around the country, would go forth and create a Marketing Buzz for Random House titles. Out of all this bedlam, for me, two things eventually grew: a career in writing ads for books, and a love for the novels of David Lodge.

That day in the diner was only my second "Meet Your RH Sales Rep" session, so there was plenty for me and Don to talk about. When he went on to suggest that I arrange a launch event for *Home Truths* – the new novella by this already renowned local author – I agreed enthusiastically. Then, after weeks of frantic planning, I met David Lodge in the over-crowded and over-heated Arts Faculty Senior Common Room, where he talked and read from *Home Truths*. The event took place in the same SCR from where he had recently retired after decades of academia, and also the same SCR where much of the action in the Rummidge trilogy took place. After that day, I read as many of his novels as I could.

I soon found that I could not enter a Rummidge novel without first being confronted by one of Lodge's disclaimers: "Perhaps I should explain, for the benefit of readers who have not been here before, that Rummidge is an imaginary city, with imaginary universities and imaginary factories, inhab-ited by imaginary people, which occupies, for the purposes of fiction, the space where Birmingham is to be found on maps of the so-called real world."[2] As he also explains in a later criti-cal work, the two places differ in various ways: "Rummidge is more dourly provincial ... The University of Rummidge ... is a much smaller and much dimmer place," and, "its undis-tinguished English Department could not conceivably be confused with this large and flourishing school of English ... in which I have had the privilege of working for most of my professional life."[3] Similarly, Rummidge's town centre has an extreme kind of grimness about it which in fairness, now seems exaggerated. Think of the kind of muddy brown cityscape you're used to seeing in *The Office*. Imagine Brent-ville; the soul-destroying trading estate and its perpetually grey environs, and you're starting to get the picture.

Despite these differences, I can't help finding that the campus descriptions have an undeniable likeness to my mem-ories of the real Birmingham. There is a passage in *Small World* which, although it is told from the voyeuristic perspective of the character Philip Swallow, still conjures up the essence of a balmy summer term at Birmingham. Philip gazes out of his office window, at the sun which "blazed down from a cloud-less sky on the library steps and the grass quadrangle." He watches the girls in their summer dresses, "strewn all over the lawns," while the boys lounged in clusters around them, "skimming frisbees ... eyeing the girls." He watches as the young students sun themselves and wrestle playfully, "in a thinly disguised mime of copulation ...." And he admires the way "the compulsion of spring had laid its irresistible spell upon these young bodies ...."[4]

Of course we did *some* work. But as everyone knows, there is a world of amusement to be had in between all the academia; in those times when the "books and ring-binders lay neglected on the greensward." University, as well as a time for expanding the mind and stuffing your head full of specialist knowledge, is also a time of discovery, of chasing the spark of new relationships, forming new friendships; of following dreams even as they are still forming. Philip was right; in those days it really was like a "spell" had been cast in the air.

Speaking in Jane Austen's *Emma*, Mrs Elton pontificates, "One has no great hopes from Birmingham. I always say there is something direful in the sound." Negative perceptions of Birmingham like this still abound today; and as Lodge admits in his author's note, Rummidge owes something to these prejudices. In the opening to *Small World*, he describes how the academic staff, having arrived in Rummidge for a conference, "glumly unpacked their suitcases" in their study-bedrooms. He describes how they surveyed the "stained and broken furniture," the, "cracked and pitted walls," and the many fade mark patterns which were the tell-tale signs of "posters hurriedly removed by their youthful owners at the commencement of the Easter vacation." Disappointedly, they tested the springs of the narrow single beds which, "sagged dejectedly in the middle, deprived of all resilience by the battering of a decade's horseplay and copulation ..."[5]

The intention may be to caricature Birmingham through the dour grimness of Rummidge. However, what may seem to be a dilapidated Martineau Hall from the perspective of the characters, instead reads to me like a mirror image of the real Mason Hall of Residence on which it is based, and where I spent my first year in Birmingham. What this passage really projects is a sense of who passed through this room before the academics, before Lodge. Who plastered the walls with pin-ups and then had to hastily rip them down again? Who made the springs in the bed sag, and how? Between the lines, there is an almost nostalgic portrayal of the joyful shabbiness of student life. The wanton bliss we all took in the idea of "roughing it," all the time knowing (or hoping) that it was only temporary. Student days are the only days when living in freezing, squalid conditions can have a sense of fun about them. The party continued even when in our second year, we upgraded from Mason to a tiny, mould-riddled house in the student vacuum that was affectionately dubbed Smelly Oak.

What begins with Lodge taking a gentle jibe at Birmingham being rough around the edges, ends up being a nod towards the more universal student experience, to which students from any major city would relate. As is the case with most large university towns, there is a striking disparity between Birmingham city centre and the more sheltered campus life, tucked safely away in suburban Edgbaston. But the two worlds are never more intertwined than they are in Lodge's campus trilogy, which has at its heart exactly this polarity between academia and the so-called "real world."

Recently I went back up the M40 to see how much had changed, and to go in search of Lodge's own writings on the matter of Rummidge vs. Birmingham. Six years on, sitting once again in the musty but homely third floor of the university library, I put down my chewed BIC® Biro and browsed the shelves of the English Literature section. I scanned the non-fiction shelves for Lodge's many works of literary criticism, then leafed through the dozens of best-selling novels by the same hand. After a while I began to realise I wasn't going to find what I was looking for on any of these shelves. Nice though it was to be back, I wasn't that awe-inspired, bookish student anymore – I realised I wasn't going to find the answer to this question on a page.

"You could never call it elegant or beautiful. It never will be," Lodge said, after agreeing to meet me again. "It simply doesn't have the cultural riches and architectural interest of London, and for a second city it has always seemed a little impoverished." Despite being born and bred in South London, Lodge has now lived in Birmingham longer than any other city. And although he'll never feel quite like a native, he told me he certainly has no wish to move, and now thinks of himself as a kind of "adopted Brummie," having written about it so often in a "fictional disguise." As any Brummie knows, (whether you're a native or just a dishevelled student passing through) there are many secret charms to Britain's second city. And, even as most balti-swigging students eventually evolve into more refined human beings, so "Brum" has also improved itself drastically in the thirty years since Rummidge was conceived.

As Lodge observes, there is always much to do there; "more than most people have time for," and you can easily afford a more civilised quality of life than you'd manage in London. The last ten years in particular have seen huge improvements to the city centre – Lodge highlights the Centenary Square development as the most significant, in creating a central public attraction for the city's people to visit.

Lodge once noted that Mrs Elton is notorious for being one of Austen's most obnoxious characters, so much so that we ought to take anything she says with a sprinkling of salt. But there's other ways to see that she is wrong. Go and wander along the meandering canals in the city centre. Stroll into Brindley Place, with its water-side culture of cafés, theatres and art galleries. Drop in to the new Mail Box and Bull Ring shopping centres. Or take any bus down the Bristol Road and go to the green campus quadrangle. Stand under "Old Joe" – the University clock tower – on a sunny day, and listen to him chime.

Legend has it that some undergraduates applied to study at Birmingham as a result of having watched the television adaptation of *Nice Work*. Maybe they were furnishing a hope that they might be taught by a lecturer like Dr. Robyn Penrose, the inspirational heroine of the novel. Or perhaps they were pleasantly surprised by the scenery, as I was on my first visit;

seeing what the characters Robyn and Vic in *Nice Work* see
when they gaze out of Robyn's office window:

> "The students in their summer finery were scattered like
> petals over the green lawns, reading, talking, necking,
> or listening to their discoursing teachers. The sun shone
> upon the façade of the library, whose glazed revolving
> doors flashed intermittently like the beams of a light-
> house as it fanned readers in and out, and shone upon
> the buildings of diverse shapes and sizes ... It shone on
> the botanical gardens, and on the sports centre and the
> playing fields and the running track ... It shone on the
> Great Hall where the university orchestra and choir
> were due to perform ... and on the Student Union with
> its Council Chamber and newspaper offices, and on the
> art gallery ... It seemed to Robyn more than ever that
> the University was the ideal type of a human commu-
> nity, where work and play, culture and nature, were in
> perfect harmony."[6]

Written over thirteen years earlier about fictional Rummidge,
this affectionate eulogy seemed even more poignant when
Professor Lodge chose to read it out on our graduation day in
2001. As it happened, he was being crowned Doctor of Letters
on the same day, having been involved with the University
ever since his academic career began there in 1960. His words
served then – as they do now – as a stirring snapshot in time.
There we were in the *real* Great Hall – elegantly gowned, and
praying inwardly that we wouldn't trip up in our heels on the
grand staircase when our time came. Sitting listening to
Lodge's fictional portrayal of that time and place, nostalgia
binding us to his every word, suddenly the similarity between
Rummidge and Birmingham was uncanny.

But times change. Lodge isn't writing about Rummidge
any more – he's moved on, along with the rest of us. His most
recent academic novel *Thinks ...* is set in the University of
Gloucester. His hair is a little thinner than when I first met
him. I'm not quite so scared of my own shadow as I was then;

and the university itself feels different today from the one I knew five years ago. The computer revolution is the first big change to hit you when you're back on campus – you can't go ten yards without bumping into a Cyber Cluster of some sort. And, after three years of working for Lodge's publishers, I'm now also heading somewhere pretty different.

But it's nice to think that, somehow, Lodge's Rummidge helped me to find some direction, helped me to decide what I wanted to do. Or was it Birmingham? Either way, my memories of life at university, and the years beyond have all been enriched by Lodge's writing. Rummidge, although an imaginary world, was rooted topographically in the reality in which my own three-year adventure was set. So much so that it must now be difficult for any Birmingham alumni not to mistake one for the other. As Lodge admits in an article written ten years after the last page of *Nice Work*, "The membrane between fact and fiction, between 'Birmingham' and 'Rummidge' has undoubtedly become thinner and more transparent with the passing of time."[7] For me, looking back, the membrane is barely there at all.

Notes

1   David Lodge, *Small World*, author's note, Secker & Warburg, 1984.

2   David Lodge, *Nice Work*, author's note, Secker & Warburg, 1984.

3   David Lodge, "Fact and Fiction in the Novel," in *The Practice of Writing*, Secker & Warburg, 1996, p. 34.

4   Lodge, *Small World,* op. cit., p. 158.

5   Ibid., p. 3.

6   Lodge, *Nice Work*, op. cit., p. 249.

7   Lodge, *The Practice of Writing*, op. cit., p. 34.

MURDOCH

F.W.

PAUL

LISTER

ABBOTT

KEITH

WATERHOUSE

ALAN
GARNER

DYLAN
THOMAS

DAVID LODGE

WILLIAM

SHAKESPEARE

WILL SELF

EDWARD

THOMAS

JULIAN

REY.W AUDRY

JASPER
FFORDES

JOHN MI

PATRICK

BARNES

HAMILTON

HNS

T.S

HILAIRE BE

RICHARD

TILMAN LONG

MARY BUTTS

VIRGINIA

WOOLF

CHAR

THOMASHARDY

Unriddling the World

Alan Garner and Cheshire

by John Mitchinson

> "The purpose of the storyteller is to relate the truth in a manner that is simple: to integrate without reduction; for it is rarely possible to declare the truth as it is, because the Universe presents itself as a Mystery. We have to find parables; we have to tell stories to unriddle the world."
>
> ("Aback of Beyond," *The Voice that Thunders*, 1997)

You catch a glimpse of the escarpment of Alderley Edge from the south just before Junction 18 on the M6. It's the first inkling of the real North Country beginning, the land of high moors, long horizons, moss, peat, grit. On a clear day that stretch of the motorway reveals the rounded spine of the Pennines, the high, distant mountains of North Wales and, eventually, looming out of the sea, the sublime peaks of the Lake District.

I don't like motorways much, but I love that road to the high country. Even the names of the bland service stations have a poetry to them – Keele, Sandbach, Charnock Richard, Tebay, Shap – Saxon, Norse and Norman words that fix the ebb and flow of settlement and culture that has shaped the landscape. I grew up on the other side of the country but the North West drew me then as it does now. For nearly twenty years I've lived in the softer pastures of the South, tending my ground but dreaming of those hills.

This story starts, as many stories do, with a place glimpsed on the way to somewhere else. Alderley Edge has become infamous as home to the country's highest concentration of millionaires. It is a small, preternaturally tidy, east Cheshire village laid waste by too much money and too little taste. AA Gill captures the odd melancholy of downtown Alderley: "They're not bad people. All they've done is follow the instructions on the box and in the glossy magazines. Got on and consumed, cut their lawns, learnt to ski."

But there is another Alderley Edge: an eroded fault scarp, 600 feet high composed largely of the Keuper and Bunter Triassic sandstones, a place rich in minerals and riddled with mines that have been worked since the Bronze Age. It is across this ancient but scrupulously "real" landscape that Alan Garner set loose two urban children in a pair of novels that redefined writing for children. *The Weirdstone of Brisingamen* (1960) and *The Moon of Gomrath* (1963) turned a whole generation on to myth and literature and the deep, unsettling power of the land. Garner fired young imaginations like no other writer. Even in the early books he seemed not to be writing "for children," still less "for young adults." He was a myth-maker, a visionary who fashioned stories out of the oldest material of all: fear, pain, joy, awe: the deep sediments of childhood. And at the heart of those early books, there stood The Edge, a place he calls "both physically and emotionally dangerous ... as full of continuity and function as a cathedral."

Alan Garner is a "Cheshire" writer. His family has lived and worked in and around Alderley Edge for at least five centuries. His father's family were rural craftsmen and he has taken on the craftsman's mantle, using his hands in a different medium but with the same painstaking attention to quality and use. But the "Cheshire" Garner knows and writes about is not the County Palatinate which, though ancient in terms of English history, is only a fleeting political shadow on the tessellation of fields, walls and hills that make up his "bone country." For "Alan Garner's Cheshire," read "Alan Garner's Back Garden." That's what feeds him and his work. But what a back garden:

> "At the edge of the garden, cobbles have been dumped to clear the field. Others made a yard and paths. They are multicoloured and beautiful. They have been brought from the Lake District, from Ireland; they have been scooped from the bottom of the sea. The rolling fields are the slurry, the detritus of the ice: ice 1,200 feet thick.
>
> Some of the cobbles are quite different from the others. They have the shape of flatirons: smooth underneath, with one end pointed, the other blunt. Their tops are domed, and their upper surfaces pocked as if by sand-blasting. Yet not "as if." It was sand that blasted them. These cobbles are "ventefacts." For hundreds of years they sat on the ground here in permafrost in a polar desert, where neither snow nor rain fell, but an endless wind blew.
>
> The ice had gone, and into this land people returned after an absence of 12,000 years."
>
> (Alan Garner, *The Times*, 23 July 2003)

This is Garnerworld, not Cheshire – the long view of deep time made real by his imagination, his meticulous research and his craftsman's mastery of prose.

He has lived and worked in the same house since 1957. He discovered it as a twenty-two-year-old Classics scholar who'd given up on his Oxford degree in order to discover if he could write. To do so he needed a place to live. The cottage he had been sent to see was a soulless modern bungalow but as he was cycling back home to Alderley he came across a battered sign advertising "Seventeenth Century Cottage For Sale." Climbing the steep hill leading to the back gate the first thing he noticed was the long roofline. Once the whole structure was revealed, he saw what few others would have recognised. Through all the dilapidations and later accretions, the brick and the tin roof, he was staring at a timber-framed medieval hall. His destiny was set: he had to live there. He would write much later: "If I have any real occupation it is to be here." Penniless, unemployed, it didn't look hopeful but his father, quite uncharacteristically, yet sensing his son's craftsmanly stubbornness, found him the £510 to buy it. All Garner's books have been written in what was once the buttery.

This sounds idyllic. The writer's cosy rural nest; the ancient house inhabited by the collector of folktales; the very model of a children's writer's home. But Garner's home isn't much like that. It's no more restful or benign than his work. Like the work, it is strong, complex, confusing, archetypal, unforgettable. It's rattled every few minutes by the Manchester to Crewe mainline which forms the boundary to his back garden. Less than a mile away the giant eye of the Jodrell Bank telescope is open to the sky. In one of the neat synchronicities that trail in Garner's wake, the year he moved in was also the year the world's most powerful terrestrial telescope of the time became operational, the only telescope able to track Sputnik 1, also launched that year.

The house was semi-derelict for a long time, made habitable slowly. In the early seventies Garner added a Tudor timber-framed apothecary's house scheduled for demolition in a town twenty miles away. He masterminded the dismantling and reconstruction of its hundreds of beams, turning the whole project into a three-dimensional jigsaw puzzle. It is built around a central chimney, open to the sky, and a fire place where eight people can sit in a circle around the fire. It throbs with a strong, unsettling energy. The first spring after its reconstruction the perimeter of the building was garlanded with opium poppies and other medicinal herbs and flowers that had sprouted from ancient seeds shaken from the beams.

So much for what you can see. The Garners (Alan is inseparable from his wife and soul-mate Griselda) are probably unique in having saved and catalogued every significant piece of stone, metal, flint, every tiny potsherd that fifty years of gardening and digging have turned up. Alan knows each beam and flagstone in his house, not a detail has escaped his sceptical attention. Five years ago discrete excavations began. Combining what Alan already knew with speculative visits from the best archaeologists and historians in the country, a picture has emerged of ten thousand years of continuous habitation. Beyond that – and this is Alan's story to tell – it now seems likely that Garner's novels are written in the middle of a ritual site. A sacred place.

That probably sounds too tidy, too like an Alan Garner novel. Well, here's another story. The young Garner was a runner. He was out on the high moors training one summer's afternoon in the early 1950s when he slipped down a steep bank and felt a flat stone against his backside. Pulling away the tussocks of grass he found the stone inscribed with the following words: "Here John Turner was cast away in a heavy snowstorm in or about the year 1755." He cleared more earth and managed to get his hand behind the stone. There was more writing. With his fingers he read: "The print of a woman's shoe was found by his side in the snow where he lay dead."

The solution to that strange and troubling riddle is the subject of his latest novel, *Thursbitch* (2003). With its predecessor, *Strandloper* (1996) it is the second book in a loose trilogy which will cement Garner's reputation as one of our greatest living writers.

The research for these books is humbling in its scope and intensity. To write *Thursbitch* Garner had to acquire a scholar's knowledge of the history and development of the eighteenth century salt trade; the passage of goods along the Silk Route; the pathology of plague; Neolithic astronomy; Mithraism; the rites of Dionysus; the Mesopotamian cult of the bull; the Eleusinian Mysteries; the geomorphology of the Western Pennines; the history of Non-Conformism in the Macclesfield area. But the story – the emotional momentum – all started in the hills, with a thump on the arse.

Thursbitch is a real place; a valley, high up in the South Western Pennines. It's an Old English name meaning "Valley of the Demon" and it's an appropriately bleak and fearful place. My wife and I walked it with Alan and Griselda one cold spring afternoon. They were keen to show us what they'd found. These were stones, mostly. Standing stones, stones half buried in the turf, stones used as gateposts or lying in the moss. It was only when you looked more closely, felt the fluting that been chiselled into them, plotted them on a map and ran the computer projections that the full truth emerged. Forgotten and abandoned in the valley there emerged a late Neolithic cathedral with stones and natural features in a sequence of alignments that suggested a complex stellar, lunar and solar cult. No plaques, no tour guides, no car park. Just us, and the valley, and its forgotten stones.

It was a life-changing day. For the first time I grasped just how little we know of the past. Most archaeologists are cheese-testers plunging their drills into the heart of a vast Stilton. You get flavour and texture but absolutely no sense of the size or shape of the whole cheese. I suspect, up there in Thursbitch, we have the remains of a very large cheese and one that was sustaining its population long after the arrival of Christianity. It also gave me the clearest evidence yet of how different Alan's methods are from most writers'. Instead of finding things "out there" and then turning them into a story, Alan starts with the story. Then he digs and, mysteriously, he finds.

At the heart of Garner's work is the power that places exert. Why are we drawn to some rather than others? What makes us drive up the M6 to spend time among the hills or find ourselves undone by dread in a valley like Thursbitch or write all our books in one small room? Is it possible that the places themselves demand our attention and presence? The idea of a "sentient landscape" has resonated with many readers of Garner's work, especially *Thursbitch*. There is now a rich seam of contemporary archaeology dedicated to understanding the ritual function of natural places, as distinct from built monuments. As Sal, the geologist in the novel, remarks: "Some places have to be treated with respect, though that doesn't get written up in the literature."

What makes a place sacred? The simple answer is: *we* do. The slow accretions left behind by human imagination and its interaction with the landscape, millennia of association, ritual and story make places significant. But are they the sole cause? Most of us, on the right day, at the right time, standing on a hill, staring into a river, looking at the night sky, entering a cave have felt Wordsworth's "sense of something far more deeply interfused." It's not for nothing that the oldest words in a language always name these places. And unlike so much else, they change little; their constancy gives us an immediate link with the past.

This sense of places "meaning" something is a common thread in human culture, as solidly attested as our need for food, sex and shelter. Perhaps it is an adaptive advantage hardwired within *Homo sapiens sapiens*, one which helped lead us out of the forest and into language. Because language is the tool that we have made places with, whatever drew us to them in the first place. We tell stories and the landscape changes; it becomes richer and more significant as each generation adds its own inflections to the tale. But it is just possible that we are simply the conduits, the sounding boards, for the place to tell its own story.

No one understands, or relishes, this paradox more than Alan Garner:

> "The first stars were showing, their sounds the echoes of the moon, and the moonlight on the brook rippled up to him. As in the day, he took of the valley and the sky and the valley and the sky took of him; but now all was lapped in a greater silence, and in it and from it he heard something in front of him, and a rustling and a plashing in the mist.
> Jack stood firm and waited. The rustling and the plashing drew near, the mist snorted, and of it and from it came a bull, a great white bull, marked only by a red stripe along its muzzle, dark in the moon."
>
> (*Thursbitch*, p. 52)

You'll have to read the book to find out what happens. But here is something rare: a modern writer who stays in one place so he can reach back to where all stories start, in the journey to "a mystical earth, a mystical geography, a mystical sequence of Time, a mystical history, and, through the individual, a mystical and personal responsibility for the universe."

Notes

Alan Garner's first six novels and most of his fairytale collections are available in paperback from HarperCollins. *Strandloper* (1996) and *Thursbitch* are Harvill Paperbacks. The passage from *The Times* was taken from Garner's review of Stephen Mithen's *After the Ice* (Weidenfeld & Nicolson, 2003). All other quotes come from Garner's indispensable collection of essays and autobiography, *The Voice that Thunders* (Harvill, 1997). This is currently out of print, but second-hand copies are available through Amazon. Snap them up; you won't regret it. A very useful resource is the unofficial Alan Garner website http://members. ozemail.com.au/~xenophon. It is full of biographical information, reviews, interviews, articles, photographs and links, and some valuable background to the research that underpins the later novels.

VAN
MORR·
ISON

HUGH
MILLER
STUART
MURR

A Sense of Ulster

Van Morrison's Belfast

by Stephen Brown

Belfast is a beautiful city. Or, to be more precise, Belfast is a city in a beautiful setting. Situated at the head of Belfast Lough, an estuarine processional way, our compact conurbation is encircled by escarpments, rugged Antrim Plateau on one side, rolling Castlereagh Hills on the other. Home to half a million people, Belfast began life as a muddy ford at the mouth of the River Lagan, burgeoned into one of the mighty workshops of the world-wide British Empire and like many of its GB equivalents – Glasgow, Cardiff, Liverpool, *et al* – is resorting to the ubiquitous urban Botox of arts festivals, dockside redevelopments and glittering shopping malls in a desperate attempt to stave off post-industrial senescence.

Locally, there is much debate about the most beautiful view of the city's situational splendours. For some, it's the seaward approaches, where the ever-increasing constriction of the Lough is offset by the ever-increasing altitude of the swaddling hills. For others, it's the outlook from the shoulders of Samson and Goliath, the giant yellow cranes that stand guard over Belfast's once gargantuan shipyard, birthplace of the *Titanic* and symbol of Ulster's obsolescent engineering capabilities. For yet others, the most singular sight is reserved for visitors driving in from the International Airport; specifically, a wonderful wide-screen windscreen moment when the humdrum motorway crests the encircling escarpment and plunges precipitously into the Belfast basin beneath. The conurbation spread-eagles from harbour to horizon, lagoon-like Belfast Lough to the left, black smudges of city centre high rise to the right. Most first-time visitors find it hard to reconcile the stunning vista below them with their mental image of a malevolent metropolitan war zone. But then again, Belfast is nothing if not contradictory, as the majority of its citizens will testify.

Of course, one doesn't need to travel to Belfast in order to appreciate its congenital contradictions. They are crystallised in the work of Van Morrison, the city's pre-eminent musical export.[1] In many ways, indeed, Van the Man is a better guide to the perennial paradoxes of Belfast than any number of citybreaks, guided tours or shoe-leather-sapping circuits on Shanks' Pony. Ulster culture, after all, is predominantly musical and literary rather than visual. There are very few buildings of note in Belfast, the City Hall, Opera House and Queen's University possibly excepted. World-renowned actors and artists are somewhat rarer still. However, our literary and musical scenes are preternaturally vibrant, as are those on the "noisy island" as a whole.[2] Ireland is the Sizewell B of the music business, a veritable fast breeder reactor, and although U2 irradiates the globe like a dismantled atomic bomb, the artiste with the longest half-life is the Belfast Cowboy himself, George Ivan Morrison.

Born and brought up in the Ulster Protestant heartland of East Belfast, Van Morrison was steeped from childhood in a musical marinade of Muddy Waters, Leadbelly, Jimmie Rodgers and just about every shade of the Blues, thanks to his music-loving father who spent time in the USA and amassed an enormous record collection.[3] By the age of eleven, Van was playing harmonica, saxophone, guitar etc in makeshift schoolyard ensembles and, after paying his dues in a cavalcade of semi-professional showbands, skiffle groups and R 'n' B bands, he formed the legendary Them in 1964. A series of rowdy hit singles swiftly transpired, though the machinations of the music business brought Belfast's premier beat boom band to a premature end. Van repaired to New York, where he recorded the signature late-sixties album "Astral Weeks," which proved to be the first in a sequence of seminal solo recordings, most notably "Moondance," "Tupelo Honey," "St Dominic's Preview" and a live album of staggering brilliance, "It's Too Late to Stop Now." This remarkable burst of creativity was followed by a fallow period of introspective self-discovery and attempts to get in touch with the spiritual wellsprings of his musical muse. After a three-year hiatus, Morrison returned to form with "Wavelength," "Into the Music," "Enlightenment" and "Inarticulate Speech of the Heart," which were quickly eclipsed by a continuous string of late-eighties classics including "Irish Heartbeat," "Avalon Sunset" and the inevitable best-selling "Best Of." By the early 1990s, Van the Man was happily ensconced in Dublin, secure in his status as a Hall of Fame- inducted living legend and producing an album a year, or thereabouts. As a rule, these excursions alternated between Morrison's musical roots – skiffle, blues, country, gospel, *et al* – and variations on his trademark, Celtic-inflected template, aka Caledonian Soul.

Van the Man is justly renowned for his prodigious musical ability, a mellifluous meld of everything from big band jazz to Irish traditional, to say nothing of a voice that has turned the unmistakable Ulster gulder into an art form.[4] But perhaps his single greatest gift is a truly unique sense of place. Whether it be the rural idyll of Old, Old Woodstock, the sheets of Snow in San Anselmo, bouncing along the boardwalk in Venice USA, politely asking the way to The Eternal Kansas City, or breaking in a new pair of shoes by Going Down Geneva's lakeside, he is blessed with the geographical equivalent of perfect pitch. When Van encapsulates the Streets of Arklow, evokes Summertime in England, sips cider in the Somerset shade, or gambols merrily among the Cotswolds' Rolling Hills, he transports his listeners – right there, right then – on a Vanlose Stairway of song.

For most people, the quintessence of Morrison's genius loci is "Coney Island," a contemplative conversational summary of a musical journey to a mythical Irish place where the *craic* is good, time stands still and potted herrings are polished off before dinner. But for residents of Northern Ireland, George Ivan Morrison is revered for his ability to capture the urban landscape, specifically the rose-tinted streets of his childhood stomping ground, East Belfast. Cyprus Avenue, Hyndford Street, Orangefield or the voices echoing across the Beechie River, late at night, are inordinately meaningful to the inhabitants of a place most of us love and hate simultaneously. Thus, when Van recalls pastie suppers at Davey's chipper; or the ice cream cones from Fusco's; or the man who played the saw outside the City Hall; or the six bells chime of St Donard's Church; or the desperate Belfast diet of gravy rings, barmbracks, wagon wheels, snowballs; or the tangible, almost oppressive, silence of Sundays in the torpid inner city; or, for that matter, throws in a familiar street name – Sandy Row, Fitzroy Avenue, Cherry Valley – he is tapping into, and drawing inspiration from, the collective Ulster unconscious, one that we all share but cannot adequately articulate. More than that, he is part of the ineradicable soundtrack of our lives. I lost my virginity to Van Morrison. Not the man himself, you understand. His music, specifically "Madame George" (the first verse, come to think of it). I was in the audience for his unforgettable "homecoming" gig in 1979, when he played "St Dominic's Preview" and the line "long way to Belfast City too" was greeted with a roar that almost ripped the roof off the concert hall and still sends shivers down my spine as I write this essay, twenty-seven years later. I will never forget catching Scorsese's celebrated rockumentary, "The Last Waltz," when Van the Man unleashed "Caravan" and literally wiped the floor with Bob Dylan, Neil Young, Eric Clapton and every other occupant of rock's top table. Better yet, I took my teenage, Kanye West-fixated daughter to see him last week, much against her supposedly superior judgement. She had a Damascene musical moment and is not only the latest convert to the cause of Caledonian Soul, but has the commemorative T-shirt to prove it. The circle of song remains unbroken.

Let me put it this way: it's not very often you're proud to be from Northern Ireland, not when you've been through what we've been through in recent decades, but when George Ivan Morrison is in full flight, it's hard not to take collateral pride in his astonishing artistic accomplishments. He's one of us. We are the people. For God and Ulster.

So powerful, indeed, is Morrison's sense of place that guided tours of the Vanscape are regularly organised, usually as part of local arts festivals. It is not unusual to find windswept tourists absorbing the arboreal atmosphere of Cyprus Avenue or attempting to make sense of the circuitous cross-country journey outlined in "Coney Island." Disappointment or frustration is the inevitable outcome. The nondescript nature of the actual locations cannot compare with the nostalgic magic of the Morrisonian invocations. When the William Blake of East Belfast imbues them with bucolic beauty – his brilliant ability to see the world in a grain of Sandy Row – we are transported from the workaday everyday to the cosmic threshold of the Celtic sublime. Van's Avalon may be off the Beersbridge Road and his Garden of Eden somewhere in the vicinity of East Bread Street, but don't try looking for them. The troubadours, likewise, may well be coming through town. Don't hold your breath, however. Celtic Ray won't be found on Bloomfield Avenue, believe me, though counterfeit Celtic RayBans might.

Morrison, then, doesn't simply capture our *sense* of place, he embodies the *spirit* of the place. Spirituality, indeed, is the single most important component of the Belfast Cowboy's cosmos. Although he is renowned for his happy wanderings along the highways and byways of New Age belief systems, from Steiner to Scientology, he keeps circling back to the evangelical Protestantism that permeates East Belfast, most notably in his sprawling double album "Hymns to the Silence." Being born again is a recurring theme in his lyrics – right back to the title track of "Astral Weeks" – and his incantatory streams of consciousness are nothing less than the musical equivalent of personal Pentecostal testimonials. Singing in tongues, so to speak. I was lost but now I'm found. Glory, glory, hallelujah.

Piety is central to A Sense of Ulster, today's sinful secular society notwithstanding. And Van Morrison, in many ways, is a stereotypical Ulsterman. Granted, the very idea of a "stereotypical Ulsterman" is deeply suspect, given the enormous variety of traditions in Northern Ireland, let alone genders, generations and geographical subdivisions (rural/urban, east/west, etc). Nevertheless, many maintain that Morrison is blessed with some, arguably all, of the personality traits associated with Ulstermen in general and working class Protestants in particular.[5] Blunt, boorish, brusque, truculent, taciturn, tenacious, pugnacious, prickly, paranoid, uncompromising, unco-operative and downright uncouth are just some of the less than flattering terms used to describe Van's irascible behaviour. This is the man who is not averse to storming off stage in high dudgeon or berating his audiences for their abyssal ignorance. This is the man who rudely refused to attend his induction into the Rock and Roll Hall of Fame and threatened legal action against local admirers who wanted to adorn his childhood home with a Van-lived-here commemorative plaque. This is the man who has written more songs about the iniquities of the music business and so-called friends who've sold him out than he has about moving on up along the ancient avenue to the higher ground where the back street jelly roll is in the garden wet with rain on golden autumn days like this when the healing has begun, begun, begun, begun, begun, begun, begun. And that's saying something.

The Ulster incarnate analogy is undeniably trite, not least because Van Morrison patently lacks the religious bigotry that is associated with rabid Protestantism. However, if the comparison is even briefly entertained,[6] then the positive side of the hoary Ulster cliché must also be acknowledged. In this regard, there are two archetypal personality traits that Morrison possesses in abundance. The first of these is industriousness. Whatever else is said about the Belfast Cowboy – and My-Van-Hell stories are legion – it cannot be denied that his work ethic is prodigious. He has enjoyed one of the longest and most illustrious careers in popular music. He started out at the same time as The Beatles and The Stones, but unlike many of his beat boom contemporaries the sexagenarian Ulsterman remains extraordinarily active. On average, he has produced an album a year for forty-odd years and a treasure trove of unreleased material is mouldering in the archives.[7] Many of his latter-day albums, admittedly, are formulaic retreads but they always contain a smattering of bone fide Celtic soul classics. We may live in a sated, sybaritic, post-industrial society but in Belfast at least hard workers are still highly regarded. Van Morrison, *pace* "Cleaning Windows," is a working man in his prime and that counts for an awful lot in our part of the world.

What is not highly regarded in Northern Ireland – well nigh unforgivable, in fact – is humourlessness. Ready wit is one of the province's most prized possessions. Belfast, believe it or not, is a very funny city (and I *do* mean funny ha-ha). George Ivan Morrison, if not exactly a bundle of laughs, is much more mirthful than many might imagine or indeed his media image intimates. From his childhood love of "The Goon Show," through his teenage showband comedy routines, to his heavily-accented Belfast banter on the fade of "Cleaning Windows," to his jaunty Benny Hill-style saxophone solo on "Higher Ground," to his yodelling homage to Carry On movies on last year's "Magic Time," which ends with a howl of studio laughter, Van Morrison is true to his jocose Ulster heritage. Seriously.

Serious play, in short, is Van Morrison's raison d'etre. He is inherently contradictory, just like the city of his birth: beautiful, bestial, benign, benighted, bedazzling, bellicose, beloved, beleaguered Belfast. Make no mistake, Van the Man is a hero in my home town. A flawed hero, to be sure, though we prefer our heroes flawed round here.[8] We love Belfast because of its flaws, not despite them. George Ivan Morrison may not be an ambassador for the city, much less an advertisement, but by God he's its apotheosis.

Notes

1   Barry Douglas, David Holmes, James Galway and Ruby Murray notwithstanding.

2   On the Irish music scene generally, see Gerry Smith, *Noisy Island: A Short History of Irish Popular Music,* Cork University Press, 2005.

3   There are many biographies of Van Morrison. The most recent is Johnny Rogan, *Van Morrison: No Surrender* , Secker & Warburg, 2005.

4   "Gulder" is an Ulster colloquialism for "loud shout." Van Morrison is the gulderer's gulderer.

5   These are cogently summarised in Geoffrey Beattie, *Protestant Boy,* Granta, 2004.

6   Rogan's biography (op. cit., note 3) is predicated on this very premise. He argues, in essence, that Van the Man is channelling The Big Man (Rev. Ian Paisley).

7   When the box set is released it'll be the size of a coffin.

8   Ulster's lionisation of George Best, Alex Higgins, Josef Locke and the *Titanic* attests to this tendency.

How to Find Your Voice in Burnley

Raising a glass to Paul Abbott

by Rob Williams

[*Ext. Burnley Town Centre. Day*]
A rusty white Cortina moves slowly out of town, steering through police horses and football fans heading to Turf Moor for the match. Inside the car, the DRIVER, *a tired-looking middle-aged Asian man, and his passenger, an inebriated younger man – a* STRANGER *to the area – are thrown around by every new pothole as they enter increasingly untidy suburbs.*

DRIVER
This Healey Wood.

STRANGER
I don't want to go to Healey Wood. I've already been here.

DRIVER
Where you want to go?

STRANGER
I've told you … What's your name?

DRIVER (*Turning as he stops at junction*)
Eh?

STRANGER
Your mate just shouted "Uncle." What's your proper name?

DRIVER
Uncle.

STRANGER (*Slumping back into seat*)
I told you where I need to get, Uncle. Coal Clough.

UNCLE
Why you want to go Coal Clough? Bad area you know.

STRANGER
Yeah well everywhere I've been someone's said "Bad area."

UNCLE
Some bad areas in Burnley, innit.

STRANGER
Where do you live, Uncle?

UNCLE
Duke Bar. That's bad area if you're white. This bad area if you're me. You get me?

STRANGER
But you'll pick me up though? I don't know where the fuck I am anymore.

UNCLE
No card, innit.

STRANGER
But …

(*The* STRANGER'S *attention snaps left as the car is overtaken by a child of no more than twelve, helmet-less, screaming down the road on an off-road motorbike.*)

UNCLE
Why you want to go Coal Clough?

STRANGER
I told you. I'm looking for someone.

[*Ext. Streets of Coal Clough. Day*]
The STRANGER *cuts a solitary figure shambling down and then up a painfully steep street, made tiny by the wild misty hills of the South Pennines ahead and the mill chimneys of the town to his rear. The camera cuts between his breathlessness (conspicuous on this bitterly cold yet sunny afternoon), his wide glassy eyes (disconcerted at the amount of sky suddenly available ever since changing trains at Preston) and his uneven steps – echoing loudly through the cobbled gulleys between identical rows of back-to-back houses crowding the narrow roads. It might be a sandier-brick Coronation Street, if every fourth house weren't boarded up and the streets weren't deserted but for a few groups of scruffy kids kicking a football or playing on their bikes. They watch the stranger suspiciously. He's looking lost now. A net curtain twitches. He stops to light a cigarette. Traffic noise pulls his attention to an adjoining road.*

[*Int. Pub. Day*]
The camera roams around a busy neighbourhood pub that with its claret gold-patterned carpet and dark wood furniture, resembles the home of a working class family with middle class aspirations. A gas heater fires out its warmth as the racing on the TV fights with S Club 7 on the jukebox: Reach for the Stars. *The music appears even more incongruous as the camera surveys the patrons: includ-*

ing an alarmingly thin, heavily tattooed MAN IN HIS FIFTIES, *sitting next to a* HUGE YOUNGER WOMAN *with "Seek and Destroy" emblazoned across her Pennine-like chest; a crowd of* MIDDLE-AGED MEN *at the bar watching the racing – all in jeans and jumpers – all loud, all white; a* PAIR OF MEN *in England rugby shirts with* TWO WOMEN *dressed for a grab-a-granny nightclub rather than an afternoon in the local; and the* STRANGER, *on whom the camera rests, standing alone at the bar with a cigarette in his mouth and an almost empty pint of Guinness in front him. A small, stocky* MAN OF PENSIONABLE AGE *arrives next to him and reaches over the bar. The barmaid, a short woman instantly recognisable as the* LANDLADY, *hands the man a clipboard.*

LANDLADY
All paid up, Jim?

JIM
Just checking now. Alan been in, Pam?

PAM
Why, has he won?
(*It seems* PAM *has grown accustomed to receiving no response from* JIM.)
Another one, love?
(*The* STRANGER *takes a moment to realise that* PAM *is talking to him.*)

STRANGER
Yeh. Thanks. And one for yourself.

PAM
I'm alright. Here for the football, are you?

STRANGER
No. I'm … looking for someone.
(*He waits for* PAM *to ask who. She doesn't.*)
Paul Abbott. Do you know him?

(PAM *weighs the money in her hand, shaking her head.*)

PAM
Do you know him, Jim? Paul Abbott.

(JIM *shakes his head without looking up from the tote sheet.*)

STRANGER
He used to live round here. He's the bloke who writes *Shameless*.

PAM
Our Richard watches that. I've not seen it. Do you watch that Gary, that *Shameless*?

(GARY, who up until now has been standing with his back to the STRANGER, barely turns his head.)

GARY
I have done. It's set round here.

PAM
Honest?

STRANGER
Well, it's filmed in Manchester but –

GARY
It's set round here.

STRANGER
Yeh …

(GARY *looks the* STRANGER *up and down before turning back to the racing.*)

He grew up round here and he's still got family in the area, I think.

PAM
What do you want him for?

JIM (*Still without looking up*)
Wossername knows the family. Barry's Angie. Reckons it's all true.

PAM
Honest?

GARY (*Turning sharply*)
So it is set round here, in't it.

STRANGER
Yeh.
(*To Jim*)
Has it changed much?

JIM
Where?

STRANGER
Round here. Have you lived here long?

JIM (*Reluctantly raising his head*)
Me? No. 'Bout forty years.

STRANGER
Can I buy you a drink?

JIM
No.

STRANGER
Right.

PAM (*At the other end of the bar, serving one of the glamorous women*)
Do you watch that *Shameless*, Sue?

SUE *screws her face like she's gulped vinegar rather than gin as a rush of arctic air announces the entrance of a* BIG BALD MAN *with a thick moustache and immediate presence. He is greeted warmly by the entire pub as* KEITH. KEITH *stands just behind* GARY *and the* STRANGER, *resting a tattooed hand on the bar.* PAM *pulls* KEITH'S *pint without being asked – a guest ale with a home-made label that the* STRANGER *can't make out any more than the fading green letters on the huge hand.*

JIM
Father in-law got mugged outside here last week.

STRANGER
Did he? Erm, shit. Is he alright?

JIM
Would you be alright if you were eighty-six and some cunt's bust two of your ribs for seven quid?

STRANGER
No.

JIM
Well then.

(*As he massages his head the* STRANGER *glimpses* KEITH, *laughing through his nose and mumbling to* GARY.)

Benefit town this is now. Fucking benefit town.

(*The* STRANGER *and* GARY *have to shuffle along the bar as* KEITH *pushes his bulk between them; the* STRANGER *very aware of* KEITH'S *eyes on him.*)

PAM
Two pound, Keith.

KEITH (*Searching his pockets, eyes still on the* STRANGER)
Who you looking for, lad?

STRANGER
Well I'm not exactly ... Paul Abbott?

KEITH
Him off the telly? I know him.

STRANGER
Do you?

KEITH
Calling me a liar?

STRANGER
No. I ... I knew he grew up round here.

KEITH
That's how I know him, in't it. How much, Pam?

STRANGER
I'll get that. And another Guinness, please. And one for
yourself erm, Pam.

(PAM *smiles thinly and takes the money. Frank Sinatra gives way
to Neil Diamond on the jukebox and at least half the pub
starts singing along:* Love On The Rocks (Live Version). *The TV
channel has been switched in favour of Sky's minute-by-minute
football service.*)

KEITH (*Sipping his pint and winking at various customers as they
catch his eye*)
What d'you wanna know then? Cheers, by the way.

STRANGER
Cheers. Erm, just a bit more about the area.

KEITH
Journalist are you?

STRANGER
No.

KEITH
Student?

STRANGER
No. Abbott ...

KEITH
Paul.

STRANGER
Paul, yeh. He reckons research gets in the way of a good story.

KEITH
Fuck you doing here then?

STRANGER
I'm interested.

KEITH
In what?

STRANGER
In how you can come out of background like his, seventh of eight kids, mum and dad gone by the time you're eleven, brought up by your sister, you try and kill yourself at fifteen so they section you, divorced by twenty one ... And instead of ending up in prison or McDonald's duty manager, you go on to write some of the best British TV of the last twenty years. *Cracker, Clocking Off, State of Play* –

KEITH

Either you find a way to laugh at the shit or it buries you. Simple. Ask us a difficult one.

STRANGER

He reckons writing saved his life.

KEITH

Aye well that sounds suspiciously like a load of bollocks to me but he's a good lad is Paul, so I'll take his word for it.
(*Enjoying the disinterested sniggers of* GARY *and* JIM.)
What's he up to now?

STRANGER

Living in Manchester, I think. Writing a rock opera about the race riots.

KEITH

You should talk to young Kev over there. He's BNP. Stood outside the Duke of York night it went up.
(*Shouts*)
That's right in't it, Kev. You're BNP.

KEV

Fuck off!

KEITH

He's so tight is Kev, if he finds a plaster he cuts his self ...
Where you from, lad?

STRANGER

Birmingham. Living in London. I'll have to watch the time.

KEITH

Never mind time you'll have to watch your back round here now it's getting dark. Fucking rucksack. You look like a tourist.

STRANGER
Get many tourists round here, do you?

KEITH
That's what I'm tellin' you. No. We having another? It's thirsty work is this research.

STRANGER
I'll do it.

(PAM *pulls another round.* KEITH *and the* STRANGER *lean further into the bar.*)

KEITH
Aye, it's a good do is *Shameless*. But it's not real. Or it's real enough for your fucking *Guardian* readers, but it's not really *real*. With me?

STRANGER
His thing ... Paul's ... is that drama should reflect society, but not necessarily literally. There's no reality in most TV, just fucking escapism. But there's real drama in everyone's life, every day.

KEITH
Oh aye? Done much scaffoldin', have you?

STRANGER
Makes you laugh out loud at mental illness and alcoholism and even paedophilia, then breaks your heart, sometimes in the same scene, till you can't help but realise that no one's life's ordinary.

KEITH
'Cept for Jim's of course. Your life's ordinary as fuck, in't it Jim?

JIM
Eh?

STRANGER
But the thing I love most about him is the faith he puts in you to cope with it all, work out what's "real" and what's not and make sense of it. He believes in his audience. How many writers of anything can you say that about?

KEITH
Plenty of tits an' all, *Shameless*. Tasty that Karen, in't she?

STRANGER (*Grinning stupidly*)
Yeh.

KEITH
Hold up.
(*Shouts*)
How those Clarets doin', Smithy? Still nil–nil?
(*To the* STRANGER)
He's like Frank off "Shameless," old Smithy. You'll never see him wi'out a pint and a fag on and he's more kids than Dr Barnardo's.

STRANGER
If desperation's a crime, I'm a fucking lifer.

KEITH
Most folk round here, they don't want much. Bit of a drink, bit of a laugh and the odd million quid off European Lottery. Is that too much to ask?

STRANGER
Did you see that survey the other week, the one where they tried to find the funniest region in the UK? Lancashire came out second.

KEITH
What come first?

STRANGER
London.

KEITH
Aye well it's a laugh-a-fucking-minute down there, in't it. Wouldn't get a pint down there for the price you're payin' here, would you?

STRANGER
Nope.

KEITH
Right, so get 'em in then while I have a piss. Might be cheap up here but you can't expect me to do your homework for bloody free, can you.

(KEITH *leers at a* YOUNG CHINESE GIRL *in passing as she enters the pub and begins trying to sell* DVDs *to drinkers out of a plastic Lidl bag. The* STRANGER *checks the time on his phone, struggling to focus.*)

PAM
Alright there, love?

STRANGER
Plot won't sustain drama, Pam. But character will.

PAM
(*Watching Sky*)
Aye. Same again?

Cut to:

[*Int. Pub Toilet*]
The STRANGER *sways comically at the open urinal to the dulled yet nonetheless relentless tune of The Proclaimers' I'm Gonna Be (500 Miles) playing in the bar. The camera jerks along with him as we read the word-processed sign posted at eye level: "In the interests of the safety of our customers CCTV has now been installed throughout these premises. So smile."*
The STRANGER *smiles.*

Cut to:

[*Int. Pub. Evening*]
The camera swims around the room, the picture in and out of focus. The lights are on now, the jukebox is dominant and the clientele has changed. Yet KEITH *and the* STRANGER *are exactly where we left them: at the bar, now totally reliant on its solidity for support,* KEITH'S *hand resting on the* STRANGER'S *back. As he talks, the camera switches between the* STRANGER'S *wet mouth, his half-closed eyes, and* KEITH'S *nodding head.*

STRANGER
But Keith. Keith. Keith. TV drama's not theatre or a film that wasn't good enough to get made. It's special. You let it into your life in a unique sort of ...

(*The* STRANGER *is distracted by the sparkling red lips of a* WOMAN OF ABOUT FORTY *across the bar. He smiles suggestively at her. Then finds* KEITH *shaking his head in deadpan warning – straightening the* STRANGER'S *face in an instant.*)

... way. Imagine you're a scriptwriter. You know someone's paid to go to the cinema or watch a DVD, so they've already invested in it. But TV. If you haven't grabbed us by the throat in the first sixty seconds, the remote control'll kill all your ideas, everything ...

KEITH
Agree.

STRANGER
I mean, even books. Novels, like. If Dickens was alive, who's to say he wouldn't just go: "Fuck this, if society can't be arsed with these big thick things I keep churning out, I'm off to write for Eastenders." You know?

KEITH
Corrie.

STRANGER
Corrie then.

KEITH
Fucking Dickens. Jesus ... Are we having a whiskey me and you, or what?

STRANGER
And a cigar. Yeh.

(KEITH *summons* PAM *and points at the* STRANGER, *who pulls his wallet yet again out of his jeans as if it's an arrow stuck in his leg.*)

Then I need to phone Uncle.

KEITH
You've an uncle lives in Burnley?

STRANGER
Not *my* uncle. Just "Uncle." He's a cabbie. But I've lost his card. No. He never had a card. Put his number in me phone.

KEITH
He'll not be a cabbie you fucking London tart. Where'd he pick you up?

STRANGER
I think I've missed me train.

KEITH
Outside a pub were you? In town?

(*The* STRANGER *shapes to object, then doesn't. Both start laughing.*
A YOUNG MAN *next to them shouts into his phone: "Never mind 'I've
not had me tea,' get a bag of Quavers and get yourself fucking down
here."* PAM *delivers two big whiskies.*)

KEITH
To what's his face then, your man …

STRANGER
Paul.

KEITH
To Paul. Aye.

STRANGER
(*Pausing with the tumbler to his lips*)
You don't know him at all, do you?

KEITH
Who?

STRANGER
Paul. Abbott.

KEITH
(*Sipping at his whiskey with raised eyebrows*)
I definitely used to know a lad called Abbott. But I think his
name was Andy. And he got hit by a truck near Accrington
years ago. Full of slot machines it were, on't way to Blackpool.
Dead now, Andy.
Does it matter?

STRANGER
(*Also with raised eyebrows*)
No.

URDOCH
F.W.
LISTER
PAUL
ABBOTT
KEITH
WATERHOUSE
ALAN
GARNER
DAVID
LODGE
DYLAN
THOMAS
WILLIAM
SHAKESPEARE
WILL
SELF
JOHN
MILTON
HAROLD
PINTER
EDWARD
THOMAS
JULIAN
BARNES
PATRICK
HAMILTON
REV W
AWDRY
HILAIRE
BELLOC
T.S.
ELIOT
JASPER
FFORDE
MARY
BUTTS
VIRGINIA
WOOLF
CHARLES
LONG
HARDY

I'm Grim Up North

Lying reminiscences with Keith Waterhouse's Billy Liar

by Roger Horberry

You know when people say it's grim up north? They're right. My advice to anxious urbanites thinking of relocation is think carefully. What do you value? Where will you find it? My problem is the people – tattooed, moustachioed nosebiters choking the Saturday streets and drinking themselves rabid on two for the price of one bottles of Bud Ice. The men are even worse. I exaggerate of course but take it from me, anyone with a metropolitan frame of mind (and using a phrase like that strongly suggests I fall into that category) will soon come up against the limitations of small town northern life.

An explanation is in order. If it's so awful then why am I here? It began with my own escape to London, although I've no real memory of this momentous event. Looking back it seemed the obvious thing to do, but looking back is an unreliable exercise. Nevertheless, one Saturday in September 1988 I must have gone south to start a new life in, er, Walthamstow. Perhaps it was because the Big Move was so inevitable that it didn't warrant thought. Perhaps it was because all my friends were in London already and that anyone with a shred of ambition was heading south. Either way, I wasn't acting on my own. I was following a script, one that had a profound effect on me when I first read it. *Billy Liar* was its name and this is the story of how it changed my life.

Six or seven years earlier I'd bought a copy of *Billy Liar* from a second-hand bookshop in Nottingham's Victoria Centre market. I took it home, lay on my bed and read. In those pages I didn't find a story, I found myself. It wasn't a book, it was a mirror. I kept wanting to shout "Yes, that's *exactly* how I feel." It was a revelation, an epiphany, a Big Bang whose faint echo I can still hear today.

First, some background. *Billy Liar* was written by Keith Waterhouse and published in 1959. It's set in the fictional – but all too real – Yorkshire town of Stradhoughton, located somewhere in West Yorkshire vaguely adjacent to the Dales. The action takes place over the course of a day (a Saturday in September please note). It begins with triumph in Billy's dream world and ends with tragedy in the real world. It's funny yet sad, light-hearted yet serious. Anyone who's ever experienced the dead hand of small town life – frustrated by the inward looking people around you, longing to escape but fearful of the consequences – will identify with Billy's story.

It's a beautifully written book. Rich imagery abounds. A character is described as having "grown old with quick experience, like forced rhubarb." A torn bench sprouts dirty foam lining "like brains." Unable to give one of his hateful girlfriends a frank honest look, Billy settles for a "frank honest profile." I think we've all been there.

For a main character Billy is sparsely drawn. We're given little information about his appearance, although he clearly belongs to a world where young men went from short trousers to suits more or less overnight. We're not told exactly how old he is, although references to time spent at technical college and his easy admittance to pubs would suggest Billy is eighteen or nineteen. Allusions to fashion and music locate the novel in the mid to late fifties, so quite how Billy avoided National Service isn't clear. Instead Billy works for local undertakers Shadrack and Duxbury. Not surprisingly he dreams of escaping to London to write comedy, live in a Chelsea studio and dabble in bohemia.

So far, so entertaining, but it was the last chapter that really struck me. When Billy's web of intrigue tears apart he makes a run for it, but at the last moment, train ticket to London in hand, he turns and heads home with rather more spring in his step than someone in that situation should feel entitled to. Was it the brave or the cowardly thing to do? Should we scorn or rejoice? Is Waterhouse saying we can never really escape, or simply wrapping up his tale in the least predictable way he could find? I'm still not sure, but I remember being absolutely stunned when I first read it. I wanted to grab Billy by the collars and scream into his face *"do it!"*. That feeling never quite left me.

Naturally, I came to think of myself as a bit of a Billy, but with one important difference – the actual lying bit in *Billy Liar* isn't really me. I'm a dreamer, but I'm not much of a liar. I lack guile. I am deficient in cunning. The moment an untruth has left my lips, those present can see through my pretence as though it were a particularly well-polished prism. Unlike Billy, whose practised deceit is the cause of so much trouble, I learned in childhood to tell the truth, not because it was morally right, but because I was so incredibly bad at the alternative.

No, the reason *Billy Liar* hit home was my background. I was born and brought up in the north Notts badlands; despite this, Stradhoughton seemed frighteningly similar to the towns I knew – Mansfield, Sutton-in-Ashfield, Kirkby-in-Ashfield, then later Ilkeston, Heanor, Eastwood. Dear God, even now their names cause me to quake. As an awkward adolescent more interested in books than beer these towns were a fine place to receive a kicking. Wherever we lived (and we moved often) I felt no connection with the place – a resident but never quite at home.

That wasn't the only reason I identified with Billy. His borderline obsessive-compulsive behaviour, his ham-fisted efforts at self-improvement – that was pure me. Billy aches for modern, metropolitan parents, the sort who swear, drink martinis and above all read – ungrateful as it sounds, me too. I remember visiting a friend's parents' house after starting college and being struck by the fact they had *books*. We had no such suspicious things at home. *Billy Liar* touched me so deeply because it captured the sense of small town ennui so perfectly. The claustrophobia, the boredom, the grey Sunday afternoon gloom that never seemed to brighten. My particular small towns weren't in Yorkshire, although culturally they were pure north (ask DH Lawrence or Alan Silitoe). Attitude, not postcode, is what counts.

Determined not to repeat Billy's mistake (if that's the right word) I moved to the brilliant incandescence of London. What a relief. Here was a place where anything seemed possible, where difference – not similarity – was celebrated. I'd achieved the anonymity that Liz, Billy's best-of-three girl-friend, so craves. She wants to be invisible, without having to explain everything all the time. Like Liz (a rather flat character in many ways) I wanted no ties, no expectations, and that's exactly what I got.

Best of all it was so easy. Billy tortures himself with doubt about his ability to survive in the capital – his bowels "filled with quick flushing terror" at the thought – but I don't remember any such hesitation (although having a support network of friends obviously helped enormously). He goes to the brink, suitcase in hand, but can't bring himself to jump. Perhaps his connection to the north is too strong, perhaps he thinks too much (OK, he *definitely* thinks too much), perhaps he's just too young, but whatever the reason he bottles it and slinks away in those closing pages. For me that's the whole point of the book. Billy chafes against the limitations of his world just as I chafed against mine. However (and this is the important bit), his failure to act inspired me not to make the same mistake. I learnt from Billy. He showed me the way, even if he didn't take it himself. Would I have jumped on that train to London in the final pages? Reader, I did.

And so it was that for thirteen years I lived a London life. I worked, married, bought a flat, had a child. Unwilling and unable to shell out an extra quarter of a million for another bedroom we did what any sane reader must judge absurd: we moved to bloody Yorkshire. You'd have thought, given all I've written, that I would have learned my lesson and chosen a soft, shandy-drinking southern hotspot like Brighton, Bath or somewhere else beginning with B. But no. I went north. Despite everything I knew (or thought I knew) about the place, I went back. Just like Billy.

By now you might be thinking, "You're no better than he was. Billy couldn't break away and neither could you. You spent a few wild years down south – so what? You came back." Guilty as charged, only it's not that clear cut. Like Billy, my feelings for Yorkshire are complex. For every plus there's a minus – self-reliance vs. smug self-satisfaction, a strong sense of identity vs. knowing your place. And above it all, class. Billy's mother captures this perfectly when she says, "We're just ordinary folk." Speak for yourself, love. Billy's Yorkshire – like mine – produces some excellent qualities in its people, but the oft-heard assertion that it somehow represents "the real world" is nonsense. It's no more or less real than anywhere else. The north is a frame of mind not everyone can share – Billy doesn't and I couldn't (still can't). Billy rails against the "lying reminiscences" of the older generation and quite right too. Their ramblings recall an England that never was, a collective hallucination. It's the supreme irony of *Billy Liar* that in the end (almost) all the other characters are shown up as liars, while Billy catches at least a glimpse of the truth.

How does this explain my return? It doesn't, except to say I came to believe my own lying reminiscences and convinced myself that where I'd come from wasn't that bad. Like most people, I've an almost unlimited capacity for self-deception. I hoped the north had changed, I hoped I'd changed, but I was wrong on both counts. Half a decade later I'm getting used to the place, the same way a lifer gets used to prison, but is it home? Never. I'm as uncomfortable today as I was at sixteen, only now my options are more limited. None of which is *Billy Liar's* fault. I loved this slight book as an angry young man stuck in the sticks wondering what to do with my life, and I still love it as a grumpy old man stuck in Yorkshire with distinctly mixed feelings about the place. What *Billy Liar* really did all those years ago was give me courage. Billy gave me permission to believe I didn't have be a younger version of my dad (not that Horberry Snr ever seemed too keen on that happening). Billy's failure to act became my go ahead to do so, a neat theory only slightly ruined by my return and subsequent ambivalence. I need to read it again.

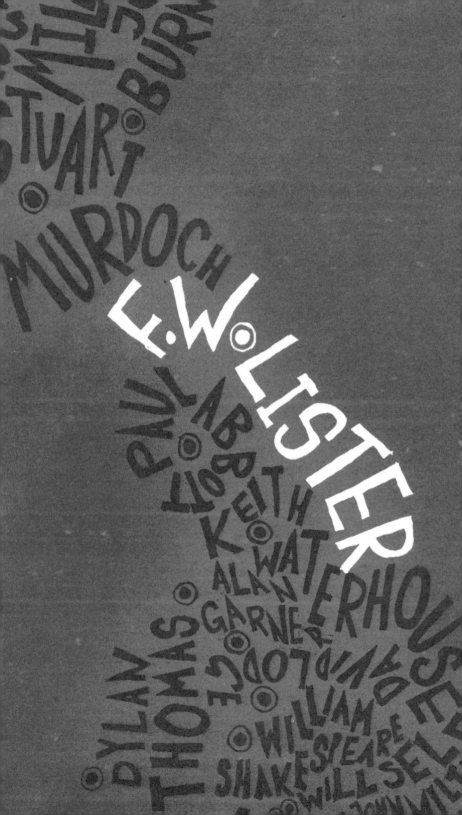

Variations on a Serenade to Teesborough

Links that bind FW Lister, my Dad and me

by Sarah McCartney

I last saw my dad on platform four of Newcastle Central Station as my train left for King's Cross. There he was, wrapped up in his tweed hat and coat, woollen scarf, leather gloves, smart shoes, shirt and tie as always, towering above my mum, who was also bundled up against the north wind.

He had tears in his eyes as he always did when I left. As the time came for me to set off for London, he would think of more and more stuff to talk about: football, books, places we'd visited when I was a kid, piano music, plays, anything so he didn't have to think about our being 275 miles apart once again. My mum would already be thinking about what to cook for dinner. He looked old and tired as he smiled and waved.

"I always wonder if it will be the last time I see them," I said to Nick.

The last time we spoke, we argued. He called just after we'd got back from holiday. Like most dads he usually left the 'phone calls to my mum. This time he gave me one of his lectures. They came once every couple of years; he would store up everything he thought I was doing wrong, every mistake I'd made, all my faults, my failures and it would all flood out in one terrible, unstoppable drenching. He used to think it was for my own good. I don't remember the details, only that this one was about money. What did I think I was doing, going away on expensive holidays while I was re-mortgaging my flat to pay credit card bills? We both got cross. He calmed down when I yelled, "I'm only angry because I know you're right!" Then we were able to talk more reasonably about other things. I remember promising him that I would never have a mortgage more than 50 per cent of my property value. You need to know that my dad was a building society manager for twenty years. Saving was very important to him. Keeping his bank accounts accurate to the last penny occupied much of his retirement. Making sure that my mum would be "comfortable" if he died and that my sister and I wouldn't get into too much of a financial scrape were the things that worried him most in his last years.

We also had a chat about a book he'd given me for Christmas, *The Wind That Blows*. "I bet you've not even opened it, have you?" he said. "I have! I've read 30 pages!" I protested. True, but I had struggled with the first chunk of FW Lister's novel, the part about life on a naval destroyer in wartime. Three weeks later my dad died in his sleep. It took me another three years before I could pick up the book and start again.

I began to understand my dad a bit better when I started to read his books. I borrowed his copy of *The L-Shaped Room*. It helped me to see things his way. The progressive 1950s take on sex before marriage, illegitimate children, how children "turned" homosexual, inter-religious unions, immigration, communism, a complete set of modern moral values. All there in a novel. It was better than a film because there was no screen to separate me from the action. Reading it, I was right there, in an L-shaped room with them. I could begin to see that my parents' views had been very modern once; without that book I'm not sure I would have made the connection.

Three days after my dad died my mum collapsed; a few minutes later she rejoined us but had left most of her memory behind. In the first series of *24*, Jack Bauer's wife Teri lost her memory from shock. People criticised the story as unrealistic. We know better. What was unrealistic was the speed at which Teri got hers back. Post-traumatic amnesia. The mind chooses not to remember.

My mother would not be left alone for a moment. She was frantic each time she remembered where she was, but nothing else. Each time we reminded her what had happened she was desolate; each time she forgot again a fog closed around her. It was shift work: me, Ruthie, her sister Viv, bailed out by friends and neighbours. The humour was black. We had no time to think or talk about my dad. Sometimes we'd have silence, a five minute break, then the little voice would pipe up, "Where's Alan?" and we'd start all over again.

She was also electing not to sleep in case she never woke up again. Fair enough, understandable under the circumstances. When she finally nodded off we would catch up with our own sleep or find something to distract us. I chose books.

My dad had given me a copy of *The Moving Toyshop* by Edmund Crispin. What a marvellous book: stuffed with gung-ho bright young things and low, thuggish criminal types and amateur sleuth Professor Gervase Fen who drove his unreliable, Italian two-seater recklessly around Oxford. Penguin had reissued a stack of its early crime novels and my dad was keen to share his rediscovered passion for Crispin and Marjory Allingham.

I found four green Penguins on his bookshelf, took them and dunked myself in "cosy crime." My mum had her way of escaping reality. I'd found one in Albert Campion and his assistant, Lugg. This way the connection with my dad didn't have to be over. We could still share common experiences. Three years later, after I had read the entire works of Allingham and Crispin, I picked up *The Wind That Blows*.

FW Lister wrote four novels. The first, *These Four Shall Die*, is set in Roman Britain at Hadrian's Wall. I haven't read it yet. The next two are set in the 1930s in County Durham (*Shadow Over Spennylam*) and Teesside (*Portrait of a Man*); if you want to know the way people lived and thought between the wars, during fascism, after the Russian Revolution, before the nuclear world, read them.

The Wind That Blows, published in 1948, tells the tale of Joe Smith, his wartime experiences at sea and the shore leave he's been longing for in Middlesbrough (or rather Teesborough) after a harrowing survival and long recovery from a torpedo attack.

I'd always assumed that I had a lot in common with my dad. We were working class from the North East; we liked mostly the same things: films, theatre, playing music, Middlesbrough FC, going out shopping, hunting flea markets and junk stalls for treasure. He had been searching bookstalls for years looking for *The Wind That Blows* and was tickled pink to get his piano player's hands on two copies at his favourite second hand bookshop, Barter Books in Alnwick, £3.60 each. My mum was convinced that the dust jacket illustrator also worked for Vogue in the 1950s. My dad recollected being very impressed when he read it at the time; he didn't say much about it, except that he'd been hunting it down for years. He wanted me to read it for myself, come back and report. Reading it, and realising that I'd never lived anywhere that resembled that world, light dawned that we'd led very different lives. I discovered that I wasn't proper working class at all. That was a bit distressing.

One thing I should explain. My dad had two completely separate lives in the 1940s. The first was at home with his mam, dad and great aunt. Grandad was a crane driver at the ICI and Grandma worked in shops until she married. Grandad came back from World War I and had no job, like so many of them, but they married all the same and lived with Aunt Henrietta until he got work. At home my dad listened to the radio, played billiards, read the *Beano* and supported the Labour Party. He had a scholarship to Middlesbrough Grammar School.

258

War broke out and half the school was evacuated to the Teesdale countryside, dished out amongst local families and educated in the Bowes Museum, Barnard Castle. He was moved to avoid the bombs aimed at Middlesbrough's docks, one of which lands in Joe's street in *The Wind That Blows*. Oddly, my dad's best friend John was moved from Tyneside to Saltburn (Lister's Saltscar, where Joe spends all his money on the glamorous but faithless Inez) which got more hits than his home town of Gateshead.

My dad found himself in a huge, elegant house in a picturesque village, the guest of Dr. Hawthorne, his second wife and his grown up daughter, Mamie. He had his own L-shaped room. Here he listened to the radio, played the piano and endless games of village green cricket, read the *Observer* and supported the Liberal party. Mamie taught him to play on their Steinway in the library. By the time he left, he was composing his own music, some of which I have safely stored in my piano stool.

As the threat fizzled to an end in England, he went back to the family's terrace house in Stockton-on-Tees. He kept up his piano playing and qualified to be a teacher while working at the town hall, then the Middlesbrough branch of the Halifax Building Society. There can't have been many other crane drivers whose sixteen-year old lads were writing ballades, serenatas and fantasias in G. He was dragged off to the navy for his national service. Here he learned not to volunteer for anything, that many officers were posh but thick as two short planks, and that aeroplanes were dangerous. He never set foot on a ship. His friend John, who had signed up for the army hoping to do very little and stay near home, was posted to Yokohama.

My dad had seen genuine middle class life first hand as a welcome guest, but it wasn't really his to join. The Hawthornes showed him Edmund Crispin, but if he wanted to read about home there was FW Lister.

Reading these novels is not a comfy ride. It's also nigh on impossible to read all three. Abebooks have *The Wind That Blows*; my copy of *Shadow Over Spennylam* cost me £46. *Portrait of a Man* finally got me through the doors of Humanities 1 at the British Library. They fetched it from Boston Spa and I established myself at seat 2777.

At the reception desk, the chap looked at my card. Ominously he returned with two books. They were all about Irish horticulture.

"These are not my books."
"Sarah McCarthy?"
"Sarah McCartney!"

He chuckled and came back with a faded aquamarine hardback. I don't mind not owning it as long as I know I can visit.

Portrait of a Man is set in Inglehow (that's Marske by the Sea where my Auntie Pamela lived). The Man is a headmaster, Will Hackett. There's always a wise older man in FW's books. One of the few things I do know about him is that he trained as a teacher at St John's in York and was headmaster of a Teesside village school. In *The Wind That Blows* it's the headmaster who tries to get Joe to see sense; in *Shadow Over Spennylam* it's the Methodist minister, then the football coach and finally the Church of England vicar with the sound advice and wise words. (But we never listen until it's too late, do we?)

In *Shadow Over Spennylam* we meet Tom Coulson, one of four brothers in a working class family. Tom is a fitter at a steelworks about to lay off half its workforce. As this is FW Lister, you know that Tom or his dad will be drawing dole pretty soon. Everything goes wrong that can, with the occasional gleam of sunshine through the clouds. After chucking his characters down a pit, FW leaves them enough rope to clamber out if they're tough enough.

He must have had a terrifying mother-in-law. Joe Smith has Mary Woodham's middle class mother to deal with and Tom has the formidable Mrs Lowton, mother of chaste, religious Jenny, followed by Mavis's ma, the slovenly Mrs Evans. For each of his well-to-do heroines there is her opposite number: Inez, the sophisticated wild child who will hang around with any man with a car and a full wallet, and Mavis, common as muck, done up like a film star, looking for a quick ticket out of her miserable home. Perhaps things will turn out reasonably in the end but you can be certain it will all get very complicated along the way. These books are full of characters, places and difficult situations which my dad's and grandad's friends and families lived though. They are fascinating, painfully compulsive. People never said what they meant and emotions were inappropriate at the tea table.

You hope that when Tom Coulson plays for Spennylam Star, observed by the Aston Villa scout with the papers in his pocket, he will score a blinder and get signed up there and then. Yes, he scores a blinder, but this is FW Lister and he's writing about life without hope in a town without a future. We are not reading *Sunshine Over Spennylam*. The chapter in which that football match unfolds has more suspense than any blockbusting bestseller. This could have happened to any of us. He writes about tragedies which happen in everyone's life, but blimey, he really does pack them in! He takes a whole street's disasters and gives them all to one family. He lets us see them coming, but there is no way to steer round them.

For northern lads, FW Lister must have been like reading their own secret diaries. Had anyone written a novel set in Middlesbrough before this? Why are they out of print and forgotten? Maybe it's because the bravery, virtue and honest toil in these tales are loaded down with undiluted hypocrisy, drunkenness, injustice, violence, betrayal, sex, unemployment and poverty. There's also a lot about God and religion, more than current taste decrees.

In his twenties my dad was on the lookout for someone like Mary Woodham, elegant, good looking, well brought up, demure. When he saw my mum for the first time, he knew he'd found her. Now that I've read *The Wind That Blows*, I understand his dislike of overly made-up women, public displays of affection and common behaviour. He'd met too many like Inez. My mum wasn't always demure. I see now why the engagement was almost ended when, dressed in her smart grey coat and Danish silver, she attracted his attention with a piercing whistle which brought central Middlesbrough to a halt.

I think FW Lister probably married a lovely girl like Mary too, learned to live with the disdainful mother-in-law, her snobbery and self-righteousness, got on well with her long-suffering dad and was a great headmaster – but I don't know. Everything I know about him comes from the dust jacket of *The Wind That Blows*, first edition 1948.

What else is there?

Anyone?

Notes

FW Lister, *Portrait of a Man*, Frederick Muller Ltd, 1933.

FW Lister, *Shadow Over Spennylam: A Tale of the Depressed Areas*, Frederick Muller Ltd, 1938.

FW Lister, *The Wind That Blows*, Frederick Muller Ltd, 1948.

R.L. STEVENSON
HUGH MILLER
JOHN BURNSIDE
STUART MURDOCH
PAUL ABBOTT

The Rules of Modernity

Not taking the bus round Glasgow with Stuart Murdoch

by Neil Taylor

Books were never my friends.

Records were. *Are*. Not actual records, you understand; not big vinyl things. I've never had that nostalgia for the physical – I'm a child of Thatcher, I can't remember an industry that made things, so I don't need to have them in my hands. Much better, in the case of records, to have them in your head. In fact, nowadays, mine live in the sky. In my house of broadband, and wi-fi, and iTunes, I like to think that every bit of music is already there, in the air, waiting to be caught in my white plastic box of butterflies.

Put it down to being an only child, if you like. I think I do now, if I didn't then. Because records are the sound of company. For other people, books always seemed to be a refuge, somewhere to escape from the chatter of family life, or a marauding bullying brother. But I never wanted to escape. I wanted to invite my entertainment in.

Now I read. It seems the right thing to do on solo journeys by bus and train. But once I'm home, my first loyalty is to records. And for ten years, a particular loyalty to records by one band, mostly written by one man: Stuart Murdoch, of Belle & Sebastian.

I got to know these songs when I was living abroad. I was happy enough. But now I see the echoes of my only childhood in that year. On my own again, this time an ocean away from family and friends, adrift in an unrecognisable strain of a language I thought I knew. I chat away, but no one quite gets me. In fact, I start to feel like a cardboard cut-out version of myself. I can talk about my day at work, what I'm doing at the weekend, "It's a really nice restaurant, and not too dear." But anything beyond a GCSE role play is hard work. I want to tell them about me, to make a joke, to discuss what I think of their politics, but I'm marooned. Everything I say comes out as straight fact.

While I was there, people sent me packages. The things I missed were details, drizzles, tastes, Lucozade, Lancashire cheese (I've never felt so British as I did then). And from Emma I got little square packages. Records. Records from the fringe of their native land, and even more out of place here.

But in those early Belle & Sebastian records, in the emotional sub-zeroes of Québec, I made friends. Stuart, of course. A Scottish voice, and a British one. It's there in his turns of phrase, and his humour, and the cultural countryside he takes me walking in: Radio 4, Man About the House, Debenhams. The characters, too; Belle & Seb songs have a cast. Lisa, who goes blind; Lisa's friend, who's abused; Anthony, bullied at school; Sukie, the kid who hangs out in the graveyard; String Bean Jean; Lazy Line Painter Jane. These characters turn up in different songs, sometimes together, sometimes alone. The songs are *rarely* about just them, but it's like they walk past as Stuart sings. Then there's Belle and Sebastian themselves. Not the ones from the original French children's story, but the ones from Stuart's imagination. The ones who met outside Hillhead Underground Station (one of the stories from the record sleeves says so). I've always assumed Stuart and Sebastian are one and the same.

It seems to me like a lot of writers are always writing about the same thing. Different voices, and different situations, but the same thing. Stuart's sketches are nearly always about the uncool school kid who learns to be confident in who they are. They don't change to fit in; they find the world changing and find their corner of it. The road comes up to meet them. They don't flower; instead the poppies that grew tall with adolescent cool shrivel in the glare of an adult sun, leaving our heroes to bask in the light.

Glasgow is one of Stuart's characters, too. Its places namechecked with that easy familiarity my parents use of Blackburn; another place I have an imaginary bond with. So Stuart sings of the river, the Easterhouse, the church on the hill, and school discos. Never having been there, in the Canadian snow I invented my own Glasgow. It was a city of dinge, of grease (I think that's all the cafés in the songs). It is usually grey, and dark. I see the cast in bedsits, or children's homes, or hospitals, or maybe just on city buses. So I decide it's time we met.

* * *

"Wow, New York, just like I pictured it!" (That's Stevie Wonder's "Living for the City.") Glasgow isn't. But there is something oddly New York about it. I think it's because I leave Queen Street train station to the planned grid of American streets, to sirens wailing, and to traffic roaring over the brows of little hills I can't see beyond. But after a few town centre blocks, I've been here before. Not here exactly, but places too like it. The station with its Smith's and Costa's, the pedestrianised precinct of big shops and lousy water features. This could be the middle of Leeds, or Birmingham. Not much sign of the hipsters.

Of course, Stuart would want me to take the bus away from the centre. It's what he and his characters are always doing. But buses are the most intimidating way of moving round somewhere new. They announce their destination, but rarely their route (maybe they're as shy as their visitors). So for the stranger, they're baffling. Of course, when it's your own city, your own bus, all of this becomes second nature. You stop fretting about the route and listen to the people on board. That's why I like people talking loudly on mobile phones. I like that they give me licence to listen. Of course, I have to fill in the gaps. But instead of making my judgements on clothes and faces, I get a string of clues to eavesdrop on. Meeting on Sauchiehall Street. Bored of the old men's pub. Fish and chips.

Yeah, you take the bus to get to know people, without having to do the work yourself. Without the embarrassing list of small talk questions. You just join the dots. It strikes me that a lot of Stuart's songs are dot-joining. I know he has a predilection for graffiti – it's given him the name of a song, an album, and an early band. I guess graffiti is the line from the middle of a story you don't get to hear. The writer writes the story instead.

So I don't take the bus. I walk. I want to meet the place as much as the people. I start at Hillhead, and I'm heading for Novar Drive, where the band made their early records in the church hall, the church hall over which Stuart lived. The name fits with my fancy: It has the feel of sixties space-age optimism, like London's Skylon, or the aching self-consciousness of all Britain's Mandela Ways. On Novar Drive in 2006, I imagine tenements, kids at bus shelters, shuttered-up shops, ASBOs. The sixties dream soured.

On the way, I'm looking for The Grosvenor too, the café where many of the early songs unfolded. It looks promising. All I have is a road name which is difficult to find on a map. And turning the corner, I'm confronted with concrete and cobbles, and a litter-strewn street. It feels right, but the illusion doesn't last long. Suddenly, the street is strung with fairy lights above my head, and I am theme pubbed to within an inch of my life. You can see it would once have been pretty, but now it's just, well, twee. Just what Belle & Seb are always accused of. (They're not. There's too much bite, his cute lines too acute. But this is.) Maybe I need to see it at night. Maybe it needs a drunken fight against the whitewashed walls. I open the door.

The Grosvenor is not a café now, but an arthouse cinema. Here I find the hipsters: university kids queuing to see the gay cowboys. It has a café, but not what I want. There's too much chrome, it's too expertly lit, the fruit is far too shiny. I've been here before, too – this time in Greenwich, in Cambridge, in Nottingham. I can only stay seconds. This just doesn't seem like the place to write a song. It's the place to write muzak. I keep my fingers crossed for Novar Drive.

There's a Belle & Seb song called "Expectations," and mine were wrong. It dawns on me that I'm in the poshest part of town. Did I know Glasgow had a posh bit? You don't get to see it on the telly. Glasgow is murder, thick accents and gallows humour. But not here: Glasgow's West End is wide streets, big houses, panini, cappuccino. There are no tenements. There are big bay windowed houses. They are grey, yes, but not depressing. This is hard-working Victorian grit. I peer in. Some of what I see matches my mind's eye, right enough. Nasty beige carpets, and three bar electric fires which look danger-ously wired. But this is not the poor area I imagined. It is the closest us middle class types get to poverty – it is studenthood. Sure there's the odd old person – just now I'm walking past a gentleman in a suit, mustard waistcoat, and peaked mustard pocket handkerchief – but he is outnumbered by the bereted girls of Belle & Seb gigs. It's all they can do not to analyse poetry on the street. There's the odd shop that feels right – a charity shop, and a card shop that looks like a charity shop, and an old ladies' shop, selling tweedy two pieces and vinyl accessories which seem to match with slightly psychopathic efficiency. Oddly, the shop is called "Rage" (I can't hear the old ladies saying it). But these three are paraded next to a wine shop – not an off licence, definitely a wine shop. And a coffee shop. With wi-fi. I sigh. I check my email.

Of course, I should have known this, really. I mean, I knew he was at Glasgow University. Most of them were, and it's just round the corner. So it makes sense that these are not the tales I imagined of lonely childhoods, or the wayward unem-ployed. They had time on their hands because they were students. He's even said he likes to sing about University as "school," like the San Franciscan it seems he would have loved to have been. I suppose I ignored it. When I listened, I took his "schools" to be true to life, British, tales of woe in the secondary modern. I have been comprehensively misled.

I like it though. I'd like to live here, or have lived here, or been a student here. There are well kept terraces, views across the city, and home cooked carrot cake. Even the buses are brand new. Double deckers with digital displays that say they're "transforming travel." No one will be drinking cider from a carrier bag on the back seat of them (it'd be hard to write a song too, while the infomercials are looping along inside). And Novar Drive is nice. I see the church hall, but can't get in. Next door, six "luxury flats" are on the rise.

I don't feel cheated, just wrong. I can't complain. In a way it should be reassuring. Stuart is from my milieu. Middle class former student, catholic record collection with a taste for the bohemian. Has it always been like this? Would he come back here and be surprised (like my mum and dad when the back streets they used to know lead to retail parks)? There's gentrification everywhere. Where I live, too. I can't complain. I'm to blame. I love my broadband, my organic fruit, my smoothies, my unknown parliamentary neighbours.

You can hear it in the records too: they've gentrified. Where once there were wayward harmonies, fluffed lyrics, too much echo from the church hall, or the sound of someone unzipping a cardy in the opening bars, now there are pop producers and shiny surfaces. It causes no end of grief from the fans. They blog their way through regretful nostalgia of times past. But they are not the students they once were either. They are buying Tesco Finest and working in ad agencies. They are going to the gigs but staying in their seats. "It's very loud, isn't it? I can hardly hear the recorder."

To me, though, this is just so much packaging. Stuart is still there, his songs full of little moments of beauty and humour, squeezed into half sentences. There are no great story arcs; even when epic they're no more than five minutes. Epics of the everyday. But there is always delight in the details: a sudden view of orthopaedic shoes, of "tartan garments," of black washing turned grey at the launderette. Stuart's writing gives me tiny smidgens of joy, the sort of joy you might get perfectly catching a jam jar which has chosen to jump from a cupboard, or when the things you're buying in a shop come to exactly ten pounds, or when you see someone at a gig who you never knew liked the same music as you. My response to these divinely tiny joys is fantastically out of proportion to the things that cause them. That's why Stuart can throw away a line about the wannabe actress who can't act her way out of a paper bag, and leave me smiling for the rest of the day.

* * *

I get on the underground. It throws me, because it's not the tube. Living in London it's easy to forget that there's anything else. Taking this bullety train is like visiting a foreign city. The seats are different, the ticket barriers different. I am abroad. I wonder if the people on the train know I'm writing notes about them? I'm looking for the characters in the songs. Not *them* them of course, but their types, the happy misfits, unafraid to be quietly different, to talk of Marx while walking into Matalan.

I think I see them. A kid reading photocopied sheets from "The Rules of Modernity." He has grey corduroy flares on which are swallowing his shoes, the kind of round, smooth trainers that look like big balls of cheese. I only know they're there because he has his legs crossed. If they were flat on the floor he'd look like an elephant, his legs unankled, straight down until they hit the deck. The man next to him is in a sort of suit, but his trousers have a flare, too. I can't tell if this is fashion, or a silent hint of the non-conformity of Lisa, or String Bean Jean, or Judy (and her dream of horses). I give him the benefit of the doubt. I get off, and head for the bus.

R.L. STEVENSON
GEORGE MACKAY BROWN
HUGH MILLER
JOHN BURNSIDE
STUART MURDOCH

Wet Sand and Gasoline

Beachcombing in Fife with John Burnside

by Richard Clayton

On a bright midwinter morning, the Fife coast gleams. Calling this corner of the ancient kingdom "a fringe of gold on a beggar's mantle,"[1] James II of Scotland clearly knew his real estate. The "East Neuk" is a beautiful sleeve of farmland – hemmed to the south by the Firth of Forth – with fishing villages every couple of miles until it elbows the North Sea at Fife Ness. Most things about the place – the seclusion, the tissue-papery sunlight and the sea mist known as the haar – seem quietly miraculous.

Standing on the shore of St Andrews Bay, just around the headland, I'm toe-to-tide with otherness. Despite the Tornados thundering in and out of RAF Leuchars, the sea has an immemorial power to captivate – holding sway over joggers, dog-walkers, even freelance journalists; each of us drawn along the ruminative strand of West Sands.

No surprise, then, that east Fife could claim to be the UK's most poetic habitat, on a leading poets per capita basis. Douglas Dunn's tenure at St Andrews University has much to do with it. But I like to think there's something in the air that makes John Burnside, Robert Crawford, Kathleen Jamie and Don Paterson live and work nearby. Lyrical and meditative, Burnside's poetry develops its own meteorology for the area – and that's the climate I'm here to experience.

* * *

"strange things come/to those who live/by water"

Poets seldom cross the news radar – the only blips being prize-days or whenever Andrew Motion keeps a straight face about the laureateship – but "History," a poem that observes father and son, in September 2001, "gathering shells / and pebbles / finding evidence of life in all this / driftwork,"[2] is perhaps the most resonant 9/11 reflection that I've read. References are oblique, and there's nothing kneejerk or preachy about the sentiments. Rather, Burnside portrays events as a shock to some wider ecosystem – "we trade so much to know the virtual / we scarcely register the drift and tug / of other bodies."[3] Irrespective of politics, he implies, we've all grown estranged from the natural regulations of the world.

It's not the sort of message, if message it is, that's actively condensed by the media bubble. But Burnside speaks to many of the issues percolating in editorial conference rooms: whether and how to reduce our demands on the planet; the role of religious belief in secular societies; the dislocation and rootlessness that modern life can engender. Of course, he doesn't offer bullet points – handy hints on energy efficiency or what to do when the oil dries up – or, indeed, any doom-laden bulletin. Instead, his poems pick a path through the terrain he's made his own: what it means to dwell on the earth.

If that sounds grandly philosophical, it's actually funda-mentally simple. Burnside moves like a beachcomber: attentive, rigorous and aware that "strange things come / to those who live / by water."[4] He might have strong views about what he finds, yet his search is contingent, restless (punctua-tion hardly breaks his stride), improvised. Beachcombing is both a method and an attitude of mind, where "the trick is in the making / not the made."[5] It's also a useful metaphor for thinking about Burnside's writing and sense of place – particularly in *The Asylum Dance*, the collection that won the 2000 Whitbread Poetry Prize, and his two subsequent volumes, *The Light Trap* and *The Good Neighbour*.

* * *

"the light above the firth"

It's so easy, as a fleeting visitor, to arrive somewhere and infer all sorts of immanent truths from first impressions. Coming from the city to the East Neuk, a rose-tinted perspective is inevitable. The fishing boats clank and bob in Pittenweem harbour. The crustacean I was eye-to-antenna with earlier may figure in my bowl of cullen skink at the West End Bar. Gulls do "flicker"[6] overhead, and "the medieval lull / of inland farms"[7] bends time as I walk the fields.

Yet having lived in rural Dorset, I'm wary of the curse of the quaint: how the outsider can ignore workaday realities. Not just those times when the rain won't stop and the mind is muddied. But also that people have businesses to run, familiar cares and internet accounts. Nevertheless, I can't help swooning over the sunsets I've seen in Fife: half a dozen bands of colour (mint, orange, raspberry, blackcurrant, lemon and lime ice-cream) resolving into purple dusk. Or the dawn, rippling out of the haar, apple-soft. It's hard not to regard such phenomena as benevolent.

Burnside pinpoints this special effect in *The Asylum Dance*. The poem Ports begins: "Our dwelling place / the light above the firth."[8] As both a geographic marker and a means of revelation, it illuminates what he strives to understand about "the notion of home"[9] and, consequently, "the painful gravity of being settled"[10] – since he isn't readily grounded. Security and co-habitation bring limitations and "the dread of belonging,"[11] as Burnside writes in The Good Neighbour.

Sometimes, "the shape of the wind on an empty street / is all you know of home."[12] At others, "home is a reason"[13] (people to return to and responsibilities), or else it's bundled with the mesh of information – "shipping forecasts / gossip / theorems"[14] – that creates a local culture. Social identity, however, isn't his primary concern. His yardsticks are seasonal, semi-mystical, talismanic. Repeating the tropes of light and dark, Burnside explores how the self reaches its accommodation with nature.

Occasionally, reading him can be like listening to a secular sermon: I yearn for some wriggle room. But his environmentalism – his charting "the brilliant commonplace / of all we take for granted"[15] – makes me sit still and pay attention.

* * *

"an earth-tide in the spine"

Like the protagonists of his poem Adam and Eve, Burnside is "stunned with a local wonder"[16] at the beauty of his surroundings. But his canvas is larger than Fife alone. "Somewhere behind it all," he maintains, lies "another world of charge and borderline / an earth-tide in the spine."[17]

For Burnside, the spine is a sensory organ, a divining rod that links him, physically, with the planet's "deeper pulse."[18] It's the bell-wether of his green credentials. He writes of being "aware of everything / aware of shoals and stars / shifting around you / endlessly / entwined,"[19] evoking what the scientist James Lovelock calls Gaia, the hypothesis that the earth and all its life forms are one, self-sustaining organism.

After 2005 – a year in which, as the headlines screamed, "nature struck back" – the idea that humanity could be more humble in the face of elemental forces is not mere eco-babble but practical advice. In his latest book, *Nature Cure*,[20] Richard Mabey claims we're increasingly "out of kilter with the rest of creation," and that redressing the balance isn't simply about "household management writ large." I imagine Burnside agrees.

In essays and poetry, he aligns himself with indigenous people – groups such as the Sami, still better known as Lapps, from whom he borrows the myth of the earth's living pulse; the concept being that the Creator placed the beating heart of two-year-old reindeer at the planet's core, and as long as people hear this rhythm "all will be well."[21] But Burnside fears it's become almost inaudible.

Instead of patronising indigenous people, he believes "we moderns"[22] can learn from them. "Where I come from," Burnside wrote in 2003, "home means something that mistakes itself for permanence: it means possession, it means consumption."[23] In other words, tenancy rather than ownership should be the contract we make with the earth – coexistence not conquest. Arguably, parts of *The Good Neighbour* become too pedagogic in this respect. Generally, however, Burnside's writing is sensuous enough to dilute the lecture. In a poem for Harald Gaski, the Sami activist and writer, Burnside celebrates "their works provisional, their dreams immense, / their children raised in memory and song."[24] Metaphorically, the Sami are beachcombers, too.

Such post-colonial kinship doesn't seem faddish because Burnside also taps a native strain of British nature poetry, stretching back beyond the English Romantics to the Scots Gaelic bards. People have extolled the "renovating virtue"[25] (in Wordsworth's phrase) of the Great Outdoors ever since there was an indoors to leave behind. It's simply that now, in the age of mass tourism, the problem is "how to be alive / in all this gazed-upon and cherished world / and do no harm."[26]

* * *

"prayers that stay unanswered"

Writing in 1966, a hundred years after Thomas Hardy resigned himself to "Crass Casualty"[27] governing the universe, the critic EDH Johnson lamented that "the study of natural history could never again address man's moral and aesthetic faculties."[28] Well, never say never again. While I've no wish to legitimise the neocon mantra "intelligent design," it's as natural history that its advocates seek to present it. (Lord knows what Johnson would think of that – I found his book, *The Poetry of Earth*, completely by chance. It had once belonged to my aunt.) Nature writing is indisputably the locus of Burnside's moral and aesthetic faculties. But he nips the Creationist fallacy in the bud. "Where logic seems apparent …," observes a poem called The Hay Devil, "we go too far / imagining a god / of purposes."[29] That's not to say religion is absent in his work. Far from it, religious discourse pervades his writing and, indeed, the words I've used to write about him and Fife. Yet it's more cultural hand-me-down, I think, than genuflection.

Vestiges of religious language remain the most apt to describe our consciousness of nature. Perhaps this is because, as Richard Mabey suggests, "all natural metaphors are miniature creation myths, allusions to how things came to be, a confirmation of the unity of life."[30] But it's as much a literary as a theological inheritance. Although the East Neuk has me in raptures, it doesn't send me hurrying to the kirk.

Having outgrown childhood religion ("I could see / their omnipresent God was neither / here nor there"[31]), Burnside retains his capacity for awe. Realising science can't measure metaphysical experience, he senses a universal hunger for grand narrative: "something in the world we cannot name / though each of us negotiates the form / it happens to assume."[32] His great moral endeavour, then, is to search for an idea of order – "something vast / that holds us all and never lets us slip"[33] to replace or compensate for "prayers that stay unanswered."[34]

Christian symbolism is acknowledged in the poem Kestrel, which refers directly to Gerard Manley Hopkins's Victorian classic The Windhover. "Though I am no believer," Burnside writes, "I could find / the blue-bleak ember of an old / significance, the promise that remains unsayable."[35] However, his own rattlebag of beliefs contains earthy, "pagan"[36] sympathies, a Buddhist-like emphasis on reincarnation and an almost shamanic sensitivity to "the otherlife of things."[37]

* * *

"the promise of elsewhere"

Walking the coast path from Anstruther, where Burnside lives, to Elie, with its wide mouth of sand, I feel recharged within. It's that wish-you-weren't-here moment of spiritual right-sizing, away from the rat race, that many urbanites crave. For Burnside, however, that's only stage one of reconnecting with nature. He doesn't strip off and paint himself with woad, at least as far as I know, but there's another setting to which he believes our lyric receivers can be tuned.

"Of course we escape," he writes in The Good Neighbour, "even the sound of rain ... is loophole enough ... for all the given versions of the self."[38] What he wants to get back to is a "primal emptiness"[39] of being. From this clean slate, perception can start again. "Radical illumination"[40] is Burnside's slightly hippyish phrase for how "we understand / another life resides, / older than time / and dizzy with momentum,"[41] alongside us, in the here and now.

At its most mystical, "the promise of elsewhere"[42] signifies aboriginal dream-time and a forensic snapshot of evolutionary process – "one broad presence that proceeds / by craft and guesswork."[43] This is quite a tangle of metaphors: partly indigenous myth, partly ecological theory, partly the Christian idea that Kingdom of Heaven is at hand. But there's no need for dogma. Burnside's best writing reflects just how much mystery we are never likely to unravel:

> "Nothing explains the pull and lurch of the sky,
> how, sooner or later, each of us goes to answer;
> no logic stills the heartbeat in the earth:
> it never stops, it knits within the bone,
> a world around the world we understand
> waiting to be recovered and given names."[44]

* * *

"a word for everything"

Naming is Burnside's sacred rite: "whenever we think of home/ we come to this"[45] – whether it's "a handful of birds and plants,"[46] a street such as Tolbooth Wynd or plaice "the colour of orangeade"[47] on a fishmonger's counter – knowing the names of things is what distinguishes home from something foreign. Beyond basic familiarity, however, names are also the way to animate personality, and to classify the environment's ceaseless "skitter and glide."[48] A couple of poems in *The Good Neighbour* record Burnside's young son vocalising what he can see, "one object at a time"[49] – a step defined as "the commencement of the soul's / unfolding / self-invention / in a world / that shifts and turns."[50]

That wonderful, symbiotic observation echoes a point the critic Jonathan Bate has made. Burnside's work, he says, "turns on the paradox that we are both a part of and apart from nature."[51] Tellingly, the figure of Adam, the original namer and natural historian, appears regularly. Just as beach-combing is a game of rediscovery – identifying "these slow / dank angels"[52] that the sea gives up – so Burnside tries to find "a word for everything … hallowed and round as a pearl."[53] Yet he knows his efforts to fix meanings are subject to the sheer flux of matter, its Ovidian transformations.

Burnside's poetry works in "the gap between a sound / and silence."[54] Sometimes, as he writes in a new poem (published in *Poetry Review* last autumn), the latter is "the only good reply"[55] to the beauty of Fife or any other landscape. After all, there's nothing inherently consoling about it – the sublime doesn't reside in coastal topography: it's in our minds. Often, we settle for "that cold and salty pact / the body has with things unlike itself,"[56] and only when we create "a sufficiency of names"[57] – a vocabulary nuanced enough – does language begin to bridge the gap.

* * *

WET SAND AND GASOLINE

Back on the beach, staring at the sea has brought me to a "vivid standstill":[58] the same feeling I get from reading Burnside. Poetry doesn't need to supply homilies. These insights may be "no more or less correct than anything / we use to make a dwelling in the world."[59] But, in a time of throwaway soundbites, they're sustainable. As I head towards the car – the sky darkening – something seems renewed.

Notes

1   Taken from a tourist information sign in Pittenweem.

2   John Burnside, "History," *The Light Trap,* Jonathan Cape, 2002, p. 40.

3   Ibid., p. 41.

4   John Burnside, "The Unprovable Fact: A Tayside Inventory," *The Asylum Dance,* Jonathan Cape, 2000, p. 69.

5   Burnside, "Koi," *The Light Trap,* op. cit., p. 3.

6   Burnside, "Ports," *The Asylum Dance,* op. cit., p, 1.

7   Burnside, "The Unprovable Fact: A Tayside Inventory," op. cit., p. 71.

8   Burnside, "Ports," op.cit., p. 1.

9   John Burnside, "Settlements," *The Asylum Dance,* op. cit., p. 29.

10   Ibid..

11   John Burnside, "Annunciation with Zero Point Field," *The Good Neighbour,* Jonathan Cape, 2005, p. 10.

12   Burnside, "Homage to Cy Twombly," *The Good Neighbour,* op. cit., p. 31.

13   Burnside, "The Hay Devil," *The Asylum Dance,* op. cit., p. 50.

14   Burnside, "Ports," op. cit., p. 1.

15   Burnside, "The Painter Fabritius ...," *The Good Neighbour,* op. cit., p. 78.

16   Burnside, "Adam and Eve," *The Asylum Dance,* op. cit., p. 20.

17   Burnside, "Sense Data," *The Asylum Dance,* op. cit., p. 12.

18   Ibid.

19   Burnside, "Ports," op. cit., p. 3.

20   John Burnside, *Nature Cure,* Chatto & Windus, 2005.

21   John Burnside, "Journey to the centre of the earth," *Guardian,* 18 October 2003.

22   Ibid.

23   Ibid.

24   Burnside, "By Kautokeino," *The Good Neighbour,* op. cit., p. 41.

25   William Wordsworth, "The Prelude," excerpted on The Wordsworth Trust website, www.wordsworth.org.uk

26   Burnside, "History," *The Light Trap,* op. cit, p. 42.

27   Thomas Hardy, "Hap," cited by Johnson, below.

28   EDH Johnson (ed.), "Introduction," *The Poetry of Earth: A Collection of English Nature Writings from Gilbert White of Selbourne to Richard Jefferies,* Gollancz, 1966.

29   Burnside, "The Hay Devil," op. cit., p. 46.

30   Burnside, *Nature Cure,* op. cit.

31 Burnside, "Fields," op. cit., p. 41.

32 Burnside, "The Painter Fabritius ...," op. cit., p. 83.

33 Burnside, "One Hand Clapping," op. cit., p. 12.

34 Burnside, "Settlements," op. cit., p. 29.

35 Burnside, "Kestrel," op. cit., p. 63.

36 Burnside, "Blue," op. cit., p. 45.

37 Burnside, "Fields," op. cit., p. 42.

38 Burnside, "Annunciation with a Garland of Self-Heal," op. cit., p. 33.

39 Burnside, "De Humani Corporis Fabrica," op. cit., p. 5.

40 John Burnside, "Travelling into the Quotidian: Some notes on Allison Funk's 'Heartland' poems," *Poetry Review,* Volume 95:2, Summer 2005.

41 Burnside, "Of Gravity and Light," *The Light Trap,* op. cit., p. 35.

42 Burnside, "Haar," *The Good Neighbour,* op. cit., p. 19.

43 Burnside, "Animals," *The Light Trap,* op. cit., p. 19.

44 Burnside, "By Kautokeino," *The Good Neighbour,* op. cit., p. 43.

45 Burnside, "Ports," op. cit., p. 1.

46 Ibid.

47 Ibid.

48 Burnside, "One Hand Clapping," *The Good Neighbour,* op. cit., p. 12.

49 Burnside, "Pentecost," *The Good Neighbour,* op. cit., p. 25.

50 Burnside, "De Anima," *The Good Neighbour,* op. cit., p. 36.

51 Jonathan Bate, "Eco Laurels," *Guardian,* 25 November 2002.

52 Burnside, "The Unprovable Fact: A Tayside Inventory," *The Asylum Dance,* op. cit., p. 68.

53 Burnside, "One Hand Clapping," *The Good Neighbour,* op. cit., p. 12.

54 Burnside, "Ports," *The Asylum Dance,* op. cit., p. 3.

55 John Burnside, "Responses to Augustine of Hippo," *Poetry Review,* Volume 95:3, Autumn 2005.

56 Ibid.

57 Burnside, "Adam and Eve," *The Asylum Dance,* op. cit., p. 22.

58 Burnside, "The Unprovable Fact: A Tayside Inventory," *The Asylum Dance,* op. cit., p. 67.

58 Burnside, "Ports," *The Asylum Dance,* op. cit., p. 8.

R·L·
STEV·
ENSON

HUGH MILLER

JOHN BURNSIDE

STUART

MURDOCH

VAN
MORR·
ISON

F.W.

PAUL

Kidnapped

Stevenson, the Highlands and a story under every stone

by Jamie Jauncey

The first edition of *Kidnapped* sits on my desk. It's slightly shabby now, but when it was published in 1886, its dark green cloth cover and gold lettering would have glowed with the promise of what lay inside. The first surprise would have been its folding map, titled:

SKETCH of the CRUISE
of the
BRIG COVENANT
And the probable course of
DAVID BALFOUR'S WANDERINGS

The very way the red lines bestrode the deep gouges of sea-lochs and wound among the stark contours of the mountains would have left one in no doubt that this was to be adventure of a high order.

Today, each time I pick up the book I think of Robert Louis Stevenson holding an identical copy, flicking through the pages with long pale fingers, fretting about the reception that would greet his latest work. It feels like a 120-year old talisman with the power to summon him to my side, his vast imagination and love of story spilling almost palpably from the rough-edged, hand-cut pages.

This treasure came to me through my mother's family. Her great-uncle, an extraordinary individual called RB Cunninghame Graham, knew Stevenson in Paris in 1877. "Don Roberto," as my great-great uncle was known, was a fellow author; an aristocrat who helped Keir Hardie found the Labour Party; an adventurer and horseman and lover of South America, of whom his friend, the novelist Joseph Conrad, said: "When I think of Cunninghame Graham I feel as if I have lived all my life in a dark hole without seeing or knowing anything." A character, in fact, worthy of Stevenson's creation, although that is another story ...

I was born in 1949, a biblical ninety-nine years after Stevenson. I grew up in his Edinburgh, among the fine Georgian houses of the New Town, the gardens and crescents with their spring crocuses and pungent autumn bonfires. Both Great King Street, where we lived until I was two years old, and our next flat, in Forres Street, where my father continued to keep his advocate's chambers for many years after we had moved to the country, were within walking distance of Stevenson's childhood home at 17 Heriot Row.

Had his ghost haunted the New Town of my early childhood, it would have found much that seemed familiar. The streets were still cobbled and I remember the pride I felt at the manly clatter of my first pair of leather-soled shoes on the granite setts. Gas lamps hissed above the pavements. A woman with a barrel-organ drawn by a Shetland pony turned her handle for pennies under our tall windows. Rag-and-bone men clopped by on their carts, and when the wind blew from the south the thick smell of malt and hops drifted up from the city's breweries, as it had done for more than a century. This was the palette from which my first years of life were coloured, although today they seem almost sepia.

Then, in a manner of speaking, I was kidnapped. In September 1957, just before my eighth birthday, I was plucked from the genteel comfort of the New Town and dispatched to a large, foursquare stone house on a windy promontory at Dunbar, thirty miles away down the east coast, where the draughts whistled through the dormitory windows and there was nothing but salt to put on our porridge.

Incarcerated there with fifty other boys, I might have longed with all my being for the familiarity of Forres Street's high-ceilinged rooms, the view across Moray Place and out over the Firth of Forth to the hazy hills of Fife. But in a private part of my imagination the place I went to was the Highlands.

My father's parents lived in Perthshire, and we visited them often. We travelled to Wester Ross in the far north-west on holidays. The journey to my other grandparents, on the Clyde, took us along the edge of the Trossachs and past Loch Lomond. The grandeur and romance and melancholy of the Highland landscape had already lodged deeply in my consciousness; and although the Scots on both sides of my family were Lowlanders, I felt a powerful affinity for all things Highland. To this day, the scent of freshly split pine logs and the treacly reek of peat make my heart lurch.

The romance of Scottish history, though little yet of its misery, had also worked its way into my imagination. We knew about Bonnie Prince Charlie and Culloden, and the idea of being chased through the heather by Redcoats had been firmly planted in my mind by songs and stories. When the ultimate Jacobite adventure finally came my way, I was, so to speak, ripe for plucking.

I don't now recall whether I first read *Kidnapped*, or had it read to me, or heard it adapted for the radio, but I was ten or eleven at the time and it gripped me at once and without remorse. Even the names of the characters had a peculiar resonance, for there were Balfours and Stewarts and Campbells at my school, latter-day kinsmen of Davie and Alan Breck and the Red Fox; and I knew well that these families were not just intricately bound up with the great events of Scottish history, but deeply connected with the landscape that Stevenson described, and which I also knew: from the brackeny Borders valleys of Davie's childhood, to the still, birch-fringed lochs of Alan Breck's Appin, to the great Campbell stronghold of Inveraray Castle.

Closer to home, meanwhile, there was Uncle Ebenezer Balfour (did Stevenson borrow that miserly first name from Dickens?) and all the horror of his unfinished staircase. On a stormy night, how little it took for the grim House of Shaws and our darkened, gale-battered east-coast mansion to become one in my imagination. As for the moment when Davie realises that he has been tricked by the wicked old man and is to be sold for labour in the plantations of Carolina, his feelings of abandonment and despair plucked madly at my heart strings.

By this time we had moved from Edinburgh to my grandparents' house. Here it was the hills of western Perthshire, Ben Chonzie and Ben Halton and Ben Vorlich, that dominated the skyline and my imagination. I missed them terribly when I returned to rolling, red-earthed East Lothian at the end of each holidays, and the thought of them lent extra poignancy to tales of the Highlands.

The move north brought with it a new holiday activity. I began going out with my father on shooting expeditions. Now, instead of looking at the hills, I spent long days walking into them. Like Davie and Alan, albeit as pursuers rather than pursued, we laboured across shelterless shoulders with freezing rain stinging our cheeks and dripping down the backs of our necks, or sweltered in August heat that had us longing for the next burn where we could fling ourselves down in the dusty, honey-scented heather and lap up the cool water from cupped hands. Sometimes, just as Davie cursed Alan during their flight across the moors, I cursed my father for pushing me close to what felt like the limits of exhaustion.

During one holidays I was taken on an educational cruise run by the National Trust for Scotland which almost exactly followed the route of the brig *Covenant*, leaving from South Queensferry on the Forth, where Davie was put to sea against his will, and sailing all the way round the coast of Scotland to land at Greenock on the Clyde.

By the time we had left Stornoway and were through the Minch I had got over my seasickness and sat on deck to watch the hills of Assynt and Torridon, Knoydart and Morar slide by in brilliant sunlight, gulls clouding our wake. Happily, the *Dunera*, a retired troop ship, did not founder off the coast of Mull but made it safely to harbour in Greenock.

What I didn't know then was that Stevenson's father had taken him on an almost identical trip in 1869 in the Northern Lighthouse Board's steamer *Pharos V*. This had provided much of the material for the sea voyage in *Kidnapped*, including the unusual scene of eviction he witnessed as the *Pharos* took on board a party of emigrants who, almost half a century after the end of the clearances proper, were being moved off their land to make way for a deer forest.

Nor did I know that, in a further curious twist, my own father would later serve for seven years as one of the Commissioners for Northern Lighthouses and make the annual trip in the *Pharos VIII* to inspect those lonely outposts and bring cheer to the keepers (none of whom today remain, for the very last of Scotland's 212 lighthouses, including all those built by Stevenson's grandfather and uncle, was automated in 1998).

Back on land, it seemed to me that with their rich, assonant Gaelic names, the hills were starting to become like people I knew, the shrouding mist and dark woods, tumbling, rocky rivers and humpbacked Wade bridges, their personal belongings. Their individuality was all the more pronounced for the emptiness of the landscape in which they loomed. But it hadn't always been so.

Stevenson set *Kidnapped* in 1751, five years after the catastrophic end of the Jacobite uprising at Culloden. It was, in effect, the beginning of the end of Highland society. But although Hanoverian repression and desperate poverty were already conspiring to drive people from the land, there would still have been crofting "townships" in the glens through which Davie and Alan fled; while higher up, the hills would have been dotted with sheilings where folk went with their beasts for the summer grazing.

By the time Stevenson himself came to know the Highlands, however, the clearances were complete, Victoria had already been ensconced at Balmoral for several years, and

North Britain had become a place where industrialists with social aspirations developed grouse moors and deer forests and entertained guests in baronial lodges.

The management of the Highland landscape as a huge empty recreation ground had begun, and the absence of civilisation would certainly have encouraged Stevenson to dramatise what he found there. For like all Victorians, he revelled in the melodramatic notion of the sublime, the thin line upon which one thrillingly confirmed one's own existence: a pace forward and nature would overwhelm one with terror, a pace back and she would transport one with delight. So, for example, Davie, the Lowlander, speaks of Appin being "full of prodigious wild and dreadful prospects."

Here we differ. I have felt that sense of awe in nature, but never in the Highlands. They can be beautiful, bleak, desolate, enfolding, enchanting, unforgiving – people die in the Scottish hills every year, and it pays to be respectful of the shifting weather, the knife-edged ridges, the treacherous, scree-clad slopes. But for all that, I have always found something comfortingly familiar about even the gloomiest, most sheer-sided west coast glen.

What I found more unsettling, as I grew older and came to know more of it, was the history that everywhere in the Highlands seeps from the peat and wreaths the hilltops. One summer evening in my teens, I walked out to a remote bothy in the hills with my best friend, David as it happens. We spent the night there and I hardly slept a wink for the sound of voices on the wind.

Stevenson undoubtedly heard them too. The voice of James Stewart of Duror, hanged in chains at Ballachulish after his wrongful conviction by a jury of Campbells for the murder of the King's factor, Colin Campbell of Glenure, the Red Fox; a murder almost certainly committed at the instigation, if not the hand, of his kinsman Alan Breck. Or of the fugitive Jacobite chieftain Cluny Macpherson hiding out in his "cage" high up among the distant crags of Ben Alder. Or of Robin Oig, son of the outlaw Rob Roy Macgregor, playing the pipes on the Braes of Balquhidder.

These were the real voices and places around which Stevenson wove his story, writing it in tautly-framed instalments for serialisation in *Young Folks* magazine. From the very first hearing, its energy and rhythm entered my bloodstream and lodged there.

Stevenson wrote *Kidnapped* in Bournemouth at the house he named Skerryvore, after the most beautiful of all the family lighthouses. I wrote my first three novels in London; and it's obvious to me now that they all feature journeys of either quest or pursuit through mountainous landscapes. Perhaps one cultivates a stronger sense of place *in absentia*.

A year after *Kidnapped* was published, Stevenson left England on the journey that would end in his death in Samoa, seven years later, in 1894. He was only forty-four. My own self-imposed exile lasted just short of twenty years and on my return, aged forty-one, I deliberately planted myself and my family off the beaten track in a gentle glen in Highland Perthshire.

During the seven years we spent there I underwent the complicated experience of rediscovering a Scotland vastly changed in some respects, as a country on the brink of political devolution; scarcely changed at all in others, as our view of the fortress-like Beinn a' Ghlo, and the forty miles of wilderness beyond it, constantly reminded me.

Being among the hills again, hearing the river at night through our bedroom window, re-awoke that sense of history as something omnipresent in the landscape, and with it returned the narrative pulse. It was a kind of unconscious preparation for my fourth novel, *The Witness*, which strongly echoes *Kidnapped* as young John MacNeil and the child known to him only as Ninian flee through the Cairngorm and Monadhliath mountains in a troubled Scotland of the near future. It seems more than coincidence that, after a tortuous journey of its own, the book should finally have found a publisher in the week before I sat down to write this essay.

As I look north now, I have to ask myself whether it is possible to view the landscape before me as something distinct from what I know to have taken place in it. For it seems as if

Stevenson's own story and the story of Davie and Alan, my story and the story of John and Ninian, are all interwoven as strands in the greater story of what it means to be Scottish and to have fallen under the spell of the Highlands. I believe it is impossible to be in love with the Highlands without being in love with narrative; and when these hills and glens provide the backdrop for one's own life, one cannot ignore the sense of being part of their unfolding tale.

No matter how empty this beautiful, proud, mournful country may sometimes seem, there's a story under every stone. And if you can't find one, or be part of one, you have to make one up for yourself.

R. L.
STEV-
ENSON

HUGH
MILLER

JOHN
BURNSIDE

STUART
MURDOCH

VAN
MORR-
ISON

F.W.

PAUL

Cromarty and the Black Isle

Hugh Miller's voices

by Ali Smith

It is 1969. I'm about seven years old. I am sitting in my parents' bedroom on the ottoman at the end of their bed, upstairs in our house in St Valery Avenue in Inverness. We live in the capital of the Highlands, I know, because my mother told me. My mother says we are descended from Rob Roy McGregor, a famous cattle thief and outlaw who stole from the rich to give to the poor. My mother, although she is northern Irish, is very proud of her children being Scottish. So is my father, though he is English, from near Lincoln. My father says he bought a ticket to come to the Highlands and has never been able to afford the return ticket home.

I'm reading a book I picked up downstairs in the living room, it's called something like *True Tales of the Highlands*. In it, I'm about to read a story that I will find so haunting that I won't be able to sleep for several nights, and when I pick up cutlery at the dinette table before every meal for what will be months, I will drive my parents mad by asking them, every time – until they lose their patience with me completely and I'm made to stop it – to tell me what the knife and the fork I'm holding in my hands are made of.

Two young men, two friends, are out on a walk through a wood, and they come upon a hoard of money just lying there on the ground. They can't believe their luck. They decide to split it between them. But on their way home, one of them picks up a large rock and hits the other one over the head with it. When his friend falls to the ground he hits him again, until his skull is broken. Then he takes the money out of his friend's pack, and buries him and the stone he killed him with under a pile of similar stones.

Ten years later and he is a rich and respected man. Every day he wakes up and looks in the mirror and shakes his head, unable to believe the secret he knows about himself.

One day he sits down to eat at a grand restaurant in the city. He orders the most expensive thing on the menu. But when he looks down at the finely carved bone handles of the knife and the fork in his hands, he finds his hands are covered in blood.

Then the bones in his hand speak.

What do the bones say? I can't remember. I had completely forgotten this story, and the very profound effect it had on me at the time, until a couple of Decembers ago when I'd gone up home to see my father (who is now in his eighties and who now lives out on the Black Isle), who'd had to go into hospital in Inverness. So I was staying at home, but not at home – in a hotel, and it was surreally mild for December in Inverness, thirteen degrees most days, and I was hanging around the haunts I used to visit and the places now totally gone, and I went to the museum, to see if the stuffed wildcat was still there. It was.

In the Museum shop, I picked up and flicked through *Scenes and Legends of the North of Scotland* (1835), the first book written by Hugh Miller, the geologist, when he was the manager of the tiny bank in the town he was born in not far from Inverness, in Cromarty, on the Black Isle (a few miles from where my father now lives).

A small boy's father is a sea-captain. He is caught in a bad storm and is about to drown at sea.

The boy, his two infant sisters, and his mother, who's sitting there sewing away at the fireplace, have no idea, are miles away, safe at home. The boy's mother is a seamstress. She does a lot of the local sewing, especially shroud-work. (Soon both her daughters will die too, both very young, and her son will be distraught when he hears her tell an acquaintance that she'd rather have lost the boy and kept one of the girls, that it would have made for a different life for her.)

She feels a draught. Go and shut the door, Hugh, she says.

Her son is five years old. When he gets to the door he sees, in the air, a disembodied hand and arm, reaching out. It seems to be a woman's hand and arm, though it has no body attached to it, and it is lit up, dripping with water, floating in the air by itself. The boy is terrified.

The Black Isle isn't an isle at all; it's an isthmus, a peninsula, nearly ten miles wide, over twenty miles long, just north of Inverness. Is it called the Black Isle because of the colour of its good dark farming soil? Or because of something to do with black magic and witchcraft? Or because at certain times of the year, if you look at it from across the other side of the Moray Firth, it looks a deep black colour? Black's not the only colour the Black Isle goes; one hot and perfect summer I saw richer purples and deeper golds in the fields of the Black Isle than I've ever seen anywhere in the world.

It sounds lyrical. Actually the Highlands, it strikes me, is an impossible blend of lyricism and measured austerity, patrolled by hooky-beaked seagulls the size of Jack Russell dogs; the kind of place where someone has shot the faces off the angels in the Catholic part of Tomnahurich cemetery with an air rifle. When I worked at the tourist office in Inverness when I was a teenager, we were regularly at a loss as to what to tell tourists they could do on a Sunday because everything shut, religiously, on a Sunday, and we used to suggest they drive themselves out along the Aberdeen road just to get a good view of the Black Isle; even then, when we were adolescently callous about the sheer beauty of the place, we knew it was a sight to see. My father has lived on the Black Isle now since my mother died in 1990. When I visit I see its sheer impossible versatility, its cliffs and moors and beaches and woods and marshes and heaths, how it's studded in its beautiful little bays with village after village protected by the dolphins and seals in the firths, and strung between a faerie glen, a tree above a well where the people in the know come to hang rags so that what they want will come true, and, of course, church after church after church.

A fisherman was walking home happily to Cromarty on the Inverness road, after visiting a friend in the upper parish. "The night was still and calm, and a thick mantle of dull yellowish clouds, which descended on every side from the centre to the horizon, so obscured the light of the moon, though at full, that beyond the hedges which bounded the road all objects seemed blended together without colour or outline." *Out of nowhere he heard a terrible noise, like a huge pack of maddened, snarling hounds somewhere very near him, just beyond that hedge; he put his hands in his pockets but there was nothing but the last of the crumbs from the food he'd had on the boat. He held the crumbs out anyway, thinking they might appease the dogs. But there were no dogs; there was only a man, walking beside him beyond the hedge, keeping up with him, and the baying noise had stopped. Good, he thought; the dogs must belong to him, so I'm fine. But when he reached the gap in the hedge, he saw the figure grow and grow until it dropped on four legs and turned itself into a huge black horse.*

He quickened his pace. The horse did too. He slowed, stood still. The horse did too. He walked his usual speed. The horse walked beside him. He saw it was an ugly kind of a horse, black-shaggy and limping, and when he reached the cemetery, a couple of hundred yards out of the town, the creature stopped, the air filled with sudden blinding light, like lightning, and "on recovering his sight, he found that he was alone."

Or how about this one:

A spring lay between two farms. One hot day two farmworkers came, from their opposite directions on the different farms, to drink from it. One reached the spring first, drank from it, and, when he saw the other approaching, grabbed up a handful of mud and threw it in the water. Try drinking that, he said.

But the spring began to boil, and sank into the ground right in front of their eyes. "Next day at noon the heap of grey sand which had been incessantly rising and falling within it, in a little conical jet, for years before, had become as dry as the dust of the fields; and the strip of white flowering cresses which skirted either side of *the runnel that had issued from it, lay withering in the sun. What rendered the matter still more extraordinary, it was found that a powerful spring had burst out on the opposite side of the firth, which at this place is nearly five miles in breadth, a few hours after the Cromarty one had disappeared."*

The farmer who'd flung the mud in the spring found that no one would speak to him anymore. Everybody thought he was cursed. So he went to see an old person who lived in a nearby parish and was known locally as a seer. You've insulted the water, the seer told him. Go back at exactly the same time as you did so, clean the place with a clean piece of linen towelling, then lie down beside it and wait.

The farmer did as he was told. He lay above the hollow on the ground where the cresses were withered, until the sun was almost down, and the water came spurting back with a force, then settled down and ran as before. *"We recognise in this singular tradition a kind of soul or naiad of the spring, susceptible of offence, and conscious of the attentions paid to it."*

The latter of these stories is one of the first in *Scenes and Legends of the North of Scotland*, which Hugh Miller wrote in his thirties and which brought him the start of a great deal of success. He died in Edinburgh on Christmas Eve in 1856, aged only fifty-four. He committed suicide, shot himself with a revolver. He had become hugely famous, a Victorian renaissance man: a folklorist, historian, poet, newspaper editor and writer; a geologist to whose lectures in the Scottish and English capitals thousands of people thronged; a rhetorician keen to modernise Church legislation; a central figure in the troubled and fiery formation of the Free Church; and most of all, a theologian determined to reconcile, as intelligently and scientifically as possible, ideas on creation and evolution with biblical tract. He died just a couple of years before Darwin would send much of his theorising the way of all flesh, with his *Origin of Species*; it is truly terrible not to know, not to be able to see, how Miller would have responded to Darwin.

Everything Miller worked on, everything he wrote, reveals his keenness to reconcile things which he knows are simply irreconcilable. "It is possible," as he wrote in his autobiographical volume, *My Schools and Schoolmasters*, "for two histories of the same period and individual, to be at once true to fact, and unlike each other in the scenes which they describe and the events which they record."

An old, old shepherd was totally deaf – so deaf that, though he was a pious man, it was simply not necessary for him to go to church on a Sunday anymore since he couldn't hear anything anyway. One Sunday, having sent his herdboy to Church, he took his sheep and his Bible and went down to a grassy hollow, and "with his Bible spread out before him on a hillock of thyme and moss, which served him for a desk, and sheltered on either hand from the sun and wind by a thicket of sweetbriar and sloethorn, he was engaged in reading," when he heard something.

He raised his head, looked at the leaves. They were waving in silence, as usual, in the light wind.

He began to read again, and again he heard something – a low airy rush of noise. He looked up.

A lady in a long green dress was standing in front of him, a dress that covered her feet but that left her incredibly beautiful shoulders and breasts completely bare. "The old man laid his hand on the book, and raising himself from his elbow, fixed his eyes on the face of the lady.

*"Old man," she said, "I see you are reading the Book. Please tell me. Is there anything in it to help or to save **us**?"*

"The gospel of this book," said the man, "is addressed to the lost children of Adam, but to the creatures of no other race." The lady shrieked as he spoke, and gliding away with the rapidity of a swallow on the wing, disappeared amid the recesses of the hollow."

Miller is a great storyteller. Off she goes, *a swallow on the wing*. The power of his storytelling leaps over its own moral import, wiry as a fox. The power lies in the detail which makes the supernatural – and the fierce challenge between the supernatural and the righteous – as real as day. Never mind that the lady in green is banished – she exists; and the old man, all hands and elbows, saw her beautiful nakedness. In the same way, a water naiad can be apologised to with clean linen, and the visual effect of a moonless night will be described every bit as fully and carefully as, and possibly even more carefully than, a devilish beast.

He grew up in Cromarty, which was at that point a quite prosperous port (and prosperity is cyclic in Cromarty, which was most recently buoyed up yet again by the lucrative oil industry in the 1970s). He was a clever but troubled child who never settled to schoolwork. He took an apprenticeship early, as a stonemason, which made him ill for life, ruined his lungs. Some of the gravestones in Cromarty churchyard were carved by him.

Scenes and Legends is a formidably layered history of the place and its irreconcilabilities and versatilities of spirit – a collection of written and oral histories, especially the latter, into a stratification of stories and voices which make up Miller's own. "Old greyheaded men, and especially old women, became my books" in the research for it, he says, and fills it with recordings he sees as not just similar to a perennial plant-life, "but also as a species of produce which the harvests of future centuries may fail to supply."

I read this book between visits to my father in Raigmore Hospital in Inverness, where he was being treated because his skin had turned incurably scaly, wouldn't stop flaking off. Nurses were moisturising him heavily every day then wrapping him tightly in linen to rebalance his skin. I would go up and spend the afternoon with him, chatting, or looking out the huge hospital windows over the dusk shadow of the Black Isle as he dozed. (My father is a keen angler. "I'm maybe turning into a salmon," he said and we laughed.) Then I'd go back to the hotel I was staying in Inverness, and lie on the bed, choose (easily) between Anne Robinson being mean to people on *The Weakest Link* on the hotel TV and Hugh Miller's *Scenes and Legends* in my hands.

Cromarty, Crummade, Chrombhte, the crooked bay, a town between two Sutors, "turrents built to command a gateway." A land dug out of the sea. A town built again, after its first version was deluged by sea. "In a burying-ground of the town, which lies embosomed in an angle of the bank, the sexton sometimes finds the dilapidated spoils of our commoner shell-fish mingling with the ruins of a nobler animal; and in another inflection of the bank, which lies a short half mile to the east of the town, there is a vast accumulation of drift-peat, many feet in thickness, and the remains of huge trees."

Miller records talking with men who saw farmed land where now you can only see sea. He tells the story of the bones of what must have been an old burial yard coming out of the sea, all blown ashore in a storm, and the local people who picked them up and carried them carefully to the new church-yard, buried them "beneath the eastern gable of the church."

He tells stories of local stubbornness, restless local ingenu-ity, local brilliance, the local writers who've gone before him, Thomas the Rhymer, and Sir Thomas Urquhart who invented his own alphabet and linguistic system, among other unbe-lievable ingenuities. He bares the roots, etymologies, meaning and foundations of the place, its "savage magnificence," the "sublimity of desolation on its shores, the effects of a conflict maintained for ages, and on a scale so gigantic." He details its superstitions, its religions, and the argument between both in a way that puts Cromarty at the thriving heart of contem-porary religious and philosophical struggle, "every tree of the wood, every tumulus of the moor. But I daresay I have imparted to the reader more of the fabulous history of Cromarty than he will well know how to be grateful for."

Miller the theologian – how Highland – could hear illegiti-mate spirit. He believed that the very rocks and earth have as important a voice as any afterlife. He was a connoisseur of fossils, an expert on time and its ravaging, a believer in the Great Chain of Being who was consumed by fragile stratifica-tion. I picked his first book up out of a little display of books all about where I'd grown up, and opened it at page 82:

"From the manner in which the bones were blended together, it seemed evident that the bodies had been thrown into the same hole, with their heads turned in opposite directions, either out of carelessness or in studied contempt. And they had, apparently, lain undis-turbed in this place for centuries. A child, by pressing its foot against the skull which had been raised entire, crushed it to pieces like the other; and the whole of the bones had become so light and porous, that when first seen by the writer, some of the smaller fragments were tumbling over the sward before a light breeze, like withered leaves, or pieces of fungous wood."

Sublimity and desolation. The bones spoke.

Northern Light

Finding George Mackay Brown and Orkney

by *Stuart Delves*

"They carved a dragon to guard their writings." Where are we? In a dark place; a tomb, no – a burial chamber. In the lamp-light there are chambers and stone ledges. Once, bones would have lain here. The guide points to the Viking runes. They were sheltering from the storm. Big men with axes and knives. Even they, with fly agaric and bull muscle, had found it hard to shift the portal stone. There was nothing to steal. The skulls had last seen sea and sand and this flotsam necklace of islands some 3,000 years before. Treasures, if there had been any, were long gone. "Here the masons built a hive." Hive is right. We are in the hive. The combs are cold now but the sun will come. One of the sailors had written of a milkmaid back home. Her warmth would have been good here. (I see her blond and blue-eyed, anxiously watching the fjord.) Outside you see the hive. In the flat, treeless landscape it could be a pod from Star Wars. But the nearby stone rings dismiss that thought. "Here the masons built a hive / That the dead lords and ladies / Might eat always honey of oblivion." Here is a poet I will listen to. Poetry is to be heard. When you read poetry, listen to yourself reading. Listening goes deeper than reading. The rhythms take us inward to the realm of vision. Maeshowe is an inward space. The sun spears in at the winter solstice, darting down the passageway and filling the chamber. But time stays at the door:

"Here masons and star watchers
Conspired: in midwinter
The good star, the sun,
Would awaken the sleepers."

I first came across the work of George Mackay Brown in my mother-in-law's house in Lauder, a small town in the Scottish Borders: *The Sun's Net and Magnus*. Short stories and novels. Magnus was a warrior and a saint. He was betrayed and cut down by a terrified cook who had drawn the short straw. Magnus was killed in cold blood. It was cold that first winter I came to stay with my new girlfriend. Before I caught the train up from Bristol I went to the Army & Navy stores and bought a fur-lined hat with earflaps. It proved to be an excessive precaution. I never wore it. It was brought out at parties or after a second bottle of wine: its ridiculous appearance never failed to cause mirth. But it was cold that first winter. And Lauder's the coldest place I've yet experienced. Colder even than Orkney. But back then I was hardly aware of Orkney. I'd come north, but Orkney was in the far north. Was it even in Scotland? The name made me think of orca whales, Prussian Blue seas. And there in my future mother-in-law's house amongst the oak shelves and the Swedish candles (she had a deep affinity with Scandinavia) were these stories.

George was my maternal grandfather's first name. He was Scottish with German ancestry. George was a popular Hanoverian name. My maternal grandmother was a Brown – a good Scottish name. Clan names were often abandoned and colours adopted after the defeat of Bonnie Prince Charlie in 1746 as a protection against reprisal. I was returning to an ancestral domain. I was hungry for all things Scottish and literature was the master key. Knowledge was bound up with the buds of love, and my new love was my muse, blond and blue-eyed ... But the irony was that the writer whom I came across that first winter, in that comfort of a new-found home, was from an archipelago of islands that are as much if not more Scandinavian than Scottish. But I wasn't to discover that for a further ten years.

For ten years my wife and I moved from place to place around the UK. Edinburgh, Kent, London, Bristol, Somerset, Devon, Inverness, Glasgow, Edinburgh and now here we are in the Scottish Borders. I always felt myself rootless, in that I could call no valley or pile of stone my home. Very different from George Mackay Brown. Brown rarely left Orkney. His roots were there, in the culture and in the blood: in the stone croft and the fisherman's boat. In his early adulthood, however, he despaired of what he thought was the islanders' neglect of their unique culture and he longed to get away.

* * *

When he was twenty-nine he did get away to study under fellow Orcadian Edwin Muir at Newbattle Abbey south of Edinburgh. Muir, himself a great poet, was Brown's touchstone. His recognition and encouragement of the younger poet's talent helped him to see himself as a real writer. Brown had already started writing journalism and guidebooks on Orkney – in fact he continued writing journalism all his life and even though he became internationally acclaimed as a poet, novelist and short story writer he maintained that some of his best writing was to be found in his newspaper columns about day-to-day life in Orkney. But in 1956 after five happy years at Newbattle – interspersed with illness – he went on to read English Language and Literature at Edinburgh University and fell in with the esteemed poetry crowd that frequented Milne's Bar and The Abbotsford in Edinburgh's Rose Street. A favourite line from one of his stories sums up that moment of buying a drink in any brightly lit bar anywhere: "the erratic jingling commerce of silver and glass across the bar."

Alexander Moffat's painting "Poet's Pub" in the Scottish National Portrait Gallery in Edinburgh captures the scene at Milne's. Twentieth century literary giant Hugh MacDiarmid holds court with Sorley MacLean, Norman MacCaig, Iain

Crichton Smith, Edwin Morgan, Robert Garioch, Sydney Goodsir Smith and George Mackay Brown in attendance. A very male literary chapter (how different would a painting of today's leading Scottish poets be with Liz Lochhead, Carol Ann Duffy, Kathleen Jamie and Jackie Kay propping up half the bar!) This was an intense time for Brown – in stark contrast to the mostly solitary existence he led otherwise in Orkney before and after – and there was one woman on the scene, Stella Cartwright, whom he remembered in a poem on her birthday some twenty years later:

"To him, she spoke sweeter than rain among roses
in summer
While poets like columns of salt stood
Round the oaken Abbotsford bar."

For Brown, Stella was very much a part of his time in Edinburgh. When she visited him in Orkney some years later Brown felt uneasy: the clash of two worlds. But there's regret in the birthday poem. He remembers her still as a "star" through "storm-clouds" and refers to himself in the fifties as a "crazy chap, high among cloud." But Brown dedicated himself totally to writing and was prepared to live simply and with few attachments to pursue his art. He had success and recognition but his newspaper columns and Orkney guides helped to sustain him. He was known and honoured in the community. In fact, he wrote for his community, revitalising and celebrating their myths, their history, their ways and turns of phrase. I have a picture of him looking out to sea, from which came much of his inspiration, came the boats of today's fishermen and yesterday's voyagers – heroes old and new of his tales and poems. So, his life wasn't glamorous, or particularly complicated. But his language was like iron and silver, starlight and granite. His vision was pure.

In the middle of our ten-year shunt about the UK, I was appointed as the Centre Director at the Arvon Foundation's Devon Centre – Totleigh Barton. Arvon was the closest I've ever got to The Abbotsford or Milne's Bar in that I was involved in a living, breathing literary tradition whereby aspirants spent an intense week with established practitioners. One of the founders, John Fairfax, was the nephew of the energetic and iconic English poet George Barker. Barker had had a magnetic personality and had naturally gathered people around him for long night discussions of that most vocational of forms – poetry – aided by wine and song (as the father of fifteen children he is well known for the women in his life and, as his widow Elspeth has wryly remarked, "each autumn, in the churchyard, a solitary specimen of the brazen mushroom *phallus impudicus* rears from his grave"). Fairfax wanted to take something of this impromptu milieu of discourse and learning and ground it in a "retreat" setting.

* * *

It was while I was the steward of Totleigh that I came across George Mackay Brown again: a book of poetry, *The Wreck of the Archangel* found in a bookcase bursting with spines between Delabole flagged floor and eleventh century rafters:

> "Prow set for Greenland, a westerly
> weeks-long, a graybeard gale
> Drove *Skarf* at Iceland,
> A bleak shore, behind it
>
> A burning mountain. One farm all night
> Thrummed with harpsong and saga
> But a hard mouth at dawn
> Bargained for cheese and eggs.
>
> The gale northerly then, a hag
> Spitting hail, herded *Skarf*
> Among Faroese yoles, rowlock-deep
> In drifts of salmon."

So begins "Sailing to Papay." I could have chosen any poem from the collection. But the page fell open on that one. And that one will do perfectly for it has many of the elements in Brown's work I find so appealing: the strong narrative drive, the vivid sense of place, the pared language, the combination of the mythic with the rudiments of life. Seamus Heaney wrote that Brown passed everything "through the eye of the needle of Orkney." Orkney, or rather Brown's use of Orkney, became my lodestar. The north had an iron pull. I had to go there.

Four or five years later I got my chance. After Totleigh my wife and I returned to Scotland with a Christmas baby in tow and in 1995 I got a job as a writer with a design consultancy in Edinburgh. Unsurprisingly, being Scotland, we worked for a number of whisky distilleries. This didn't mean, necessarily, that I got to visit them. But when I was assigned to work on Highland Park, from "the Northernmost Scotch Whisky Distillery in the world" I hoped I might get a chance. The brand name seemed very un-Orcadian but as I learnt more about the history, geography and culture of the place in order to write about the whisky that seemed by the by. Orkney was the land of the Midnight Sun, the Northern Lights, a Neolithic complex of sites, a trading post between Canada and continental Europe, a conflict zone in both World Wars. It was also a land of storytelling. And when I came to write the label for the outer box of Highland Park 25 Year Old that was to have a beautiful calligraphic treatment I wanted words that were meaningful. And words of value – each bottle retailed at £99! I turned to George Mackay Brown's "John Barleycorn" in which the barley says "Forever I flush the winters of men with wassails of corn." I was using poetry in commerce. I remember questioning my integrity but the whisky was good, made with integrity from the elements of Orkney. It felt organic and right.

Writing for Highland Park led to writing for the Orkney Tourist Board and I used Brown's words again because he was, for me, the voice of the islands. Little wonder his autobiography is called *For the Islands I Sing*. I used his line "The Orkney imagination is haunted by time" because finally I had visited and found this to be true. Nowhere else that I have visited has such a presence of history all around. Not only are there some 3,000 ancient sites on Orkney but traces of the two World Wars – the Churchill barriers, the rusting block ships, the slicks of oil from the sunken Royal Oak, the roll call of the drowned in St Magnus Cathedral in Kirkwall and the Italian Chapel at Lamb Holm built by PoWs from an old Nissan hut – are constant reminders that the present is progeny of the past. Visiting the Italian Chapel and its religious icons made from debris, driftwood, barbed wire, bully beef cans – the "rubbish and tinsel of war" as Brown put it – you can't help but be moved by such a monument to human ingenuity, faith and resilience.

* * *

Orkney, and its whisky Highland Park, were the subjects of my first sustained piece of prose writing "Hourglass." Like my adopted mentor I was writing about time – the effect of time on the whisky and the expanse of time experienced in the islands. There's a strange temporal elasticity in Orkney: a suspension. My wife and two children came with me when I did my research for the book. I have an abiding image of my children in anoraks, virtually at forty-five degrees, battling their way round the calendrical stones at The Ring of Brodgar through driving wind and rain – dwarf druids; young life in the ring of time.

George Mackay Brown used Orkney, its legends, its people, its landmarks, as the raw material for many of his poems and stories. Some material he worked on again and again wresting new insight from it. He also commented on the daily life of the islands and his place within it in his columns and journals. In his view his output was seamless. He simply wrote about where he lived. However, although rooted in the particular, his vision was universal: the mark of any great writer. For me, having come to rest in a village over 250 miles south of Orkney, having found a community that engages my energies with a history and landscape that snares my attention I find the inspiration of Brown guiding me to write with and for whatever and whomever is at hand. So Orkney is not a spiritual home for me: it's a spiritual bolt-hole. I am grateful for it and its tangential distance. Its poetry helped me find a way to connect with another corner of this world.

One day at the winter solstice I hope to stoop into the hive and womb of Maeshowe and experience – through the power of ancient geomancy – that the nadir of the sun, held for a spell in this timeless chamber, is its gradual re-birth. And if I don't recite this catechism I'll whisper it; and if I don't whisper it I'll think it: Sometimes. Sometimes when you're alone on the earth and the wind's belting you and you feel you have no roots, no claims, no reverence and that you could be blown to kingdom come and it would make no difference to anybody – in fact the world would be a slightly less messy place without you – it's good to know that you didn't just land here, that your nakedness is common to all, that you're linked by blood and language in whichever tongue it's spoken, that your darkness is my darkness and your light is my light and the light of all who've ever lived or are yet to walk alone on the hard stone of earth.

Notes:

Magnus (Hogarth Press, 1973); *Beside the Ocean of Time* (John Murray, 1994); *The Wreck of the Archangel* (John Murray, 1989); *Collected Poems* (John Murray, 2005); *For the Islands I Sing: An Autobiography* (John Murray, 1997); *Interrogation of Silence: The Writings of George Mackay Brown* by Rowena and Brian Murray (John Murray, 2004).

The Arvon Foundation www.arvonfoundation.org is a registered charity. It runs writing courses on many different kinds of writing at four houses around the country – Devon, Inverness-shire, Shropshire and Yorkshire.

Biographies

Will Awdry is an advertising writer turned creative director at Ogilvy London. "Wilbert Awdry's Wiltshire is omnipresent in the twenty-six titles of the Railway Series. The tunnel at Box has its literary echoes throughout the stories. *Troublesome Engines* (1950) features one that harbours an elephant. Other tunnels crop up in several of the books. Brian Sibley remains the written authority on the detail. Elsewhere, Google produces legions of zealous commentaries about my relation's influences and accuracy, not all them too train-spotty."

Stephen Brown is Professor of Marketing Research at the University of Ulster. "Van Morrison holds a degree from the same academic institution, though he's rather better known for his scintillating musical abilities. The Godfather of Caledonian Soul – and the grumpiest man in showbusiness, allegedly – Van Morrison's latest album is *Pay the Devil*, a homage to his country and western influences. The Belfast Cowboy rides again."

Sarah Burnett is a freelance business writer living in Edinburgh. "Thomas Hardy must be Dorset's most famous export. He's great for the county's tourism industry and one of the greatest story-tellers of the nineteenth century. Speaking today, I'd recommend you read *Tess of the d'Urbervilles*. But, as a teenager growing up in Hardy country, I wished desperately that he had lived in any other county but my own ..."

Richard Clayton is a London-based freelance journalist, until the Kingdom of Fife declares independence (assuming it would have him). He suggests that readers new to John Burnside repair, with the *Selected Poems*, to the Ship Tavern on Anstruther's water-front, where they might just catch King Creosote's twisted folk music to boot.

Rishi Dastidar works for customer experience consultancy Seren Partners in London. To pursue some of the themes in Metroland,

Rishi suggests you look for Barnes' collection of articles written for *The New Yorker,* "Letters from London: 1990–1995," which remains a fine insight into Britain in the early 1990s. *England, England* feels eerily prophetic in its analysis of a theme-park country, while providing an acidic commentary on the interplay of politics, economics and the creation of British heritage.

Jim Davies is a writer, author and design critic. "It seems there's always room for another scholarly interpretation of the bard. But you're not going to get one here. Just put any school-day preconceptions you may have aside, and take a fresh look. His range is breathtaking, his influence on the way we speak and write today profound. And for sheer kitsch, Shakespeare memorabilia can't be beaten."

Stuart Delves is co-founder of Henzteeth, Edinburgh. "Orkney is fifty-eight/fifty-nine degrees north, on the same latitude as Stavanger, Norway. Shortlisted for the Booker Prize in 1994, George Mackay Brown was the undisputed voice of Orkney, summed up by the title of his autobiography, *For the Islands I Sing.*"

William Easton is head of Berghs, Sweden's leading school of advertising, design and marketing. "Searching for Pinter in Hackney or Hackney in Pinter was a journey back in time, a rare visit to the UK and a rediscovery of words that have gone neglected too long on my bookshelves. Not a nostalgic trip down memory lane, but a journey where the spectres of violence and alienation seemed constantly present. You can never go home again!"

After several years at Interbrand, **Laura Forman** moved on to become Copy Manager at John Lewis. Now fluent in the language of haberdashery, electrical appliances and perfumery, she also has poetic leanings. She's been published in *The North, Smiths Knoll* and *The Interpreter's House* so far. Laura wants you to remember that Patrick Hamilton's *Hangover Square* is as much about pubs as *Romeo and Juliet* is about balconies. But that's no reason not to enjoy a good read at your local.

Acclaimed author **Niall Griffiths** was born in Liverpool and now lives and works in Wales, where he has just started work on his sixth novel. "The newcomer to Dylan Thomas should start with *Under Milk Wood* and the first of several big drinks, only stopping to ensure that you don't 'insult your brain' to death in a hotel room thousands of miles from home four days after your thirty-ninth birthday ..."

Justina Hart is a writer and editor. To learn more about Will Self's fascination with British roads, read his articles "Mad About Motorways" and "Do You Believe in the Westway?" in *Junk Mail*. Self's early short story collections, *The Quantity Theory of Insanity* and *Grey Area*, are a good introduction to his work.

Jonathan Holt is an editor and copywriter. He works, sometimes, in the City of London. "You may think of TS Eliot as a 'difficult' writer, but his life and verse have inspired lyrics by Bob Dylan, the Manic Street Preachers and Public Enemy, not to mention *Cats,* the musical. *The Complete Poems and Plays* is published by Faber."

Roger Horberry is a copywriter and maker of wilfully obscure music. He invites you to enjoy the John Schlesinger-directed 1963 film of *Billy Liar* starring Tom Courtenay and the far-too-good-looking-for-her-character Julie Christie, but only after you've read the book. Despite his curmudgeonly view of the north, Roger recommends the Yorkshire Sculpture Park, fish and chips on the beach at Robin Hood's Bay, drinking in The Minster in York (the pub, not the large church) and the excellent rail service south. Preferably all in one day.

Novelist, musician and business writer **Jamie Jauncey** today lives on the edge of the Highlands, a short distance from where he was born. He believes that Robert Louis Stevenson's *Kidnapped* and *Treasure Island* are equally incomparable for their storytelling genius, though for reasons of national prejudice he marginally favours *Kidnapped*.

Artist and writer of *A Walk Through Books* and *&\aslo*, **Peter Kirby** grew up raking low tide coves for, among other things, seal spines, in the dark lands of West Penwith, Cornwall. For a baptism into Richard Long, he swears by *Walking in Circles*. A second, more masochistic head plunge, is to take the OS Explorer 1:25,000 map of Dartmoor (Long's most-walked landscape) and wear out every square inch of it.

A meandering career path beginning at Penguin Books and stopping off at BBC Radio 1 led **Molly Mackey** to write for Corporate Edge, a branding, design and communications consultancy. New readers (most people!) to Mary Butts should start at *Armed with Madness* – it's a much better grail legend than *The Da Vinci Code*, but not a lot of people know that. For the more highbrow, Butts saw parallels between *Armed with Madness* and TS Eliot's *The Waste Land*, so have that in mind as you go.

Lorelei Mathias writes for an advertising agency during the day and "chick-lit" novels at night. Her first novel, *Step On It, Cupid*, was published in July 2006. If it's your first trip to Rummidge, Lorelei says that *Scenes of Academic Life* (a Pocket Penguin) provides a helpful shortcut, and is a lively potted history of Lodge's campus corpus. Once you've graduated from there, the "Rummidge trilogy" is a must. Lorelei's favourite Lodge book is actually *Thinks ...*, which after all that, isn't even set in Birmingham.

Sarah McCartney is a marketing strategist, writer and yoga teacher. "FW Lister has disappeared. All I know about him is printed on the dust jacket: he was born in Durham, served in the Navy during the war, went to St John's College in York and was a schoolmaster in Billingham. He may still be alive, but there is no one of that name in the Teesside phone book."

Richard Medrington is a writer, puppeteer and performance poet who spends a lot of time wandering and wondering. "Reading Edward Thomas's poem *Adlestrop* is like looking through the window of a stationary train and seeing a familiar face peering back at you. You raise your hand, only to realise that you're waving at your own reflection."

Robert Mighall is a senior consultant at design and branding agency Lloyd Northover. In a former life he was an academic, researching Victorian Gothic literature at Merton College, Oxford. He is currently writing a book about sunshine. To find Dickens's Kent (and yourself) read *Great Expectations* and *David Copperfield*. These are Dickens's most autobiographical novels, and the only ones written entirely in first-person narrative. Dickens grew up in Chatham, and in later life returned to Kent when he moved to Gad's Hill, a few miles from the scenes depicted in *Great Expectations*.

John Mitchinson is one of the main researchers and writers on the BBC TV show *QI* and was, for a while, Alan Garner's publisher. "Alan opened the eyes and imaginations of a whole generation, but he's writing his best work now. It's as if William Blake or Homer were still alive; his words and sentences are as shaped, weathered and enduring as millstone grit and his stories go straight to the heart of the Mystery."

Tim Rich is a writer and editor. Start with Belloc's collections of essays, says Tim: *Hills and the Sea* and *On Something*, perhaps. Or *On Nothing*. Then imbibe *The Four Men* in the sort of pub where at any moment a breathless fox-eyed old boy might crash through the door with a brace of pheasants stuffed inside his coat. *The Path to Rome* is a profound and entertaining companion for a long distance journey, such as the epic Heathfield–Eastbourne–Heathfield odyssey on the No. 52 bus.

John Simmons is the author of many books on writing for business and brands, including *Dark Angels* (the last part of The Writer's Materials trilogy). "You can visit Milton's Cottage and become a Friend to help support the wonderful place. I recommend the new Oxford edition of *Paradise Lost* with an introduction and notes by Philip Pullman. The Folio Society edition is beautifully produced with illustrations by William Blake."

Maja Pawinska Sims is a journalist and the director of Besparkle editorial and coaching. Maja says, "Jasper Fforde's four books set in Swindon stand up as self-contained stories, but I think it's best to take a rather more linear approach than Thursday might, and begin at the beginning with *The Eyre Affair*. Once you've been sucked in, check out www.jasperfforde.com."

Ali Smith grew up about forty minutes by car from Hugh Miller's Cottage, which is now a National Trust property. She is the author of three books of stories and three novels, the most recent of which, *The Accidental*, was shortlisted for the 2005 Booker Prize and won the Whitbread Novel Award. Miller was the author of, among many other books and pamphlets, *Scenes and Legends of the North of Scotland* (1837), *First Impressions of England and its People* (1846) and *The Testimony of the Rocks* (1857). "We are not only travelling, but also, as a people, living fast; and see revolutions, which were formerly the slow work of ages, matured in a few brief seasons." –Hugh Miller

Neil Taylor is Creative Director of The Writer and the author of *Search Me: The surprising success of Google* and *The Name of the Beast: The process and perils of naming products, companies and brands.* Neil's whistle-stop tour of ten years of Belle & Sebastian starts with their best early album, *If You're Feeling Sinister*, and their best later album, *Dear Catastrophe Waitress*. "And if you get to see them live, stand at the front, on the left, by Sarah and the string section."

Elise Valmorbida is a designer and writer. Her first published novel was *Matilde Waltzing*. There are more to come. Virginia's poetic imagination sparkles in *The Waves, To the Lighthouse* and *Mrs Dalloway*. "For some literary laughing, *Orlando* is the thing. Shy readers can sit in the dark and watch an inspiring film or two: *Orlando* by Sally Potter, or *Mrs Dalloway* by Marlene Gorris. Virginia's arguments in *Three Guineas* about peace and women's rights to learn, earn and own, are as relevant as ever. Today, two-thirds of the world's illiterates are female, women typically earn 25 per cent less than men doing the same work in developed and developing countries, nearly 70 per cent of the world's poor are women, there are eleven women heads of state or government ..."

Tom Wilcox escaped from Colchester to become General Manager of Whitechapel Gallery, a lecturer and a musician, formerly with Maniac Squat and now with The Chavs. He also produces records with Gillian Glover and The Fiascos and Vita. "Fans of rock lit may appreciate *Diary of a Rock 'n' Roll Star* by Ian Hunter (road anecdotes from Mott the Hoople's singer) and *Hammer of the Gods* by Stephen Davis (Led Zeppelin's debauched history). Giles Smith recommended to me *Chronicles Vol. 1* by Bob Dylan."

Penelope Williams is Creative Director at EquatorBlue Ltd. HW Tilman's *The Seven Mountain-Travel Books* is published by Diadem and by Mountaineers Books. Tim Madge's biography, *The Last Hero*, is published by Hodder & Stoughton. Bob Comlay, another of Tilman's crew, runs a fascinating website with some beautiful photographs at www.comlay.net/tilman.

Rob Williams is Creative Director at Penguin Books. Although much of Paul Abbott's work is now available on DVD, Rob reckons that in terms of defining Abbott's talent and his contribution to television drama, series one of *Shameless* is compulsory viewing. He also recommends reading Abbott's 2004 "Huw Wheldon Lecture to the Royal Television Society" and a solid few days drinking with the equally opinionated regulars of any Burnley pub. ("But do check that Burnley aren't playing Preston at home that day – it could end in tears.")

26 Letters

Illuminating the Alphabet

Edited by Freda Sack, John Simmons & Tim Rich

How often do we think about the individual letters of the alphabet? What are their histories, their personalities, their stories? What does C mean to you? Where did Z come from? How does N make you feel?

In 2004, the writing group 26 and the International Society of Typographic Designers joined forces to explore the DNA of language. Twenty-six business writers were randomly paired with twenty-six graphic designers, given one letter each and asked to create a collaborative work that celebrated, explored, questioned, elucidated or subverted that letter. In a series of diary pieces, the pairs wrote about the excitement and frustration, the research and the concepts, the relationships and the techniques that led to the finished works.

Throughout the process, the British Library acted as a resource for information and inspiration, and the resulting exhibition, "26 Letters: Illuminating the Alphabet," was displayed throughout the library building as part of the London Design Festival.

This book is a celebration of creative partnership based on a neglected aspect of our lives: the twenty-six letters that convey information, express emotion and enable us to function in the world. Amid the variety of contributions, what shines through is a love of letters, their look and their meaning, and the gift of pleasure that they offer to us all.

£14.99 in UK only
ISBN 1-904879-15-2

26 Malts

Some Joy Ride

Stuart Delves, Jamie Jauncey & Damian Mullan

What happens when you throw 26 writers together with 26 designers and give them carte blanche to create identities for 26 malt whiskies?

26 Malts tells the fascinating story of how 52 writers and designers tore up the rulebook in a groundbreaking venture between The Scotch Malt Whisky Society and the language organisation 26.

The results, revealed in full colour and described in the personal journals of the creative collaborators, defy all the conventions of whisky packaging and language. They demonstrate the power of words and images really working together.

A must for anyone with an interest in contemporary design, *26 Malts* also brings a wholly new level of appreciation to malt whisky-lovers everywhere.

£15.00 in UK only
ISBN 1-904879-61-6

From Here to Here

Stories Inspired by London's Circle Line

John Simmons, Neil Taylor, Tim Rich & Tom Lynham

"There's some great writing here, and you'll be surprised to discover a much deeper level to the London you thought you knew"
Ed Docx, author of *The Calligrapher*

Notting Hill, Baker Street, King's Cross, Westminster ... the Circle Line transports us to and from many of London's most famous places, as well as some of its obscure corners (Temple, Euston Road, Aldgate). The 31 chapters of this book, each by a different writer, explore the territory around the Circle Line's stations and the network that connects them. Through fiction, poetry, memoir and reportage, they bring to life the extraordinary spirit of this complex, demanding, inspiring city.

From Here to Here is a vibrant exploration of a place rich in stories and history, and teeming with plots and characters. It's the prefect companion for any journey, but especially one underground.

"Brace and be brisk,
Commoner, carry your heart like an egg
On a spoon, be fleet through the concourse"
From *KX* by Simon Armitage (King's Cross)

UK £12.99 | US $21.95 | CAN $29.95
ISBN 1-904879-35-7